'The increasing presence in Britain  of the world and the proliferation of ins are hugely significant develop. ial missiological issues. This well-res ly comprehensive approach, drawing om the disciplines of theology, anthrop psychology and sociology. The authors explore complex and sometimes contentious topics in a thoughtful and creative way and offer many practical suggestions to encourage partnership and multicultural initiatives.'
Dr Stuart Murray Williams

'One of the earliest missionary challenges was the crossing of cultural boundaries. The church refused to be captured by a single culture; the message was to be taken to all peoples and so the puzzle of how to express the faith in many cultures has been a perpetual theme in mission. Almost always that challenge has been picked up by practical cross-cultural partnerships expressed in deep friendships and strong teams. This book is a thorough and thoughtful examination of the challenges that come to us as these themes are confronted. It is a timely and rare contribution to a growing debate.'
Rev Dr Martin Robinson, Principal of Springdale College: Together in Mission, and the CEO of Together in Mission

'Wherever you look, people are on the move searching for a better life, whether that is freedom from life-threatening persecution or just looking for more opportunities to improve their circumstances. Migrants inevitably search out others in the same situation and keep a distance from those who are different. In this melting pot of humanity, what might church need to look like if it is to be inclusive of many diverse lifestyles and understandings of the gospel? Using the tools of social science as well as theology, this work offers an insightful analysis of the emerging situation and explores ways in which the church can embrace and celebrate differences while being faithful to the message of Jesus.'
Dr John Drane, Fellow of St John's College, University of Durham

'Effective missionary work in Britain today must involve a united movement of Christians from various ethnic and cultural heritages. True multicultural partnerships are the only way forward; nothing short of that will do. With this fascinating book, Andy Hardy and Dan Yarnell have humbly raised up a much-needed voice on a subject of growing concern among missionaries and Christians from the rest of the world, especially those living and serving in the West. Every chapter is filled with powerful insights that, if taken seriously, will make all our work a lot easier.'

Dr Harvey Kwiyani, founding director of Missio Africanus and author of Sent Forth: African Missionary Work in the West

Forming Multicultural Partnerships

Church planting in a divided society

Andy Hardy and Dan Yarnell

instant
apⵔstle

First published in Great Britain in 2015

Instant Apostle
The Barn
1 Watford House Lane
Watford
Herts
WD17 1BJ

British Library Cataloguing-in-Publication Data

A catalogue record for this book is available from the British Library

This book and all other Instant Apostle books are available from Instant Apostle:

Website: www.instantapostle.com

E-mail: info@instantapostle.com

ISBN 978-1-909728-24-0

Printed in Great Britain

Instant Apostle is a new way of getting ideas flowing, between followers of Jesus, and between those who would like to know more about His Kingdom.

It's not just about books and it's not about a one-way information flow. It's about building a community where ideas are exchanged. Ideas will be expressed at an appropriate length. Some will take the form of books. But in many cases ideas can be expressed more briefly than in a book. Short books, or pamphlets, will be an important part of what we provide. As with pamphlets of old, these are likely to be opinionated, and produced quickly so that the community can discuss them.

Well-known authors are welcome, but we also welcome new writers. We are looking for prophetic voices, authentic and original ideas, produced at any length; quick and relevant, insightful and opinionated. And as the name implies, these will be released very quickly, either as Kindle books or printed texts or both.

Join the community. Get reading, get writing and get discussing!

Contents

Dedications

Andy would like to dedicate this book to his wife Jenny and their children Tim and Lizzy who have been such a support to him in encouraging him in his writing and research. Also to all the leaders who patiently took time to help him see things through fresh eyes.

Dan would like to dedicate this book to his wife Amy, his two sons David and Josh, and to all the pioneer missional leaders with whom it is a privilege to work in seeing a new generation of multicultural expressions of the kingdom of God in our day.

Both Dan and Andy express deep thanks to all our students, to Laura for contributing to some refinement of ideas in this book and to Kelly for helping us to get the Bibliography and footnotes into the right shape.

We would also like to mention Simon for his encouragement, and Dr Ash Barker and many other students and colleagues who have helped us in numerous ways to keep on thinking about concepts found in this volume and in the ongoing research we engage with in missional studies.

Foreword

The world is changing and new conversations are needed. If the Christian faith is to be both relevant to this new world and faithful to Jesus, then the plight of millions of migrants, refugees and asylum seekers in our midst urgently needs some of our best attention and reflection. As Dan and Andy make clear in this compelling book, these are not only challenges of hospitality, but also a challenge to grasp opportunities to be evangelised anew by our new neighbours who have come to live with us in the West. These new neighbours come from the southern nations who were once evangelised by the colonial missionaries from Europe, but now Africans, Asians and South Americans are bringing the gospel back to the nations which once took the gospel to them.

Our cities are now like lakes to which many rivers and tributaries have brought diverse people within its banks. With nationalist trading barriers falling, workers from anywhere can flow into any of our cities where amazing opportunities are offered. Organisations, businesses and churches are seeking to draw the best workers from wherever they can find them too. In this broader global context we naturally find diverse and steady streams of asylum seekers, refugees and migrant workers running from poverty and persecution and naturally gravitating to the calmer waters of freer cities. The plight of transient and vulnerable people, then, is a growing and characteristic feature of today's global cities.

As I read this book further, however, our cities seemed to be an even more complex reality than a slow and steadily rising lake. The challenges include second culture children, identity, powers, reverse missionaries, competing visions and values, post-colonial realities, every resident a cross-cultural citizen, worldviews that range from pre-modern and secular to postmodern even in one family. I found myself feeling that this is less like a lake that steadily rises from new streams of people and far more like rapid, swirling tidal waters circling a delta. A delta is an area of low flat land, sometimes shaped like a triangle, typically found at the mouth of a river where it divides into several smaller rivers before flowing into the sea. Like a delta, the city sees people flow in, out and around it before they reach their final destinations. Sometimes people's lives swirl around one city, but more often now people flow down streams to other cities, back up to rural homelands for a while and then on again to another city. To push the analogy further, we know that all humans will eventually flow into death before their final eternal destinations.

What does it mean to share Christian faith and community among such a swirling tidal delta of people? How can we make our neighbourhood deltas as healthy and hospitable as possible for those who might not stay?

Andy and Dan draw insights from personal multicultural experiences with churches and Springdale College's equipping of leaders, as well as engaging biblical, theological and sociological analysis. They challenge us to see how today's growing movements of diversity can undermine so many traditional modernist models of Christian theology, leadership development and local churches. Imagined and perfected in more stable, dormant and mostly rural periods of human history, these have few answers to the chronic lack of time, stability and trust that undermines the building of life together across cultures and worldviews. A sense of belonging, so fundamental to building community and needed by churches and leaders, can so quickly be undermined by isolation, loneliness and lack of connections in cities. This can be the case as much within the tightest ethnic communities as in those with more individualistic worldviews. This can be deadly for any urban resident, but can be especially brutal on those fleeing poverty or persecution.

Rapid migrations may prove to provide an unprecedented challenge for the people of God, but also amazing opportunities. As well as the transience and rootlessness many feel, there can be the very obvious needs for housing, food, legal help and jobs that can easily overwhelm even the most compassionate churches. I know of a church in Bangkok, for example, that has grown rapidly because of the number of asylum seekers and refugees who are joining the church, but it has also lost many existing members because they couldn't cope with being 'ambushed' each week by folk in desperate need who were making up almost a third of the church. Few existing church members had the resources or experience to continue to respond each week to an increasing number of people who had fled persecution, were suffering mental and physical health and were in a desperate survival mode of existence. To its credit, the church leadership has tried to organise and respond to the needs of the newcomers and to equip existing members, but it has not been without cost.

The body of Christ has an amazing opportunity to engage in hospitality, compassion and justice in ways few others in society are motivated to do. We love not because our churches or colleges will grow bigger, but because we can become channels of God's grace and love, meeting Jesus in the faces of the ones we love. We will require God's help to find more flexible, compassionate and innovative responses to the growing needs of more diverse models of churches and training, but then God has a habit of doing this with His people who go out to the edges of society's power. Indeed, transformation often comes to the whole from those on the edges. Dare we miss out on what the Spirit is saying and doing?

It is an honour to foreword this book that draws all this to our attention, reflects thoughtfully and points to potential responses. I pray and hope that this book is read and devoured, and that it helps to start a new conversation that is much needed today.

Dr Ash Barker PhD (Founding Director and CEO Urban Neighbours of Hope)
Author of *Making Poverty Personal* and *Slum Life Rising*

Prologue

We recently went to a missionary conference in Melbourne, Australia. Our journey included a number of 'legs' to arrive there and return to the UK. As we took our first flight in cosmopolitan Birmingham, crossed time zones, landed in Dubai and then eventually wound up in Melbourne, the consistency of meeting people from many different ethnic and cultural backgrounds struck us. We encountered Indians, Pakistanis, Africans, Malaysians, Chinese, Indonesians, Arabs, Japanese, Australians, English, Americans and Canadians, to name but a few. These people represented all kinds of cultural and ethnic backgrounds. They also came from any number of religious faith persuasions – Hindu, Christian, Muslim, Buddhist, Shinto, Secularist and so on. The same mix of peoples was obvious to a greater or lesser extent at each airport on our way home as well.

The striking feature was that each airport represented a multicultural and pluralistic mixture of peoples, cultures, nations and faiths or no faith persuasions. The globalisation of the whole world's peoples who can pass each other by in many, if not most, airports of the world demonstrates the great opportunities we have to share the gospel with all nations.

And in the Western nations of the world, we find this incredible mixture and melting pot of various peoples, and the rich heritages they bring with them to live among us. We could not help but ask ourselves once more, 'How can we plant churches in the midst of diverse, multicultural communities that are made up of people from all the nations and cultures of the world?'

At present, many Western nations are continuing in their efforts to help multiple peoples in their midst live in harmony together. It is a challenge for which solutions to the issues of integration or closer relationships between peoples will not occur speedily. But the exciting thought we have both been reflecting on is, 'How can we plant multicultural churches that represent the goal of the gospel of Christ to unite all peoples, nations and tongues?' This is the exciting question we invite you to think about with us in this book. We want the kingdom of God to come on earth as it is in heaven, with all peoples joined together by the love of the one Lord who welcomes diversity and creativity to become a reality in His multicultural kingdom.

Why not join us in our imaginative journey? We hope to encourage ourselves and the people of Christ to dream of new ways of helping each other to become one new people in united, multi-ethnic churches, as we all engage together in creative, missional partnerships.

This book is a collaborative effort of love. While each of us has written the first drafts of different chapters, the other has offered critique, observation and at times correction to reach the final version. This is often how we live our lives, working together in intentional partnerships, whether we are lecturing, exploring new initiatives, writing or leading a fresh expression of church that is engaging with those for whom a more traditional approach is no longer relevant. We are passionate about God and His mission, and we are delighted to share our thoughts, insights and journey with you. We look forward to sharing with you our dream to see this happen more fully in our lifetimes, as part of the great dream of when Jesus will finally establish the kingdom of God when He comes again.

Andy Hardy and Dan Yarnell

We would value hearing from others who are exploring this important aspect of mission. If you are involved in a multicultural or multi-ethnic church plant, we would love to hear from you.

You can contact us at:
andy@springdalecollege.org.uk or danthevicarman@gmail.com

Part 1

Framing the Context of the Western Multicultural Missional Situation

Chapter 1
The Multicultural Missional Conversation

Welcome to the multicultural missional conversation on the subject of God's mission among multicultural and postmodern people in Western society. In this context the term 'conversation' means that we learn by talking with others about the methods they are using to share the gospel with the diverse cultures that are found in the West today.

We believe God is essentially a missionary God and that He desires to share His gospel through our churches, whether they be ethnic or multi-ethnic congregations, or whether they are predominately White or Black Majority Churches (WMCs or BMCs).

Whether you are originally from France, Germany, Britain, North America, Australia, India, China, Africa, South America or anywhere else, you will probably be very aware of the effects of secularisation on our Western society. Christianity has become a voice on the margins rather than having a more central influence on politics, education, medicine and business in this postmodern, consumer-driven world. You may not feel you are particularly engaged with the missional conversation. You may find yourself confused by the many varieties of ethnic cultural groups who form a significant part of the fabric of most British cities, and it probably feels like an impossible task to understand the outlooks of these diverse cultural groups. Some of them consist of first-generation migrants from a variety of cultures that are very different from Western ones. You might be a leader of a first- or second-generation ethnic church and your outlook on multicultural society may be, 'What an opportunity – there are so many people from different races and cultures with whom we can share the gospel.' You may already be very engaged in the conversation, asking questions like, 'How can we reach the people who live near our local church with the message of Jesus?'

Part of becoming aware of the various missional conversations that different ethnic churches are holding will be taking time to meet with them. The popular writer J. D. Payne begins his book *Strangers Next Door: Immigration, Migration and Mission*, by pointing out that many

Western Christians have no idea of the scale of the numbers of migrants arriving to live among us, and are even less likely to have thought about trying to meet with them for missional purposes:

> It is my desire to educate the Western church on the scope of global migrations that are taking place as the peoples of the world move to the West in search of a better way of life. At present there are large numbers of believers and unbelievers migrating to Western nations, much of the Western church is fairly ignorant as to the numbers, cultures, and beliefs of such peoples.[1]

There appears to be a little more awareness among Caucasian Christians of the rapid growth of migrant groups in the UK than in the North American scene. However, it is true that many of the WMCs we know of seem broadly unaware of the rich diversity of the large range of migrant Christian groups in the UK, and of the many struggles they face as they seek to establish themselves in the West. It is our hope, as you read this book, that you will be stimulated to get to know some of these migrant Christian groups better, as well as be encouraged to help them to be involved in the missional conversation. The key question for this conversation is, 'How can we join together to bring the gospel back to the centre of Western society?'

However, what has been written so far begs the question, 'Is there a missional conversation for our different ethnic church groups to have?' In the first place, there are forums where the missional conversation is taking place. One of these relates to the organisation Fresh Expressions, which began as an Anglican–Methodist emerging church initiative and now includes many other denominations. Inner-city church leader Michael Moynagh and Professor Philip Harrold from Trinity School of Ministry comment about the beginnings of the emerging church movement, to which Fresh Expressions has added its voice:

---

[1]. J. D. Payne, *Strangers Next Door: Immigration, Migration and Mission* (Downers Grove, IVP, 2012), p.18.

Originating in the United States, [it] consists of a smorgasbord of groups and individuals who want to find what they consider to be more authentic ways to live the Christian faith. Found mainly among the Gen X and Y generations, participants in the emerging church conversation seek to connect with popular culture, postmodern practice and philosophy, and reflect a widespread disenchantment with evangelicalism. The conversation, in which 'emergent' is a prominent sub-group, comprises 'a network of networks and has an extensive presence online and in print.'[2]

Fresh Expressions is involved in experiments and dialogues to discover effective methods to share the gospel with postmodern people who do not respond well to traditional churches. Emerging church conversations are also happening with some BMCs and Neo-Pentecostal Churches (NPCs). The questions addressed here have to do with their longer-term sustainability and their desire to take the gospel beyond their own people groups to native Westerners. In this respect, Moynagh argues that culture-specific churches (homogenous) are legitimate in a multicultural environment, just as much as multi-ethnic churches (heterogeneous) are, because people of a particular ethnic group may be best reached by people from their own group. Some second and third generation migrant believers prefer multi-ethnic churches, which represent the multicultural diversity they have become used to in places like the UK. Moynagh suggests an interesting approach for churches to consider in order to participate in the multicultural missional conversation (although he does not use the term 'multicultural'):

Culturally focused [specific] churches ... [meet] together as 'the whole church' (1 Cor. 14:23) from time to time.
New contextual churches follow this model when they focus on a specific culture but also connect up. Both should be seen as equally important. Homogeneity and heterogeneity can then be held together – for instance:

---

[2] Michael Moynagh and Philip Harrold, *Church for Every Context: A Theology for Every Practice* (London, SCM Press, 2013), p.xi.

- A local church might give birth to several culturally different congregations (perhaps mid-sized communities). The congregations would cluster together from time to time.
- Culturally distinct contextual churches might join with other churches in their locality to collaborate on mission and discipleship.
- Contextual churches from different backgrounds might come together in activities organized by a national network sharing a common spiritual tradition.
- Individuals might attend more than one 'local' church.[3]

Moynagh partly recognises the need for liaison between congregations when more than one ethnic group is part of a church-planting venture, or when congregations are part of one national network. When we speak of joining the multicultural missional conversation, we want to argue for something far broader. The need for missional conversations is assumed readily enough by other organisations as well as Fresh Expressions. These include The Gospel and Our Culture Network in the USA and in the UK; Together in Mission (TiM) in Birmingham; The Church Planting Forum which is hosted by TiM, which national church-planting leaders attend to share new ideas and good practice.

The North American missiologist Kathleen Garces-Foley adds her voice by making the case for the church to move its missional conversation towards a multi-ethnic/multicultural focus:

> Depending on how we assess the current climate, multi-ethnic churches are either the natural fruition of a general trend toward a more racially tolerant society or a progressive social force breaking new ground in forming racially inclusive public spaces. Churches are either catching up with a progressive, tolerant society, or they are a countercultural

---

[3] Moynagh and Harrold, *Church for Every Context*, p.171.

force challenging entrenched social patterns of ethnic divisions.[4]

She argues for multicultural churches as part of a necessary breakthrough in order to catch up with secular culture, which is ahead of the church in engaging with the broader multicultural society and is already seeking to break down cultural boundaries. We argue that the church should take inspiration from this eventuality because of the nature of the gospel of the kingdom, which seeks to unite all nations and cultures in Christ. Hence this chapter will set the scene for the rest of this book. It regards the need for different ethnic groups (including English churches as an ethnic group) to join with others in multicultural missional conversations. Following on from this, we will argue for these conversations to lead to cross-cultural partnerships between different ethnic Christian groups that are now living in the West. Such partnerships require us to consider planting multi-ethnic breakthrough congregations that will model the unifying power of the kingdom of God to our secular culture.

We realise that a few multi-ethnic churches already exist in the UK, which consist of people from diverse ethnic groups. This book calls us to think through how we might join together across ethnic and cultural boundaries to share in God's mission to reconcile all peoples of the earth under our one Lord. It is clear that the multicultural situation in the UK and in other Western countries requires us to explore how additional cosmopolitan fellowships may be formed.

There are many different kinds of beliefs and religious persuasions in the West. These make up the rich tapestry of what is technically termed 'pluralism'. So, 'How can we unite to bring the gospel back to the secular West, in the context of multiculturalism and religious and non-religious pluralism?' We need to be very clear in our thinking in this regard.

The church and/or the denomination you belong to may generally be made up of a majority ethnic group with a clear cultural identity. This means that most of those with you are from the same ethnic and cultural background as you are. Each category attracts people from its

---

[4] Kathleen Garces-Foley, *Crossing the Ethnic Divide: The Multiethnic Church on a Mission* (Oxford, Oxford University Press, 2007), p.11.

own culture or ethnicity. The questions that form the missional conversation start with the need for Christians to become aware of the range and variety of Christian ethnic groups living among us. Many of these groups aspire to bring the gospel back to Britain, Europe and North America. These ethnic churches are often made up of first generation migrants who have come from former British colonies to live in the UK, and who once received the gospel from the French, Spanish, Portuguese, Dutch, etc. They come to the West in order to bring the gospel back to Europe.[5] Some have called these ethnic evangelists 'reverse missionaries'.[6] It has also been spoken of as 'Mission in Reverse.' So let's start from here.

How can all of us, regardless of our ethnic persuasions, join together to bring the gospel back to the West by working more intentionally together? Because the term 'reverse mission' is technically related to people from the former colonies bringing the gospel back to the West, it may be better to just use the term 'mission' or 'missional', as native Western Christians also want to bring the gospel back to the centre of secular society. The term 'reverse mission' will be used strategically from time to time, but the word 'missional' is preferred for any attempt made jointly by ethnic and home-grown churches who want to join forces to convert Westerners.

The range of potential missionary congregations

There are numerous migrant Christians in the UK today. The *Mail Online* journalist Hugo Gye wrote an article with the header, '"British whites" are the minority for the first time as census shows number of UK immigrants has jumped by 3 million in 10 years'. It says:

- 'Just 44.9% of Londoners are White British, according to census data

---

[5] Israel Olofinjana, *Reverse in Ministry & Missions: Africans in the Dark Continent of Europe – An Historical Study of African Churches in Europe* (Milton Keynes, Author House, 2010), Chapter 3.

[6] Jonathan Bonk, *The Routledge Encyclopedia of Missions and Missionaries* (London, Routledge, 2010), p.380.

- 7.5million residents of England and Wales were foreign-born in 2011

- Census data reveal just 59% now call themselves Christian as a quarter say they have no religion and 5% are Muslim

- Less than 90% of the country is white for the first time ever

- Home ownership declines but more people have paid off their mortgages

- Marriage rate dips to record low as fewer than half are hitched'[7]

How can we work together to bring Jesus Christ back to the centre of this diverse multicultural society? The word 'diverse' expresses the creative opportunities that Christian groups have to take the message of Jesus to people of their own ethnicity who live in the West, or to the mixed race people of this society, including native Western people.

Statistics taken from the 2011 Census for the United Kingdom has 59.5% of the population considering themselves to be Christian.[8] It depends, of course, on how we define a Christian. However, taken at face value, this means that out of the population of 63,182,178 people in the UK in 2011, 37,583,962 people considered themselves to be included in this category. Of course, this survey tells us little about whether these people were practising Christians. The British Social Attitudes Survey 2009, which looks at how people classify themselves in terms of religious beliefs and denominational affiliation discovered that:

- 50.7% claimed to have no religion

- 19.9% considered themselves to be part of the Church of England

- 8.6% were Roman Catholic

---

[7] Hugo Gye, '"British whites" are the minority for the first time as census shows number of UK immigrants has jumped by 3 million in 10 years', 11 December 2012. Available at http://www.dailymail.co.uk/news/article-2246288/Census-2011-UK-immigrant-population-jumps-THREE-MILLION-10-years.html#ixzz2sefOvQap (accessed 12th August 2014).
[8] Office of National Statistics, 2011 Census for England and Wales. Available at http://www.ons.gov.uk/ons/guide-method/census/2011/index.html (accessed 12th August 2014).

- 2.2% were Presbyterian/Church of Scotland

- 1.3% were Methodist

- 1.2% were other Protestant

- 9.3% were Christian (no denomination)

- 0.4% were other Christian

- 2.4% were Muslim

- 0.9% were Hindu

- 0.8% were Sikh

- 0.4% were Jewish

- 0.3% professed to follow another religions

- 0.4% refused to take part[9]

None of these statistics indicates Christian distribution within different ethnic groups in the UK. However, more helpfully, the UK 2001 Census indicated the percentage of people in various ethnic populations in the UK who claimed to be Christians:

- 75.94% of white English, out of 100% of the total population of whites

- 85.42% of white Irish

- 62.67% of other white

- 52.46% of mixed

- 4.98% of Indian

- 1.09% of Pakistani

- 0.5% of Bangladeshi

- 13.42% of other Asian

- 73.76% of black Caribbean

- 68.87% of black African

[9] UK Data Service, 'British Social Attitudes Survey, 2009'. Available at http://discover.ukdataservice.ac.uk/catalogue?sn=6695 (accessed 12th August 2014).

- 66.61% of other black

- 25.56% of Chinese

- 32.98% of other racial groups also called themselves Christian[10]

The sociologist Anthony Giddens refers to the UK's 2001 Census of ethnic groups in England and Wales:

> The 2001 Census ... showed that people from the non-white ethnic groups had a younger age structure than the white population in the UK. The 'Mixed' group were the youngest, with half under the age of 16. 'Bangladeshi', 'Other Black' and 'Pakistani' groups also had young age structures, with more than a third of each of those groups being under the age of 16.[11]

One third of migrants are 16 years of age or under, and bring with them a deficit of age and life experience when they first come to Britain. It is quite possible that they will adapt much more quickly to life in the West because they have more time to receive a Western education, which their parents may find harder because of the need to earn a living. The good news is that these younger people will be more open to new ideas about cross-cultural mission than their parents will have time to try to understand.

What is encouraging is the high ratio of people identifying with the Christian faith in Britain, even though many of those taking part in the 2011 Census did not attend church regularly at the time of the research. It could be said that there is a lot of goodwill towards the Christian faith among many of the ethnic groups represented in this brief survey, with the highest number of those calling themselves Christians being white British, at 59%. However, it is also important to recognise that Afro-Caribbeans, black Africans, other blacks and Chinese ethnic groups in the UK have the highest ratios of Christians among them compared to smaller ethnic groups, according to the 2001 survey. It is encouraging that some ethnic Christian groups have a powerful desire to bring the gospel back to the West. For example, in a

---

10 Office of National Statistics, 2001 Census data.
11 Anthony Giddens and Anthony Sutton, *Sociology* (Cambridge, Polity, 2012), p.647.

recent piece of research we conducted, rapid growth among BMCs demonstrates that they have a strong aspiration to bring the Christian faith back to the secularised West.

Having said this, most BMCs are not multi-ethnic congregations, but are normally made up of one national group such as Nigerians or Kenyans. These groups often have a desire to share the gospel with other ethnicities in the UK's multicultural landscape, but as yet they generally have not been able to do this. The challenges facing BMCs will be discussed in a later chapter. At this stage it is enough to note the broad desire they have to share the gospel with anyone who is receptive to it. In reality, it is hard for BMCs to make significant breakthroughs among native white, Western people. It is also important to note that church growth for BMCs has normally been the result of a gathering together of people from a single group who have migrated to the West. Churches are planted for those who come from a particular home nation. Hence we find that many BMCs are thought of as Nigerian, or Kenyan or Ghanaian, and so on. They are considered to be diaspora communities, seeking to support those who come to the UK through migration, or for those who seek asylum. Generally speaking, therefore, church growth among BMCs is not highly missional in a multicultural sense of the word, as they are not multicultural congregations made up of converts from other ethnic groups. An important question to explore concerns how we might help each other form multi-ethnic, missional congregations.

Is it possible to plant multi-ethnic congregations?

Globalisation is a powerful force which has provided the means of travel and the opening of borders, and these in turn have further encouraged international migration to take place, particularly within the last 50 years. In the 1960s, the British government encouraged Caribbean people to migrate to the UK to do a variety of jobs. Subsequently, the 1970s witnessed large numbers coming from Uganda as well as India and Pakistan. The 1980s saw an increase of asylum seekers coming to the UK. These increases were largely a result of deliberate policies which partly found their political rationale with the British government seeking to honour colonial and imperial legacies. Moreover, ethnic mixing of global populations has increased as Western economies have become more affluent and non-Westerners have sought to come to seek better standards of living. Giddens considers it a foregone conclusion that this multicultural mixing of peoples is 'sure to intensify in years to come'.[12]

The biggest question facing the UK has to do with the accommodation of diverse ethnic groups into British society in order to overcome the possibilities of ethnic conflict. How can accommodation and mutual understanding be achieved to overcome conflicts caused by significantly different ideological outlooks on the world? We all face potential racial and cultural tensions because of these differences.

Giddens recognises three possible ways that such tensions can be overcome in the longer term. The first of these has to do with assimilation, as immigrants slowly abandon their original customs and practices and take on the values and norms of the majority Western culture. The second possibility is that rather than immigrant traditions being jettisoned by migrants, they become part of a melting pot, where their traditions are blended as part of a new evolving culture which will change the current Western culture into something else. Thirdly, and the possibility that leaders of ethnic groups most often argue for, is that of 'cultural pluralism'. In this case, each ethnic group is given 'full validity to exist separately, yet they can still participate in the larger society's economic and political life'.[13] The broad outgrowth of pluralism is 'multiculturalism which refers to policies that encourage cultural or ethnic groups to live in harmony with each other'.[14] And this is where it will be very useful for Christian ethnic groups to engage in the missional conversation together. How can we help imagine into being a more unified cross-cultural way of living together?

We will be making the case in the next chapter that different varieties of Christian ethnic groups in our society need to seek to unite more intentionally in cross-cultural conversations. The argument will

---

[12] Giddens and Sutton, *Sociology*, p.643.

[13] Giddens and Sutton, *Sociology*, pp.643-644.

[14] Giddens and Sutton, *Sociology*, p.644.

be framed around the gospel that unites all ethnicities and cultures so that the people of God might together imagine a new countercultural Christian society into being. However, this idea may be seriously challenged, based on some important findings that missional thinkers have identified for us to consider first.

Donald McGavran established strong evidence that people from the same ethnic-cultural group tend to more successfully win converts from their own people than missionaries from a significantly different culture to their own.[15] This principle is known as the homogenous unit principle.[16] It is interesting to note that during the long period of colonisation of Africa during the sixteenth to early twentieth centuries, only about 4% of African people came to embrace the Christian faith. Indeed, David Livingstone argued early on that converts from the same people group needed to win their own people to Christ, rather than white missionaries trying to do it. But the 4% won for Christ in Africa came to be overshadowed by the huge growth in Christian conversions in Africa during the twentieth and early twenty-first centuries.

When Pentecostalism came to birth in Azusa Street in Los Angeles in 1906, a worldwide movement of the Holy Spirit was soon to follow. By the 1970s, Nigeria witnessed Nigerian Christian leaders begin the African Initiated Church (AIC) movement.[17] Part of AIC mission policy was for blacks to evangelise other black people, rather than non-African missionaries doing so.[18] The massive Christian growth that has occurred among Pentecostals since this time is estimated to be between 400 million and 624 million. This makes Pentecostalism the fastest growing form of Christianity in the world today.[19] It bears testament to the power of the Holy Spirit as He has worked through leaders in Africa, Asia and South America to bring many millions to faith. Some missional thinkers believe that the homogenous unit principle is the

---

[15] Moynagh and Harrold, *Church for Every Context*, p.168.

[16] Moynagh and Harrold, *Church for Every Context*, p.168.

[17] Abraham Akrong, *Deconstructing Colonial Mission – New Missiological Perspectives in African Christianity*, in Adogame, A., Gerloff, R. and Hock, K. (eds.), *Christianity in Africa and the African Diaspora* (London, Continuum, 2008), p.68.

[18] Akrong, *Deconstructing Colonial Mission*, pp.67-68.

[19] Bonk, *The Routledge Encyclopedia of Missions and Missionaries*, p.332.

best way for people to be brought to faith in the first place, because it has a proven track record of success compared to other approaches. If they are right, what hope is there for those of us in the multicultural West to join together in missional conversations so that we can do mission enterprises together?

There is cause for hope. The brother-in-law of one of our colleagues at Springdale College is part of a mid-sized multi-ethnic church, made up of blacks and whites who worship together. Garces-Foley, an expert in multi-ethnic missional churches in the US, has established the principle that a church may be deemed to be multi-ethnic when at least 10% of its worshippers are from another single ethnic group.[20] Until a smaller minority reaches the 10% threshold it is much harder for others of that minority to join. She shares some very interesting case studies of a number of multi-ethnic churches that are made up of white, black, Hispanic and Asian people joining together to worship and fellowship in the US multicultural context.[21] She does not airbrush out the challenges that this causes for multi-ethnic churches, but notes that it is difficult to model the unity of the kingdom of God when significant cultural differences exist within these churches.[22]

Garces-Foley confirms that some of the multi-ethnic churches in her study feel it is worth the discomfort that their differences cause at first, as when they get beyond the pain threshold caused by their differences, people start to find it easier to celebrate their differences.[23] We would argue that it is pre-eminently worthwhile to find ways to fellowship and worship together cross culturally, in order for multicultural learning to take place. Learning will be enabled as we converse about our differences and seek ways to build bridges. By engaging in conversations about our differences we can develop strategies to overcome them, and learn to appreciate the good things that our differences can equip us to do much better together, rather than alone in our monocultural congregations. And it is important to note that people in the UK who have given up on worshipping with Christians from their own Western native culture are hardly likely to

---

[20] Garces-Foley, *Crossing the Ethnic Divide*, pp.22-24.
[21] Garces-Foley, *Crossing the Ethnic Divide*, Chapter 1.
[22] Garces-Foley, *Crossing the Ethnic Divide*, Introduction.
[23] Garces-Foley, *Crossing the Ethnic Divide*, Introduction and Chapter 1.

try to worship in an ethnic church. This means that a lot of white people are trying to find other ways of exploring faith outside Western churches, because they find that going to these churches is not attractive and feel that they are profoundly out of step with the challenges they face in their everyday lives. It must also be noted that if Western churches cannot attract such postmodern people who come from their own type of culture, it will potentially prove much harder for first or second generation migrant churches to engage in mission with native Westerners.

A useful piece of work that can help us to understand how many people actually express their faith by going to church in the UK is provided by Stoddard and Cuthbert. It must be remembered that their figures also include the ethnic Christian churches that make up a percentage of the statistics for church attendance in the UK. Their record, which is broadly accepted by experts in the field of church growth, highlights that:

- 10% of the UK's population attend church regularly (ie at least once a month)

- 10% attend church occasionally

- 20% left church for negative reasons

- 20% drifted away from church and no one followed them up when they stopped attending

- 40% have never been to church[24]

It seems fair to assume that a significant proportion of native white people are living their faith outside of churches in the UK. This assumption is made because up to 70% still identify themselves culturally as Christians, according to another official survey.[25] There is a need for some real strategic thinking to see how groups like those who have drifted away from churches can be helped to meaningfully

[24] Chris Stoddard, and Nick Cuthbert, *Church on the Edge: Principles and real life stories of 21st century mission* (Milton Keynes, Authentic, 2006), p.30.
[25] Steve Doughty, 'The make-up of modern Britain: 70% of us claim to be Christians... and only 1.5% are gay', 29th September 2011. Available at http://www.dailymail.co.uk/news/article-2043045/Modern-Britain-70-claim-Christians-1-5-gay.html (accessed 12th August 2014).

reconnect with Christian communities (ie churches and smaller missional communities).

An important political and sociological debate that is taking place has to do with the significance of faith to life in the secular public square.[26] This makes thinking through the multicultural missional conversation, as part of this debate, a critical question to reflect on so that we can provide a significant input into the whole debate. Alan Roxburgh challenges Christians to think through how we can re-enter our neighbourhoods in the context of postmodernism, and, for that matter, multiculturalism:

> The [Holy] Spirit is breaking apart a form of church that took shape in the Protestant West from the sixteenth century forward ... God is on the move. The kingdom is so much bigger than our little, tribal cultural enclaves, and the world is in crisis. The Lord of creation is out there ahead of us; he has left the temple and is calling the church to follow in a risky path leaving behind its baggage, becoming like the stranger in need, and receiving hospitality from the very ones we assume are the candidates of our evangelism plans. Luke's [the gospel writer] re-theologizing would say that the only way we can understand and practice again this kingdom message is by getting out of our churches and re-entering our neighbourhoods and communities. This is where we will discern God's future, not in our vision and mission statements or the arrogant need to start a movement in our own image. This is a time for a radical shift in the imagination and practices of our once dominant Euro-tribal churches.[27]

It is still very early in the emerging multicultural missional conversation for us to know how we can work better cross-culturally in order to conceive of how to re-enter our neighbourhoods. One thing seems certain from our experience of working alongside ethnic leaders: many have a passion to bring the gospel back to the West. It is

---

[26] Brunner Verlag, *Religion in the Public Sphere I* (Switzerland, Forum Mission, 2012), pp.253-264.
[27] Alan Roxburgh, *Missional Joining God in the Neighbourhood* (Grand Rapids, Baker Publishing Group, 2011), p.162.

important to be realistic about how quickly different ethnic groups can be mobilised to share their faith successfully with the majority secular, postmodern population. Perhaps a first step might be to consider how to share the gospel with less dissimilar ethnic cultures among other groups in the West, coming as they do from Hindu, Sikh, Buddhist, Muslim and other backgrounds. It has to be worthwhile for us to at least join together in conversations to seek what God is saying to us as His multicultural people about the mission opportunities that are open to us at present. Moreover, as we start to understand each other's challenges, we can hopefully start to imagine new ways to resource missionary congregations that working together may provide. We may also be able to start to work through our differences, and hopefully this process will help us to understand how to work cross-culturally with others who are not Christians as yet. Ultimately, it is hoped that some multi-ethnic breakthrough congregations may be planted, which will practically display to others the unifying power of the gospel of Christ.

It is not our intention to give the impression that we believe we should all disband our ethnic churches and seek to manipulate multi-ethnic churches into being. Rather, we would argue that it is worthwhile getting to know each other better, at events such as multicultural church-planting conferences or through more formal initiatives like local Churches Together in order to seek how we can join with the missionary God's desire for His kingdom to be realised as a united people who serve one Lord.[28] It will still be quite appropriate for one particular people group to plant a congregation for the people they belong to. We are not arguing for a one-size-fits-all solution. However, it will be important for us to explore together ways of planting at least some multi-ethnic churches so that we can help our society to become more accepting of multiculturalism.

There is no simple definition of the missional challenges we face in our complex multicultural and pluralistic society. But it has to be worth joining in conversations together to see how we can build bridges that can help us get to know each other better. At the heart of our argument is the big, ideal picture of the kingdom of God that

---

[28] See Revelation 7.

would have all people united by God's love. This is the goal of history which will be finally realised when Christ comes again. In the meantime, there are no perfect solutions to sharing the gospel within multicultural societies, which implies that a variety of methods will need to be utilised in order to witness to different peoples. One of those argued for in this book is the planting of multi-ethnic breakthrough congregations. Equally important will be the formation of closer ties between various Ethnic Churches (ECs) so that we can support each other better. Shared resources which come from our cross-cultural backgrounds will surely bring strength to our joint missional endeavours, whether they be formal or informal in nature.

Engagement in community life

One important blind spot that many Western Christians appear to have lost sight of is that the dominant narrative of individualism not only influences our outlook on people who no longer go to church, but it has also blinded many of us to our own deficiencies as Christian communities. Arguably, individualism has led to the disintegration of the sense of fellowship and shared community life in our Western churches. Many of our ethnic brothers and sisters still have higher values regarding the importance of shared community life, which is an important reminder for us of what our culture has done to the sense of fellowship in our churches. Individualism acting as an important influence on Western Christians can tend to make people attend church in order to have their individual needs met, rather than seeking to foster a deeper sense of shared fellowship. One excuse for not spending much time in fellowship concerns the time cost which our highly stressed Western lives impose upon us. The main Sunday worship service and the tea and biscuits that often follow it are essentially what many Westerners may consider to be fellowship. Of course, many congregations now have regular small group meetings which, encouragingly, have helped deepen the desire of Western Christians to fellowship together.

We would suggest that small group meetings are a benefit of postmodernity. Postmodern culture prefers small and intimate to large and anonymous. The missiologist Alan Roxburgh suggests that we find it hard enough to have time for our families, let alone to think about following 'the Lord of creation who is out there ahead of us',[29] working in our neighbourhoods and seeking to reconcile people to Himself. Indeed, the use of the term 'Himself' assumes an individualistic vision of God's nature, when in fact the dogma of the Trinity is suggestive that God forms people as part of His family – the Christian community (see chapter 2). It seems that too often individuals in larger churches do not know other people in their congregations very well, let alone those they live next door to. There can be a superficial sense of community in congregations where members are more like acquaintances than brothers and sisters. And this is where our multi-ethnic brothers and sisters can helpfully challenge our cultural reserve, prompting us to go deeper in our relationships with each other, and also maybe with others outside of our cultural comfort zones. However, we are not minimising the impact of secular Western life on Western or migrant peoples.

We have noticed a far deeper sense of shared community life among many of the ethnic churches we have visited. This is not to say they are perfect communities. We all have limitations that our cultural perspectives cause us to adopt, mostly unconsciously. But seeking to form friendships with our ethnic brothers and sisters can offer Western churches the opportunity to serve a kind of apprenticeship to learn how to develop deeper fellowship once more in our churches. Some ethnic churches speak about the church as a family, and they also live that out in terms of how they support each other, particularly during times of need. Shared deep fellowship is the huge strength that our ethnic brothers and sisters bring to the missional conversation in the multicultural West.

Having said this, the tendency of first generation migrant churches is to be monocultural. The breakthrough will need to be made where the value of deeper community fellowship can lead to the formation over time of multi-ethnic missional congregations who become united as forums that encourage deeper expressions of fellowship. At present, one of the missional conversations orbits around the question, 'How can we represent the all-inclusive kingdom of God by planting and

---

[29] Roxburgh, *Missional Joining God in the Neighbourhood*, p.162.

developing churches made up of diverse ethnicities and cultures who share in fellowship together?'

A friend of ours who belongs to a third generation Afro-Caribbean church that was planted in the 1960s has observed upon reading this chapter that her church has lost much of its original first generation sense of shared fellowship. In other words, the power of our individualistic secular culture is persuasive in its intrinsic propaganda of 'me first', which infects postmodern hyper-individualism. The drive to achieve things as an individual, and to push past others in order to get ahead, has changed the way the second and third generations of the Afro-Caribbean church value community in many cases. Obviously this is one view among many. However, we know of at least 20 Afro-Caribbean churches where this trend seems evident. Our friend also shared her fear that, having grown up in Britain in the 1970s and 1980s, this loss of community spirit could also become the experience of first generation migrant congregations in the future. Given that many secular postmodern 20- to 40-somethings are joining together in small friendship groups, called 'new tribes' by sociologists,[30] there seems to be an opportunity for migrant churches to seek to enter some of these small communities because they value the kinds of deeper fellowship these 'tribes' want to experience together.

This 'tribal' phenomenon is an important one for us to pause and think about. In the earlier part of the twentieth century there was a phenomenon which sociologists called 'fordism'. Fordism relates to Henry Ford's great consumer-driven need to supply as many people as possible in America with black Ford cars. It is the black cars and their mass production which is of interest here, as Ford's marketing strategy assumed that getting as many cars out there as possible that looked exactly the same was more important than providing a variety of colours and designs for consumers to purchase. Fordism was largely a product of Western culture prior to the 1950s and 1960s. It acts as a metaphor to sociologists for the modern people of the period who largely still conformed to social structures which made them think of themselves as essentially all the same. People outside their own culture were thought to be in need of becoming like them. Western

---

[30] Giddens and Sutton, *Sociology*, p.698.

modern culture was the real authentic progressive culture which people outside of it needed to become like.

However, things changed with what sociologists term 'post-fordism'. Post-fordite culture exploded into life during the 1960s, especially in the West. As time has gone on, our consumerist economies have had to catch up with the desires of postmodern people for niche products. It is no longer acceptable to clone people to accept one kind of product such as Ford did. Postmodern people see the world as a place full of colour and variety. Part of this post-fordite culture is also that people reject the notion that everyone is the same and should conform to a few nationally established ways of identifying themselves. There is suspicion of single products because they are likely to be of poor quality unless other products challenge the market to develop better products.

The 'new tribes' phenomenon has arisen in part out of post-fordism. People prefer to get together in smaller niche-like groups to explore life with those who value what their tribe stands for. There is suspicion of large corporate bodies, such as churches, that claim to have 'the product of belief' into which everyone should buy. Post-fordite new tribes want permission to develop their own beliefs, which normally come from a collection of different belief systems. This demonstrates why corporate bodies of believers and their denominations are not attractive to new tribes.

The emerging church conversation is challenging institutional churches to buck this trend by encouraging their members to become more like small tribes by meeting in smaller communities to form their spiritual identities. Emerging church planters do not want people to lose their Christian faith, but neither do they want people to lose key values that encourage Christian community participants to shape their own beliefs and practices around core Biblical beliefs they reflect on together. Moreover, they often desire that these smaller missional communities encourage people to participate in sharing the real struggles that life throws at them in the time they spend in community together. This kind of missional community is much more demanding on participants because they share private matters with each other in order to support one another better than traditional churches do. This kind of approach to missional church is proving effective with

35

postmodern seekers who value these emerging kinds of tribal churches.

During the late 1990s and early 2000s, Dan worked as the small church officer for the British Church Growth Association. In this ministry, he worked with many smaller churches from a wide variety of denominations and traditions across the UK and in other parts of the world to explore what value there could be for small churches to become missional communities. Through training events, conferences and the development of resources and input, many smaller churches began to re-envision themselves for their communities. This provided a subversive reading of church that enabled many congregations and denominations to reconsider the important contribution that was being made by these faithful expressions of the kingdom.[31] This work, in a somewhat limited way, began to anticipate the importance of smaller gatherings for new expressions of mission in the Western world. And let us not forget that postmodern, secular people are often seeking spiritual experiences to bring meaning to their lives, although mostly they are not going to churches to find answers to their questions. If charismatic ethnic second and third generation churches can find ways to share their Pentecostal spirit-sensitivity with such groups, this could be one important contribution to the mission strategy of bringing the gospel back to these Euro 'tribes' who value authentic experiences expressed in an appropriate contextualised manner with them. Having said this, there are important challenges that need to be overcome for this to happen, because of significant cultural differences that exist between migrant Christian cultures and the postmodern culture. We will consider some of these challenges in a later chapter.

John Drane has done much to help us understand how changes in society since the 1960s have led to a massive downturn in church attendance, with the majority of native white Westerners no longer supporting Christian churches because postmodern people are not looking to formalised religious practices to explore their spirituality. Interestingly, it was probably the failure of denominations in the 1950s

---

[31] Martin Robinson and Dan Yarnell, *Celebrating the Small Church* (London, Monarch, 1993), Chapter 10.

and 1960s to engage with the deep spiritual questions raised by the young people of the 1960s, and the decades following that, that led to this decline. Generation X were born from parents from the Boomer Generation, in the period 1964 to 1981. The generation that came next is known as Generation Y – made up of offspring born in 2000 onwards. This millennial generation has little or no interest in the institutional church.

The opportunity is to learn from each other, as the diverse family of God, how to become more united in our efforts to reach the people of this postmodern culture. Westerners can obtain important insights from the spiritual affinities to which non-Western cultures naturally relate, which in some ways feel very much like what postmodern people are coming to deeply value. Smaller emerging churches and missional communities, who share life together at a deeper level outside of the Sunday worship hour, will be ideal forums for postmodern seekers to loosely join in with – that is, of course, if these communities are sensitive to the kinds of questions these 'new tribes' are asking.

Moreover, we need to think much more about work-related mission in the context of postmodern life. For instance, there have been important developments of vocational Christian networks for those who work for secular companies and are in need of support for their Christian contribution to the jobs they do. These are organisations which help Christian business people to meet locally and to receive important insights from their peers in business. This is what the Christian organisation Business Matters has to say:

> We are a charitable trust set up in 2006 by a group of Christian businessmen and women who want to be of service to their neighbours in the world of work. The Trustees include two lawyers, an accountant, two IT consultants, a financial analyst and an energy consultant. They want to serve their neighbours in the workplace, but because they hold down demanding jobs and cannot make themselves

available as they would like, they have appointed a staff team.[32]

It is encouraging that different organisations like this offer their support to Christian business people. The well-known Alpha course has also developed a workplace offering:

> Alpha in the Workplace began as a one-off Alpha course run in a boardroom in Canada and soon became a model used in other companies around the world. It works extremely well for the same reason that Alpha works in churches – people find community amongst their peers in the middle of their working day. Many Alpha in the Workplace guests comment that it is a privilege to be able to take time to look at the spiritual side of life during their working week.[33]

It is these kinds of creative approaches that are required in the new postmodern secular world. People have far less time to go to things outside of work, but it is possible to be creative about support networks or direct evangelistic tools which could meet the needs of people in the middle of their busy lives. What is required of Christians is to actively listen more carefully to what the Spirit is revealing about the way people today live their lives. We need to go out to people where they are, and this means we need to discern where God wants us to go.

And it is vital that we remind ourselves that the extent to which people in the church have a living spiritual connection with the missionary God will provide the means to pick up on the vibrations of His Spirit at work among people in postmodern workplaces and neighbourhoods. The institutional church and its buildings have a place, but postmodern people tend to appreciate sharing life more organically in smaller groups that enable them to freely and openly seek answers to their questions together, however unorthodox they

---

[32] Business Matters. See http://www.businessmattersedinburgh.com/about (accessed 13th August 2014).
[33] http://www.transformworkuk.org/Groups/208894/Transform_Work_UK/Resources/ Alpha_in_the/Alpha_in_the.aspx (accessed 6th November 2014).

may seem to be to those outside of their communities. Drane comments:

> Many people have come to believe that whatever spiritual reality the churches may once have had, it has been siphoned off or suppressed in the interests of the ecclesiastical power structures, and that the professional clergy are so concerned with keeping the machinery going and maintaining their own vested interests in control and position that they too have lost touch with any kind of movement of the spirit. Even those who are sympathetic to the Church are no longer able to deny the reality of such opinions.[34]

It is important to note that the spiritual questing of people today does not often find them going to Christian churches to find answers. It is true that the decline in church attendance has now bottomed out, with somewhere between 8% and 10% of the UK population attending church. This halt in decline is largely due to the rapid growth of ethnic churches. Secular people seem to be seeking meaning to their lives through alternative kinds of spirituality. Interestingly enough, those looking to New Age forms of spirituality or other Eastern forms of mysticism are exploring a large variety of experiences on offer. Moreover, it is not just physical venues where these 'new tribes' group gather. It happens through blogs, Facebook and Twitter as much as in pubs or coffee shops.

Ethan Watters, a popular journalist for publications like *Glamour* and *The New York Times Magazine*, talks of what he calls 'Urban Tribes'.[35] He asks, 'Are friends the new family?' He makes the case that many 20- to 30-somethings in the West tend to form tribe-like friendship groups, where the value of being together in a small community with those who share similar aspirations is highly valued. They desire to be free from formal governing hierarchies. Exploration of everything that interests their members is the adventurous ideal for

---

[34] John Drane, *Do Christians Know How to be Spiritual? The Rise of New Spirituality, and the Mission of the Church* (London, Darton Longman and Todd, 2005), p.13.
[35] Ethan Watters, *Urban Tribes: Are Friends the New Family?*(Edinburgh, Bloomsbury, 2003), Chapter 1.

participants to pursue. He comments on the freedoms he himself valued during his tribal community phase of life:

> Our freedom from strict life advice has a corollary: We were freer of the consequences of our actions than other generations. Our elders couldn't punish us for ignoring advice that had never been given in the first place. Of course, we weren't free from all consequences, contracting AIDS and being hit by a bus among them ... But in general there seemed plenty of forgiveness for mistakes – plenty of time to make everything right. We could date the wrong person for years, start one career, quit, go back to school and try another. We had the sense that it could all be undone. We had moved to the city once to create a new adult self. If we wanted, we could move across town or across the country and do it again.[36]

Notice the emphasis he lays on 'the sense that it could all be undone'. An important similarity to Christian gospel-based communities that offer a fresh start for believers is a shared value between us and these 'new tribes'. The perception that Christ can undo the power of sin and its dominance over people's lives means it provides all of us with healing and new beginnings. Nothing need be written that cannot be edited or shredded in the life experiments of these tribal communities. In similar vein, the gospel offers a complete new start to life when a person puts their faith in Jesus Christ. It must not be forgotten that part of that new life means that Christian communities actively seek to develop all of their people to become true followers of Jesus (see chapter 5 on discipleship).

The significance of 'new tribes' has been a source of the modern media culture which has developed TV shows that explore this new reality. The popular US TV show *Friends* has been succeeded by new soaps such as *The Big Bang Theory*, which once again is based around a small tribe of geeks seeking their way in their American context. Small friendship tribes are the new way of being part of community life. These small communities liberate people from the demands of

---

36 Watters, *Urban Tribes*, pp.28-29.

authority figures such as are often found in churches. It is not hard to see that churches do not represent the community values of freedom to explore the horizons of the spiritual world that these informal, relationally based tribes allow and encourage, with the potential to welcome exploration of alternative spiritualities. It feels too regimented to go to church, hear someone talk at you, share a quick cup of tea and a biscuit and then go home. Where is the meaningful community life in this, where deeper life can be shared together? It is important not to assume a predominant caricature to describe church fellowship, or the lack of it.

Community participation for the 'new tribes' phenomenon includes a strong desire for people to go deeper with each other, sharing their lives because they trust each other, which enables their members to buy in deeply to caring for and supporting each other. This tribal category, made up of numerous small groupings of people, practises its own kind of forgiveness for mistakes as well as giving grace and freedom for participants to start over with a clean sheet. It is important to understand how these tribes form their communities by averring loosely held structures, where accountability comes from relationships rather than from a hierarchy and prescriptive moral code.

What these small communities of young adults show us is that the spiritual connections of their participants are probably very similar to what many small emerging Christian churches practise in the way they support their people. We believe that if our different, ethnic, exclusive congregations were to intentionally join in fellowship with smaller missional communities and make up a more multi-ethnic mix, it would become possible to make meaningful connections with some of these new tribes that value multicultural society across ethnicities, as well as the diverse possibilities such groups could offer for new experiences to be explored within them. The huge overemphasis on people primarily getting what they want as individuals out of their churches, so that their needs are met, is really part of secular culture's insidious influence that has caused Christians to adopt rather selfish outlooks. In turn, these tribes do not find this kind of individualism attractive, as one of the throwbacks has to do with a managed kind of church service which provides a worship product, rather than the opportunity to dialogue and learn based on deep friendships.

New tribes value small community life, as secular society no longer provides them with the security of the Christian metanarrative. They find the opportunity to develop their own narratives that bring meaning to them spiritually in their small groups. They are looking for meaning.

Are we ready to join some of their groups to share in the journey with them? If so, we will have to be willing to be open to question our own beliefs much more intentionally.

A shared interest in the missional conversation

What we have been saying so far emphasises the opportunities all readers, from all ethnic Christian backgrounds, have to recapture a sense of shared missional fellowship. If we seek to join in multicultural missional conversations together we may create a deeper shared vision of how to focus our attention outward, so that we can come up with new ways of fellowshipping with postmodern people, as well as with each other. Our churches can become far more sensitive to deeper spiritual intimacy with God, and this in turn will help them to follow God's heart to win others to fellowship with Him. We can join together to bring our diverse gifts into the missional conversation to share as a rich banquet of resources so that we can bring the gospel back to the centre of Western society. The book of Revelation provides a wonderful picture of how all nations and cultures will bring their richness and diversity into the kingdom of God – united as they will be through the one Spirit:

> After this I looked, and there was a great multitude that no one could count, from every nation, from all tribes and peoples and languages, standing before the throne and before the Lamb, robed in white, with palm branches in their hands. They cried out in a loud voice, saying,
> 'Salvation belongs to our God who is seated on the throne, and to the Lamb!'
> And all the angels stood around the throne and around the elders and the four living creatures, and they fell on their faces before the throne and worshipped God, singing,
> 'Amen! Blessing and glory and wisdom

and thanksgiving and honour
and power and might
be to our God for ever and ever! Amen.'
Revelation 7:9-12

This prophetic picture is the climax to what we might assume to be something to which we are already aspiring to unite as kingdom people, as we see more and more people becoming part of God's kingdom. The late Bishop Lesslie Newbigin passionately argued that the mission of God is nothing less than the universal reconciliation of all peoples who have joined together as they worship the one Lord.[37] One of the largest pieces of apologetics we can engage in will be the act of joining together in multicultural expressions of our Christian unity, which will convey a rich creative menu for seeking people to come to be fed by. This is at the heart of the missional conversation, for us together to bring the dream into reality of one family in our Lord Jesus Christ:

> in Christ Jesus you are all children of God through faith. As many of you as were baptized into Christ have clothed yourselves with Christ. There is no longer Jew or Greek, there is no longer slave or free, there is no longer male and female; for all of you are one in Christ Jesus. And if you belong to Christ, then you are Abraham's offspring, heirs according to the promise.
> *Galatians 3:26-29*

Setting an example is often a good way to demonstrate the importance of shared values, in order for us to join together as the people of God in fellowship across ethnic boundaries. One way we can do this together is by our leaders, younger and older, joining in conversations in multi-ethnic strategic planning meetings.

A forum of which we have both valued being part is that provided by our teaching ministries with students who study with Springdale College. The passion that drives our college comes from the larger vision of Together in Mission. Together in Mission is an organisation

---

[37] Lesslie Newbigin, *The Open Secret: An Introduction to the Theology of Mission* (London, SPCK, 1995), pp.64-65.

which has successfully joined Christian leaders from different ethnic backgrounds in conversations with many major church planting groups in the UK, Europe and internationally. Leaders from all kinds of ethnicities who engage in church planting are part of our Church Planting Forum. They are all helping each other to share the larger missional conversation of, 'What will it take for our different ethnic churches to unite in bringing the gospel back to the centre of secular Western society?'

The students on both our undergraduate and postgraduate degree programmes come from at least 25 different ethnic Christian backgrounds. They share in the vision of uniting together as brothers and sisters to bring the gospel back to all who make up the multicultural landscape of our Western society. Our total student body, including those on non-accredited courses, numbers about 200. Our passion is to equip men and women to spiritually discern God's mission, and for them to go out and equip others to win back the West for Christ, including all races, ethnicities and cultural groupings. This is a simple example of how important it is to educate and equip God's people to work together, as one people and one family who already belong to the same kingdom of God.

One of the largest challenges we need to embrace on a multi-ethnic level is to equip younger potential leaders to become agents of change for our churches, as well as in the ways they seek to imagine with God new ways to reach secular and multicultural people groups today.

Having articulated all of this, let's not sugar-coat the very real challenges that this calls the people of God to engage in together. It is much more comfortable for our churches to remain in the safety zone of their particular cultural groupings. It is when we actually start to intentionally get up and build relationships with other ethnic Christian groups that reality will rub up against any idealistic misapprehensions we begin with. Kathleen Garces-Foley brings an important reality check to enthusiasm for the planting of united multi-ethnic churches:

> Like many churches, Greenwood Acres Full Gospel Baptist Church wants to be a multi-ethnic church. This five-thousand member African American church in Shreveport, Louisiana, wants to be a gathering of all tribes and all the nations, as

described in the New Testament Book of Revelation. After joint ministry projects and pulpit-sharing with White churches failed to bring any non-Blacks through his doors, Bishop Fred Caldwell decided to take more drastic measures ... [He commented,] 'Our churches are too segregated, and the Lord never intended for that to happen. It's time for something radical.' ... [During one month] Greenwood Acres [had] 125 White and six Native American visitors ... I imagine this was a very exciting time at Greenwood Acres, culminating in the decision by one White couple to sign the membership book. The euphoria could not have lasted long, however, because this couple quickly faded out of sight, as did the rest of the visitors. One month ... later, Greenwood Acres was still a Black church.[38]

As discouraging as this was for Greenwood Church, Garces-Foley shows how some multi-ethnic churches are succeeding in places like New York to establish cross-cultural fellowships.

The question we may ask ourselves is, 'Why did Greenwood Acres fail to get whites to join them?' Probably the biggest obstacle was the sheer numbers of black faces which white visitors saw when they came. It is our experience that the best environment for people to be able to fellowship together, at first, is in small mission-focused groups in homes, pubs, coffee bars, etc. It is important to start small and to get to know others in groups of no more than about 16 people. When small groups of this size meet together successfully over a number of months, meaningful relationships have a chance to form. As other similar groups grow, the various groups can then meet together for larger celebration services. The danger often is that large congregations can consume the values of smaller fellowships. Both can exist together, but large congregational gatherings require a different kind of leadership than small groups.

Large gatherings require leaders who can provide structures that enable participants to value the time they spend together. This in turn follows the employment of leaders who have the experience, gifts and skills to do this. It is at this point that fellowship can be lost and people

---

[38] Garces-Foley, *Crossing the Ethnic Divide*, pp.3-4.

can lose their sense of meaningful identity because they feel they can do little to contribute to large gatherings of this sort. And here is the downside of large groups compared to smaller ones: small groups allow their members the freedom to contribute to each other's overall growth, whereas this level of contribution is largely lost in sizeable church gatherings.

However, we must not miss the opportunities that large celebration events can provide. If, let us say, 20 different small groups of about 12 members are networked together, and if each group is made up of different ethnicities, for argument's sake, then when these groups join to celebrate and worship together there is a marvellous opportunity to affirm the contributions that each group brings to such events.

We believe it is vital to find creative ways of modelling the unity of larger, multi-ethnic Christian worship events, where shared fellowship becomes a way of life at least some of the time. Among the reasons for doing this is one offered by Garces-Foley – that they provide a vital missional motivation, where people are:

> impelled in this direction by a desire to bring healing to society and [draw] upon racial reconciliation theology as they [push] their congregations to become color-conscious, multicultural, multi-ethnic churches.[39]

Garces-Foley is not alone in her enthusiasm for multicultural churches. Tom Sine, the Fuller Seminary missiologist, discusses at length the many opportunities for mission in regions of the West which offer broad ethnic tapestries. Concerning the need for churches to go beyond their monocultural make-up, he writes:

> There is another important reason to consider moving beyond a monocultural church experience. I have seen the future and, whether we recognize it or not, it looks like London, Los Angeles and Auckland. These cities reflect the wonderfully diverse cultures of our world. In fact by 2060 the United States will become the first non-European Western nation – a nation of Latinos, African Americans and Asians. Those of us

---

[39] Garces-Foley, *Crossing the Ethnic Divide*, p.158.

from European roots will just be another group. Our churches need to help people prepare to not only live in this future, but to receive and celebrate the gifts from other cultures.

God is indeed raising up new conspirators who are determined to create churches that look like God's multicultural kingdom.[40]

Sine's words seem prophetic indeed to us. Globalism and ethnic diversity is bringing richness and diversity into the Western world. Sine connects the movement towards planting multicultural churches to the emerging church movement as well. It is inspiring to read of North American churches which are already multicultural. Sine comments:

> One of the most innovative U.S. congregations in the area of ethnic diversity is a church in Southern California called Mosaic. It is comprised of 'people from all over the world who have settled in Los Angeles, California area. Their audience is multi-cultural, postmodern, pluralistic and global culture seekers.' Like the emerging church, Mosaic gives a major place in its life and mission to the arts; its group Urban Poets includes artists, dramatists and social innovators.
>
> Most of the pastors of these multicultural churches are not content to simply create interesting programmes to meet the needs of people within the building. They are intent on involving their members in word and deed ministries that impact the lives of people in their communities.[41]

Sine's book is well worth a read as it outlines many important strands in the diverse developments in the emerging church and missional church planting scenes. Mosaic may well prove to be of interest for those who are interested in planting multicultural breakthrough congregations in Britain, Europe, Australia and

---

[40] Tom Sine, *The New Conspirators: Creating the future one mustard seed at a time* (Downers Grove, IVP, 2008), p.457.
[41] Sine, *The New Conspirators*, pp.47-48.

Northern America. We would suggest it is worth visiting Mosaic's website to find out more.[42]

At this stage we have given a broad overview of some important questions related to multicultural diversity in the West, and the missional opportunities God has provided to reach out to different people groups that live in the West. In order for us to take the next step in our exploration of the multicultural missional conversation, we need to ask ourselves, 'Where can we start for our vision of what multicultural churches could do to found their identities upon?' This is essentially a theological question. We are not suggesting that we should aspire to manufacture multi-ethnic churches or to force people into taking part in missional conversations. However, we do want to raise this question now as we believe some ethnic Christian groups may be ready to take the next step of becoming multi-ethnic missional congregations, especially those made up of second and third generation families. Whether we use the term 'reverse mission' or not at this point is probably less important than asking how we can converse and debate together in order to imagine a new multicultural form of Christianity into being for the future.

Multiculturalism and the inputs from different ethnic communities is a critical political issue, and makes up the whole question of faith in the public square. Part of the challenge is to help them to develop a theology of mission, from which foundation they can conceive of new ways to form multi-ethnic congregations. The debate on the role of faith in the public square as a potential primary influence on secular Western policymaking and life will inevitably need living examples of successful multi-ethnic churches that help join people together in Jesus Christ.

The next chapter starts to think about the question, 'On what can multi-ethnic churches build their theology of mission?'

---

[42] Mosaic: A Community of Faith, Love and Hope. See http://mosaic.org/ (accessed 13th August 2014).

Group exercise

Look at a map of the area where your church is located. Do some research into the local areas where different churches are to be found. Also do some research to find out about any church planting ventures in your town or city. Mark these churches on your map. Also look for a local demographic survey, which can often be found on local government websites, to discover where different ethnic groups live in your locality. Once you have found out about the locations of churches, look up their websites and find out about them. Present your findings to your church leadership team.

- What opportunities are there for you to join with other Christians in a mission venture?

- What groups are not being reached by the gospel in your area?

- What is the Holy Spirit saying to your congregation about mission opportunities in which He may be guiding you to take part?

You may find it helpful to obtain some professional help in learning how to map your area for mission. An organisation that can do this for you is the Worship and Leadership Academy which is located in Coventry, England.[43]

---

[43] WL Academy: www.wlacademy.org.uk (accessed 13th August 2014).

Reflective exercise

To finish this chapter take a few minutes to reflect on the following questions:

- What did you find most challenging in this chapter?

- What encouraged you?

- How can you use your current knowledge about mission-focused churches in your area to help your church engage in mission conversations with them?

- What steps would it take to help your congregation understand the multicultural missional conversation?

- What steps could you take to equip your church's mission team to explore ways of dialoguing with another missional church?

Comments

Chapter 2
The Multicultural Trinity

The doctrine of the Trinity was adopted at the first Ecumenical Church Council of Nicaea (AD 323) and further developed at subsequent Church Councils. It was a development that was implied by the New Testament and which the Early Church Fathers saw the need to clarify in credal terms.[44] After the resurrection, Jesus met with His disciples (Matthew 28:16-20) and commissioned them to 'make disciples' of all nations. This commission also includes the Trinitarian baptismal formula. The church is to baptise believers in the name of the Father, the Son and the Holy Spirit. The call to baptise all nations in the name of the Trinity means that the Trinity embraces all nations and cultures of the world in the scope of its mission.

In this chapter we will use the term 'Multicultural Trinity' as a metaphor for the God who embraces all nations and cultures that now live in the West. We believe this metaphor will help us to develop an appropriate language of identity which can help churches to embrace multicultural diversity while also providing a theology to unite people in that diversity. Father, Son and Holy Spirit want the whole world to be reconciled to themselves.[45]

We will also explore how the theological understanding of the Trinity helps us formulate a theology of multicultural missional church which can unite people in their diversity. Just as the Early Church Fathers began with Christ for their theology of the Trinity, so we will begin with Him in order to develop a brief survey of our concept of the Multicultural Trinity. The church has one foundation, which is Jesus Christ the Lord. Paul said as much in his letter to the Gentile Christians at Corinth in ancient Greece:

---

[44] The word 'Trinity' is not found in the Bible – it is a word that was later used by the church fathers to describe the tripartite nature of the Godhead which they found expressed in a number of crucial passages in the New Testament.

[45] John Flett, *The Witness of God The Trinity, Missio Dei, Karl Barth, and the Nature of Christian Community* (Grand Rapids, Eerdmans, 2010), pp.57-61.

According to the grace of God given to me, like a skilled master builder I laid a foundation, and someone else is building on it. Each builder must choose with care how to build on it. For no one can lay any foundation other than the one that has been laid; that foundation is Jesus Christ. Now if anyone builds on the foundation with gold, silver, precious stones, wood, hay, straw – the work of each builder will become visible, for the Day will disclose it, because it will be revealed with fire, and the fire will test what sort of work each has done.

1 Corinthians 3:10-13

The multicultural church of Christ is established on the foundation of the incarnate Son of God, whom the Father sent and the Spirit continues to manifest to people today. Jesus was a Jew and ministered to Jews during His life and ministry in Galilee and Judea. How can Jesus the Jew embrace all nations and their races and cultures? Surely Jesus the Jew provides evidence for us to plant churches made up of people of the same or similar cultures to their own?

The Jewish identity of Jesus has often been raised by theologians as a question of the superiority of one people group over others. This 'one people group' is thought by some to be the chosen people of Israel. Charles Kraft, the well-known expert in mission and cultural studies, classically stated what the cultural philosopher Niebuhr[46] had formulated:

God-in-culture advocates see God as contained within, or at least as endorsing, one particular culture. This was, and still is, the view of many Hebrews who see God as related only to their culture. It is also the position of countless tribal groups who understand their god(s) as exclusively related to themselves.

Within Christianity a God-endorsing-my-culture perspective often stems from the God-against-culture position. It sees God as either creating, gradually developing, or endorsing a given culture or subculture, and ordaining that

[46] H. Richard Niebuhr, *Christ and Culture* (Grand Rapids, Harper Torchbooks, 1975), pp101-107.

all people everywhere if they are to be Christian be converted thereto. This concept may take the form of an absolutization of some historical culture such as Hebrew, Greco-Roman ... or, more often in the last few centuries, some form of modification of western 'civilization.' Or it may refer simply to 'Christian culture'.[47]

Jesus was born as a Jew, but the coming of the Spirit of Jesus at Pentecost propelled the Jewish messianic Christian faith outwards from Jerusalem to all the nations of the world. According to Jesus and the apostle Paul, the movement was to break boundaries and to take the gospel to all nations and cultures (Matthew 28:16-20; Ephesians 2:14).

In what ways can this insight help us to answer some of our questions about working cross culturally? How can it help us think about the approaches we take to share the gospel with other people groups in the West's multicultural society? How can it help us to overcome our ethnocentric desires to make people adopt our own cultural version of Christianity?

Jesus had a practical theology of mission as Son of God and as Son of Mankind. He did all that He saw the Father doing in His mission to save the whole world which He loves (John 5:19-20). The *missio Dei* ('God's mission') was also central to the practical theology of the apostle Paul. He was sent by the risen Lord to take the gospel to the Gentiles (Acts 9).

The word 'mission' itself is never used in the New Testament but it is powerfully conveyed in passages that speak of Christ being sent by the Father, as well as those of Christ sending the church to 'make disciples' of all nations (John 17:1-5; 20:21). This theology came out of the Old Testament and the culture of Israel.

A classic example of Yahweh sending someone on a kind of mission is the story of Abraham in Genesis 12:1-3. It is evident to most missiologists that Paul was an expert in using language in culturally relevant ways with Gentile converts (1 Corinthians 3:10-15). Moreover, another Hellenist Jew named Stephen challenged the received

---

[47] Charles Kraft, *Christianity in Culture: A Study in Dynamic Biblical Theologizing in Cross-Cultural Perspective* (Maryknoll, Orbis Books, 2002), p.107.

monocultural Jewish identity which many Jews held. The speech Stephen delivered at his trial is recorded in Acts 7. It demonstrates that the focal point of the Christian faith would no longer be the physical location of Jerusalem and its temple. Instead it makes the place of Jesus Christ at God's right hand in heaven the new locus of their attention. There is a shift of our attention from a particular place on earth where God's presence could be found to the universal presence of God in Christ, who reigns over the whole cosmos (Colossians 1:5-20). The work of the Spirit of Jesus was to be focused on the reconciliation of all peoples of the earth to God (Acts 16:6-10; John 16:12-16).

At the heart of Stephen's speech was his assertion about the displacement of the temple from its one location in Jerusalem to all locations universally, as Christ was beyond one place and was now to be present by His Spirit in all places (John 14:15-17). Christ was now at the right hand of the Father in heaven, and the kingdom of God was to be made up of all nations and cultures which His Spirit would call to follow Him:

> 'The Most High does not dwell in houses made with hands; as
> the prophet says,
> "Heaven is my throne,
> and earth my footstall.
> What kind of house will you build for me, says the Lord,
> or what is the place of my rest?
> Did not my hand make all these things?"
> 'You stiff-necked people, uncircumcised in heart and ears,
> you always resist the Holy Spirit.'
> When they heard these things, they became enraged and
> ground their teeth at Stephen. But filled with the Holy Spirit,
> he gazed into heaven and saw the glory of God and Jesus
> standing at the right hand of God.'
> *Acts 7:48-51, 54-55*

The theology of Stephen's speech is based around God's presence moving from a particular temple to the work of His universal Spirit, which means all the people of creation can commune with Him throughout the whole temple of creation. This new temple theology is recognised by various scholars, including the Anglican scholar N. T.

Wright, to be very much part of John Gospel's theology and Paul's theology, among other New Testament documents such as here in Acts. Connected to this creation temple theology is also the concept of the boundary-breaking God who is now to be met in every place in creation through His Spirit (Acts 1:8).

In Paul's letter to the Gentile believers at Ephesus he indicates that the mission of God in Christ is to break boundaries and to abolish the 'absolutization' of one Jewish race over all others as the keepers of God's mission. Many Jews in the first century had an exclusive view of themselves as the people of God, and believed that Gentiles had to become Jews like them by taking on the Jewish traditions and lifestyle before God could accept them. The kingdom of God in this respect was concerned with having Gentile proselytes becoming Torah-observing Jews. The Messiah to come from this kind of perspective envisioned a war-like Messiah overthrowing the hated Gentile nations in a last great battle, which would then be followed by the ushering in of the kingdom. However, not all Jews thought this way in Jesus' time; it was groups like the sectarian separatist Essenes who looked forward to a great battle between God's people and the Gentile nations.

In Paul's view, Jesus the Jew came to break down all boundaries that disunited racial and cultural groups (Ephesians 2:19). The aim was that all peoples could unite with the universal Christ of the Spirit, who was, and is, sent by the Father to gather all people into His multicultural kingdom (Matthew 28:16-20). The final goal of the kingdom of God, in this view, is for all peoples to be united with the Father, Son and Holy Spirit. This provides the rationale for the Multicultural Trinity. The climax will be when Jesus comes to finally complete the mission in which the church is presently engaged, as it seeks to 'make disciples' of all nations. Jesus will complete the establishment of the kingdom at His second coming (Luke 21:24-28). The Trinity is made up of persons gathered around the one being. All created persons being reshaped into the image of Christ are called to gather as part of the Trinity's family. Since the time of Jesus this has been in the process of happening. It includes all peoples uniting together in Christ to be reconciled to God, which in turn will unite a disunited world of separate peoples:

> For he has made known to us in all wisdom and insight the mystery of his will, according to his purpose which he set forth in Christ as a plan for the fulness of time, to unite all things in him, things in heaven and things on earth.
>
> *Ephesians 1: 9-10 (RSV)*

To what extent does this vision of a God who loves all peoples equally equate with those with whom we choose to worship within our churches? To what extent are we really trying to join in conversations with our brothers and sisters from other races and cultures in the multicultural missional conversation? The passages from Acts and Ephesians both demonstrate the universal plan of Father, Son and Holy Spirit to bring all races and peoples together to be part of the Trinity's one family. History teaches us that Kraft's assessment (mentioned above) that Christians themselves have 'absolutized' their own Western 'civilization', as if Western culture is part of being a Christian, demonstrates that the message of all people becoming united as the one people of God can be missed, as it was by Europe's colonial missionaries in the nineteenth and early twentieth centuries.

The days of the European empires have long gone, where, among others, the British Empire sought to take its version of 'Christian culture' into its colonies seeking to convert other peoples to adopt their Western 'Christian culture'. There was a failure to allow Christianity to embed itself into new cultures in a contextualised form that would meaningfully relate to the people of that culture. When we use the word 'contextual', it means, among other things, that Christians listen carefully to the stories of those with whom they want to share Christ so that they can share the gospel in language suited to the new people's cultural founding stories, through which they understand the world around them. The failure of the colonial missionaries was that they attempted to make converts become Westernised Christians. How could Westerners ever hope to make African peoples, with their rich and diverse cultural heritages, become European in the way they lived? Christ needed to become part of their existing cultures to transform them from within. The culture-bound version of Christianity that the British Empire epitomised was forced on to other peoples as the only meaningful form of 'Christian culture' for them to emulate.[48]

An opportunity for the multicultural West is to seek to bring Christ into varieties of ethnic minority subcultures. Numerous cultures live among us, bringing their imported home cultures to be part of the other migrant subcultures and the predominant secular Western culture. In the Old Testament, the reign of God was expressed in terms of all nations bringing their glory to Mount Zion (Isaiah 2:1-4). Mount Zion was the place from which the Messianic kings of Israel reigned (Psalm 2). Jesus the universal Lord is not to be limited in such a manner (see above). We have the opportunity to unite together through the Spirit of the Lord Jesus as one people of God made up of many peoples. This is not to deny our racial and cultural differences, which bring richness and diversity to the kingdom of God as it continues to be manifested. United missional efforts built on God's unifying love act as a sign and foretaste of what it looks like to be joined together by the one God. Our society needs to see what a difference God can make to racial and cultural divisions in Western society. A tremendous variety of culture-specific migrant Christians have joined us in the West, bringing with them their own wonderful cultural expressions of faith to enrich our lives together. To further advance this enrichment we need to start to plant some multi-ethnic breakthrough congregations as living representations of the Multicultural Trinity who unites us.

Early Gentile Christians were not racially Jews, and at first there was a large debate in which the apostle Paul engaged with his Jewish peers regarding the place of the Gentile Christian's status in relationship to the ethnic people of Israel.[49] We know from reading his letters that he sought to help churches made up of Jews and Gentiles to understand their equal status in Christ (Galatians 3:28). He pointed out to Jews and Gentiles alike that all nations were to be blessed through Abraham as the multicultural representative of all nations, through whom they would be blessed if they had a faith like his (Galatians 3:14). This recognition of equality and impartiality needs to advise the

---

[48] Akrong, *Deconstructing Colonial Mission*, pp.67-68.
[49] N. T. Wright, *Paul: Fresh Perspectives* (London, SPCK, 2005), p.36.

call for our different Christian ethnic churches to work more closely together.

When Jesus talked with the Samaritan woman at the well of Sychar, He shocked His disciples as He spoke not only to a woman but also to a much-hated Samaritan (John 4:27). Is it possible that we entertain similar divisions in the way we join churches made up of one people group who are like us? It is quite likely that we would all say in principle that we agree that different cultural groups are united by the gospel. Having said this, do our practices of meeting together match what we claim to believe? The Samaritan woman asked Jesus about the right location for people to worship, as the Jews said it was at the temple on Mount Zion, and the Samaritans had a rival temple on Mount Gerazim. Jesus' response did away with having one location to worship, making it clear that God was to become present everywhere by His Spirit. We have already made this point based on Stephen's speech. Christ said to the Samaritan woman:

> 'Woman, believe me, the hour is coming when neither on this mountain nor in Jerusalem will you worship the Father ... But the hour is coming, and now is, when the true worshipers will worship the Father in spirit and truth, for such the Father seeks to worship him.'
> John 4:21, 23 (RSV)

What has too often been missed in this passage is that the three persons of the Trinity are all referred to. This is a vital point to grasp in our discussion of uniting all peoples as part of the plan of the Multicultural Trinity for the coming kingdom. We could paraphrase this verse by saying that Father, Son and Spirit seek those who will worship Them based on a mutual shared spiritual intimacy with God. This passage implies the beginning of the end of the distinction between Jew and Samaritan. For this reason it is vital that our biblical beliefs shape us to join in the multicultural missional conversation, which is implied by the boundary-breaking activities of Jesus with the Samaritans when He also shared fellowship with the woman's whole village (John 4:39-42).

This boundary-breaking moment informs us that Jews and Samaritans will not be racially segregated in the kingdom of God. The

Messiah welcomes them and shares fellowship with them. He accepts their hospitality and offers them the 'living water' of eternal life. This provides a theology of missional hospitality for us to practise, by getting to know each other as we share food together, coming as we do from different cultures. Father, Son and Holy Spirit unite all nations and cultures to be one new people of God who can experience God's presence wherever they are to be found. Part of this joining process includes sharing in the hospitality of life-giving food. Eating together and sharing the intimacy of table fellowship is the arena where the Multicultural Trinity gives us His life-giving water. This is a vital practice to bring into the way we meet together to engage in the multicultural missional conversation. The way we develop hospitality towards our multi-ethnic brothers and sisters can help us to share dialogue together.

Having made these vital observations, we need to explore how our identities need to be shaped, made as we are in the image of Christ who seeks to unite all nations as one new humanity, because all God's people are to become one in Him.

Many peoples, one Adam

N. T. Wright has demonstrated that the creation story played a vital role in the whole theology of the Judeo-Christian faith and Jewish belief systems.[50] Genesis 1 and 2 have much to teach us about the connectedness that mankind made in God's image shares at a fundamental level. It is this recognition that also provides the scientific grounds for what joins us. Using a modern biological analogy, God created mankind with the genetic potential for all races and cultures to unite on the basis of their common likeness, because of their common genetic heritage. The human genome project,[51] which has mapped the human gene, has provided the evidence in support of this thesis. These insights provide an interesting view into the well-known narrative of

---

[50] N. T, Wright, *The New Testament and the People of God* (London, SPCK, 1993), pp.248-250.

[51] Francis Collins, *The Language of God: A Scientist Presents Evidence for Belief* (London, Pocket Books, 2007), pp.109-144.

the creation of mankind (whether we take it to be literally or poetically significant):

> Then God said, 'Let us make man in our image, after our likeness; and let them have dominion over the fish of the sea, and over the birds of the air, and over the cattle, and over all the earth, and over every creeping thing that creeps upon the earth.' So God created man in his own image, in the image of God he created him; male and female he created them. And God blessed them, and God said to them, 'Be fruitful and multiply, and fill the earth and subdue it; and have dominion over the fish of the sea and over the birds of the air and over every living thing that moves upon the earth.'
> *Genesis 1:26-28 (RSV)*

It is probably not surprising that early theologians considered the 'us' of this passage to be the Father, Son and Holy Spirit being involved in creation together. It certainly makes sense to see it in this way from verses found in passages like John 1:1-18, which declares that 'all things came into being through him, and without him [Christ] not one thing came into being'. Paul articulates this (Colossians 1:16), as do other New Testament documents.

Some Jewish theologians have pointed out that in Genesis 1:26-27 the Creator was calling on the heavenly 'sons of god' to make a contribution to the creation of mankind.[52] This is a wonderful insight into God's creative nature, in the sense that the Multicultural Trinity calls on the creatures He has already made to participate in imagining into being what He will make of the new stuff of creation. It also provides us with a beautiful insight into what the people of God can do together when we unite in the multicultural missional conversation. Among other things, it needs to be a creative conversation about how we can imagine new ways of forming multicultural communities together, as this is a part of what a theology of the kingdom of God implies in the context of passages like Matthew 24:1-14 and Matthew 28:16-20.

---

[52] We find this among Kabbalists.

When different people groups unite in conversation, one exciting possibility is for them to help to conceive of new ways in which different ethnic groups can live together in wider secular society. People can discover the beauty of joining with other racial groups and cultures to enrich each other's experiences in the public square in Western society. Many of us already love to share different cultural foods together, bearing testament to a new opportunity to seek to further enrich each other. God's multicultural Trinitarian family is made up of multiple cultures who can take courage from this celebration of differences through sharing foods to persevere in hospitality for the planting of multi-ethnic churches. Not because it is easy to do, but because by the presence of the Father, Son and Holy Spirit it becomes possible to live in harmony as we become more interconnected in a shared life together like Theirs.

This vision of the harmony of the persons of the Trinity provides the multicultural church with inspiration to model our fellowships on God's deep life joined by love in unity and in purpose. In what ways can we build our communities based on God's inner life of sacrificial love and grace? Each person of the Trinity is completely transparent with the other persons. This is what the ancient term *perichoresis* powerfully implies, with, among other things, the picture of a harmonious dance between the persons of the Trinity illustrating their interconnectivity. Applied to cross-cultural relationships, it suggests that sacrificial love will be needed in order to overcome some acute differences caused by a variety of cultural differences, which threaten the chance for different ethnic groups to develop relationships with each other.

It will take a strategic adoption of actively listening to each other to build empathy as we fellowship together in newly conceived multi-ethnic breakthrough congregations. We need to be realistic about the difficulties, and this means we need to be careful to keep on seeking the presence of Christ to equip our capacities to overcome the power of sin, which too often drives us to take the easy selfish route that will keep us in our own monocultural people group comfort zones in our
· ethnically separated churches.

Paul indicated that through the renewal of our minds we can become ever more like the Son of God, who lived in harmony with the

Father of the families of the earth (2 Corinthians 10:5; Ephesians 3:14-15). Christ the Saviour is the agent of a new creation made up of diverse peoples, which provides the rationale for us to embrace diversity as part of God's kingdom (1 Corinthians 12:20). God has called us together in this multicultural society to explore ways to unite as multi-ethnic peoples, through our shared creational likeness, as one people restored to unite and overthrow the divisions of the nations represented biblically as Babel. In the New Testament, God's people are called as communities to participate in the 'image' and 'likeness' of the Lord, who is the head of the multi-ethnic body of Christ – the church (Ephesians 5:23).

Father, Son and Holy Spirit originally made humankind to become the multicultural one people of God, to bless a fallen world together through their creative expressions of being the one people of God. What can we start to do together in order to imagine a new Western multicultural Christian society into being? The image of God in mankind is focused on the one new Adam, Jesus Christ, who unites all of us as a new diverse people (1 Corinthians 15:45; Romans 5:12-19; Ephesians 2:11-22). As the new diverse people of God, we come bearing gifts from our cultures to share with one another, as well as with peoples among whom we live in the fragmented secular world. Mankind in its racial and cultural diversity was, and is, made in the image of the Multicultural Trinity, which embraces diversity in its three persons and unity in its one substance as God. This is deep practical theology, but it is absolutely fundamental to what we believe God is calling us to dialogue about doing together, through working more closely together as multiple cultures in the name of one Lord Jesus.

How can we unite in our diversity? How can we show our fragmented multicultural society what a difference it makes to become Trinity-shaped multi-ethnic missional communities who can share life deeply together? Our vision for what such multicultural Christian communities (churches) do to build their peoples' identities on will need to come from a vision of God the Trinity. From ancient times it has been recognised that the persons of the Trinity are united in transparent trust and love in their creative diversity as one God. We are part of God's Trinitarian family that provides the potential for us to share in His unity and diversity, so that a new united society that celebrates diversity can be formed within the multicultural marketplace. Are we ready to reform our culturally limited identities to engage with others in the mission of the Trinity? In what ways can the Holy Spirit enable us to unite all races and cultures into the family of the one God?

Identity matters

Much work has been done in the field of human psychology and sociology on the relationship of a person's self-image to the role of parents and society in its formation. A common way that sociologists define the way in which children come to form their understanding of who they are is through socialisation theory. Socialisation is defined as the ways children develop the ability to live effectively in the particular society and culture into which they are born.

According to the sociologist Handel, children develop three main capacities through socialisation. The first of these is empathy. This trait requires that a person is able to put themselves in another person's position, including a good awareness of what they might feel when they are faced by any number of new situations in life. This is the trait of empathy – the child develops an ability to see things from another's perspective.

The second trait is the ability to communicate using signs and symbols in spoken language as well as body language. A person needs to be aware of how their communication can be interpreted by another person. This relates to our self-awareness in regard to the way we convey what we communicate and how it makes others behave or potentially feel when faced with interaction with us. Such awareness helps us to read people (empathy) and it helps us to adapt our behaviours, so that people can feel valued by us and comfortable to interrelate to us and with us.

Thirdly, Haralambos and Holborn discuss the importance of the development of the sense of self, which makes it possible for us to relate as adults with other adult defined selves. The person as a self, in order to be a self, has to see itself as a separate entity compared to other selves:

Drawing on the work of the symbolic interactionist Charles Horton Cooley, Handel defines this sense of self as 'the ability to take oneself as an object, to be conscious that one is an object distinct from other objects'. By distinguishing their self from others the child can begin to regulate their own conduct, evaluate their behaviour and, in time, imagine how their behaviour is viewed by others. Cooley argued that people come to possess a 'looking-glass self' – their sense of who they are becomes a reflection of how others see them.

The development of self is crucial in socialization because it enables a child to align their behaviour with that of others. Instead of simply pursuing their own desires, children start to take account of the opinion of others and to act in ways they believe will reflect well in the looking-glass that others hold up to them.'[53]

Identity formation

The psychologist Cooley's 'looking-glass self' is vital to the discussion of this chapter. The question is, 'How can insights from psychology help us to form stable multicultural Christian communities?' Exciting findings have been made by psychologists about the way human beings form their identities through participation in the communities among which they grow up. Cooley asserted the fundamental principle that children and adults tend to adapt their behaviours, thinking and feelings to win the approval of others. The first place we do this is with our parents and siblings.

Another important place where identities are formed during childhood and adolescence is in school. People tend to develop a positive self-image if they are affirmed as valued individuals in their own right. Negative self-images develop if this affirmation is not received.

We believe that the theology of God's unmerited grace and favour is built on His desire for us to develop positive self-images based on us

---

[53] Michael Haralambos, and Martin Holborn, *Sociology: Themes and Perspectives Seventh Edition* (London, HarperCollins, 2008), pp.689-690.

all sharing in the likeness of Christ. Taking this a step further, we tend to feel good about ourselves based on affirmations that we are loved and accepted for who we are, despite our faults and failings. The opinions of those closest to us will have the largest impact on how we see ourselves, as opposed to views that come from those with whom we have less significant relationships. Hence the way we are valued by others in our churches will affect how much we feel valued, significant to and integrated into a church's fellowship. This means that the way our congregational fellowship environments operate will have a direct bearing on how much each person feels valued by their peers as much as by the God they claim to serve.

Moving back to a childhood analogy will help us to develop this thinking further. Analysis of a child's confidence to explore the world and to forge meaningful relationships with parents, siblings and peers comes from, among others, the work of the classic psychotherapist Carl Rogers. He spoke of the need for us to treat each other with 'unconditional positive regard', which means we accept others in warm and accepting ways.[54] He also wrote about the need for us to use 'non-judgemental regard', which treats others in a way that does not express condemnation.[55] People tend to flourish in communities when they feel that their real selves are not being threatened by others who want to force them to change. The 'real self' is the core essence of our inner being which motivates and shapes how we feel about ourselves in relationship to others and God. In affirming communities, be they small family units, friendship groups or churches, there will be a sense that a person is valued for being themselves even when they make mistakes.

What it is vital for us to consider, if we are to successfully converse in the broader multicultural conversation, is, 'Are we quick to listen and affirm the value of each other as loved by God, and slow to focus on the differences that can alienate us?' We need to be very patient with one another and learn to accept cultural differences as a normal part of being part of the Multicultural Trinity's family. It is too often badly managed relationships between ethnic Christian groups that

---

[54] Carl Rogers, On Becoming a Person: A Therapist's View of Psychotherapy (London, Constable, 1991), pp.47, 48, 49, 63, 66, 185, 283.
[55] Rogers, On Becoming a Person, pp.47, 48, 49.

create fears which stop people talking to each other meaningfully after an initial meeting with a new group.

Rogers suggested that people develop the best relationships when they are given permission to be themselves.[56] If they make mistakes or hurt others' feelings, communities need to be quick to ignore or forgive such differences which will often be a natural part of getting to know people from a different culture. Cross-cultural missional partnerships need to include a willingness to adapt our less helpful behaviours if they cause special offence to others, which means that we will need to develop a positive attitude towards difference so that we can resolve potential conflicts before they become too obvious. This must become a strong value for ethnic churches to embrace so that it becomes ingrained enough for them to be able to transfer this level of allowance to the way they treat other ethnic Christian groups. If people are given permission to make mistakes as accepted persons of value in their own right in their own contexts, they can be helped to develop a deeper capacity for empathy which will help them to be patient with others who are not like them. If our cultural differences are criticised when we engage in cross-cultural conversations, this will feel like an attack on our deeper cultural identities.

It is at these sharp points which hurt us to the bone that we need to be the most careful to put ourselves in the place of the one who has offended us. By doing this, we will seek to understand the way others are trying to relate to us from the standpoint of their own cultural perspective. It will require us to listen carefully to them in order to understand their motives, conditioned as they are by their own outlooks on the world. It is our suggestion that most often we take offence when none was intended, and what was perceived as an offence was a result of cross-cultural differences. In order to relate to each other well, we need to learn to celebrate our cultural differences, which can often best be done by eating together.

Moreover, an important factor in how we approach overcoming our differences when we meet new people is the need for sensitive non-threatening feedback of a non-judgemental type. It is fundamental to the notion of grace and faith (see Ephesians 4:15). The best place to

---

[56] Rogers, *On Becoming a Person,* pp.31-38.

build relationships will most often be by showing hospitality to one another, as it is around the meal table that we learn the most about the richness of each other's cultures. Sharing together in this way can build understanding and a shared sense of community. It is no wonder Scripture places a high value on the meal table as the place for people to express their desires to unite together in Christ. Jesus shared table-fellowship with tax-collectors and sinners, according to the gospels (eg Luke 15:1-2). If He did this with those with whom other Jews would not share hospitality, it is clearly a high premium piece that was at the heart of His mission and ministry. From a pastoral and psychological point of view, Carl Rogers hit on something that is intrinsic to the very nature of the grace of God and the positive messages that sharing food and hospitality naturally help us to communicate to others with whom we share time. God loves His people despite their differences. Rogers was not a Christian and he did not apply his ideas to the doctrine of grace, but they resonate well with the biblical concept of grace at some important points.

New believers adopted into the family of God through Jesus Christ can learn how to treat each other with the same acceptance and grace that God offers to them (see Ephesians 4:25-32). Jesus' parable of the unforgiving servant in Matthew 18:23-35 demonstrates that forgiveness received also needs to be offered in return, or we have not really been forgiven as it has not transformed our approach to others. The man who was forgiven much did not practise forgiveness towards the poor worker for whom he was responsible. The parable is designed to help us consider the ethics of forgiveness which needs to be at the foundation of our Christian communities. People who behold in the face of Jesus the gracious welcome of God can come to treat each other with the same love which the Holy Spirit is said to pour into each person's heart as a gift of grace (2 Corinthians 4:1-5; Romans 5:5). Forgiveness will be a high-premium product for multi-ethnic Christian churches to learn to exercise towards others, who may at times be culturally insensitive in return without realising.

In other words, Cooley's 'looking-glass self' has each believer gaze into the face of God's favour, and by it he or she is given a positive self-image in the likeness of Christ. If we accept ourselves as justified by the Christ of forgiveness, we will not need to justify ourselves to others. There is one who justifies, and that is Christ. This releases us from the need to defend ourselves when we feel threatened by others' responses to us. In other words, if God's grace has been fully embedded into our hearts, then we can have confidence to treat others with the same grace that God has given to each of us.

It is very important for multi-ethnic churches to build deep foundations on the practice of grace, particularly in the ways they welcome strangers to their groups. This theology of hospitality to the stranger is enshrined at the heart of Israel's faith, and it came to full maturity in the unlimited hospitality of the grace of God expressed in Christ. The Christian community that practises this kind of affirming approach to life models the image of Christ which restores people to live with each other, based on loving acts of service which are inspired by the Spirit of Jesus. The picture of a God who is giving and grace filled as He pours out His love on His people needs to be at the heart of a Christian missional community's life practices towards outsiders.

In what ways can we join together in building up the people in our churches so that they exercise patience, grace, forgiveness and acceptance as a spiritual discipline and way of life? One motivation for doing this has to do with the inner life of the Trinity that accepts the other in the persons of the Father, Son and Holy Spirit. This deep value offers a new vision of how we treat others before our communities. It is based on accepting others even before they are willing to accept themselves. After all, that is what grace implies. It covers up a multitude of sins and defects (see James 5:20). Moreover, the mission of the Multicultural Trinity is to unite believers in their diversity as the main way in which people of no Christian faith can be attracted to the family of God, expressed by a fellowship that practises God's grace and hospitality to strangers.

The way God is pictured by persons in a community affects the image of God reflected to those who behold it in their words and behaviour. If we accept that God as Father, Son and Holy Spirit is the model of a perfect community, we can learn from examples of how the persons of the Trinity interact with each other. Jesus' relationship with His Father in heaven recorded in Scripture provides a window into how we as sons and daughters of God can model our relationships with each other and the family of the Trinity.

We would add at this point that it is not enough to simply apply psychosocial theory to a Christian community as a programme for change. We can learn from such theories, of course, but they do not actually produce such communities. It is important to understand some of the dynamics and processes which have been empirically observed to be vital for healthy functioning of people in communities, but theories do not make things actually work. At the heart of a Christian missional community is the power and presence of God who provides the fruit of the Spirit and who helps us to think and behave like Christ who came to heal all that separates us from God and others.

In what ways do we identify the sacrificial love of God at work in ourselves and others in our churches? How can we encourage each other to focus on living our lives based on servant-hearted ministry, which defined Jesus' identity according to Philippians, calling for believer's to:

> Have this mind among yourselves, which is yours in Christ Jesus, who, though he was in the form of God, did not count equality with God a thing to be grasped, but emptied himself, taking the form of a servant, being born in the likeness of men. And being found in human form he humbled himself and became obedient unto death, even death on the cross.
> *Philippians 2:5-8*

Social psychologists Hogg and Vaughan make several very helpful comments which will help us to grasp something of great importance related to understanding our proposition 'the way God is pictured by persons in a community affects the image of God reflected through a community'. Like Rogers, they are not theologians and they make no claims to be. But their comments can help us to understand some important dynamics for how people in communities can relate with each other in healthier ways. To do this, our communities first need to base their identities on the grace of God given to all who will receive it, and then they need to let it transform how they treat others.

Hogg and Vaughan make four points which will help us to understand how the sense of the self comes to be expressed in communities as the collective self. The collective self is defined as a self-aware person's recognition that they are not simply an isolated

69

individual but that they also belong in relationship with other selves with whom they share life. In terms of the multicultural missional church, this strongly implies that we need to learn to identify ourselves more collectively, because the Multicultural Trinity embraces all cultures without partiality. These cultures will inevitably be transformed by the grace of God to become graciously more open to other cultures.

In terms of the formation of multi-ethnic breakthrough congregations, the collective self will need to include the embracing of values that do not simply come from our native monocultures. If we believe the Trinity embraces all peoples and cultures, multi-ethnic churches will need to learn to celebrate what each culture brings to enrich their fellowships.

Let us now consider the four insights suggested by Hogg and Vaughan that can help us interact more effectively. This short section is a bit more technical but it will be worth the extra concentration to grasp what is written:

1. 'People do have a sense of "me", and according to symbolic interactionism the self arises out of human interaction.'[57]

Multi-ethnic churches will need to take much more time in their efforts to help their cross-cultural members to understand how their cultural perspectives have been influenced by their own cultural signs and symbols. Listening carefully to the way we use language, with an eye to what it means to each of us in terms of our own culture, will help us to understand each other's perspectives. This will be especially needful when what we say does not convey what we really mean to another member who is not from our culture.

We may need to explain what we mean more clearly, with an eye to our cultural differences. For example, when I (Andy) talk about loving my wife Jenny, I assume that we are equal to each other and that neither of us has greater authority when we make decisions. Jenny's sense of her 'me' is partly constructed by me accepting her equal status to my 'me'.

---

[57] Michael Hogg and Graham Vaughan, *Social Psychology* (Harlow, Pearson Education Limited, 2011), p.115.

Our symbols of husband and wife are encoded with this basic assumption of equality as equals, and this fits well with our modern views of the equality of the sexes. Jenny's and my sense of 'me' is based on the view that we are equal, whereas for some of our good friends from non-Western cultures, the husband's sense of 'me' puts more emphasis on his authority compared to his wife's sense of 'me', which makes her think of herself as subservient to her husband's wishes compared to her own.

Symbolic interactionism helps us to become more aware of how different cultural assumptions – of issues such as the roles of men and women – cause us to interact with specific expectations of each other, within our own cultures as well as cross culturally.

This is all over-simplified, of course. The reader probably grasps that conflict may arise in multi-ethnic churches when there is a disparity in the cultural identities shared by husbands and wives, which differ between some Western and non-Western cultures. The Multicultural Trinity embraces both types of cultural construction of the roles of men and women. It is, of course, possible for a man to abuse his wife or for a wife to abuse her husband in either cultural construction.

Culture is largely neutral, but when we seek to fellowship cross culturally, strong efforts will be required to help us respect our differences, because norms and values vary. Paul wrote of boundary breaking so that one new people of God would come into existence. This breakdown of barriers was brought about by Christ. Boundary breaking does not mean wanton disrespect of our cultural diversities, but it does require us to understand our differences and to respect them so that we can fellowship with each other graciously.

Being practical

- What would you do if a young Ethiopian non-Westernised man and a young white English woman wanted to marry each other?

- How would you help to prepare them for marriage?

- How would you help them to work through the issues of cross-cultural marriage?

- What steps would you take to help them explore their culture-specific symbols of husband and wife?

- Describe a married couple you know who have successfully worked through cultural differences. What lessons can you learn from their example to help you think through cross-cultural differences so that people can live together more harmoniously?

Comments:

---

2. 'Effective interaction also rests on being able to take the role of the other person; which of course entails "looking in from outside" and seeing oneself as others do – as a social object, "me", rather than social subject, "I".'[58]

Hogg and Vaughan demonstrate the need for people to develop the capacity not just to take on the role of another person to understand their perspective better, but also to be able to reflect on feedback from others to help them see themselves as others see them. Human beings made in the image of the Multicultural Trinity have the ability to construct their identities not as isolated individuals in one culture, but as persons who have the capacity to understand themselves in relationship to others in the multicultural community. It is also possible for us to see ourselves to some extent as others see us, and to

---

[58] Hogg and Vaughan, *Social Psychology*, p.115.

see things from others' points of view. Each of these abilities constructs the ability of the multicultural church to develop empathy among its members so they can understand each other better.

Being practical

- What practical steps would you take to help people understand each other's cultural points of view about subjects such as marriage, child-rearing practices, discipline, men's and women's roles in church, dating customs, time management, sexual practices, grief, punishment, female genital mutilation?

- Describe a situation where people successfully understood their different points of view on one of the matters above. How did this help them to move ahead together as a community?

Comments:

3. 'Because self-conception comes from seeing ourselves as others see us (the idea of the looking-glass self), there should be a strong correlation between how we rate ourselves and how others rate us.'[59] The important point to understand here is that members of the Christian community obtain much of their significance and sense of self-worth from their perception of how others view them. They most

---

[59] Hogg and Vaughan, *Social Psychology*, p.115.

often discern their value and status among others by how others treat them.

This is a vital social psychological insight, in support of our idea that people more easily see themselves as worthy of acceptance if they have accepted God's grace which completely embraces and forgives them. There can be no higher authority in the universe than God, and He is completely on every believer's side in the multicultural Christian community. This means that in the planting of multi-ethnic churches, it is vital that we express the same grace to each other as the Multicultural Trinity expresses to us without partiality. How we perceive God's complete gracious acceptance of us and of others provides the vision for how we can behave towards one another. In other words, our vision of the Trinity that has complete acceptance of otherness and diversity existing between Father, Son and Spirit needs to provide the vision for the way we live with each other as multicultural Christians in pluralist Western society. We need to form our community identities around the vision of the Multicultural Trinity if we are to really transform our churches to unite under the one Lord.

Being practical

- How would you find out about other members' feelings about themselves in your church community?

- What steps would you take to help them rate their sense of self-worth?

- What signs would you look for in order to judge how people communicate grace and acceptance to others?

- What steps would you need to take to help people develop a sense of self-worth?

- What approaches could you formulate to help people communicate acceptance and worth to others?

- Describe a community you know that is good at helping people feel their worth. What can you learn from them about how to develop communities that communicate worth to others?

4. 'The collective self is recognition that the self emerges and is shaped by social interaction.'[60]

We return full circle to the 'collective self' that is healthily integrated into a community, because the community is able to make those who live as part of it feel safe to be themselves.

Father, Son and Spirit may be said to be the ultimate 'collective self'. There is no shadow of distrust among the three persons of the one God. What one loves all love. What one values all value. Simply stated, they are completely safe within their one harmonious being. Their diversity is no threat to their unity.

The Multicultural Trinity offers our multicultural Christian conversations the vision we need to embrace and to stay focused on becoming more united in our diversity. Our multicultural Christian communities will need to base the vision for the way they live in communion with God, and among themselves, on this vision of the Multicultural Trinity.

Being practical

- What steps would you need to take to help people understand and absorb the love of God deeply into their hearts?

---

[60] Hogg and Vaughan, *Social Psychology*, p.114.

- What would you communicate to help people grasp this kind of vision of the Trinity?

- How could you help members deal with hurts caused to them that would discourage them from developing the 'collective self'?

- Describe a congregation you know that is highly caring and supportive of its people. What lessons can you take from this description to help you think of steps to help your congregation become more like this other group?

Comments:

Conclusions

What we learn from this social psychological point of view of the self is that the way others relate to us conveys a message to us, and that in turn can help us value ourselves better, accept ourselves, value others, accept others and understand others by putting ourselves in their shoes. As those new to a missional community behold themselves in the way established community members treat them as acceptable and loved by God through His grace and forgiveness, despite their shortcomings, this will impact how they interact with other community members and how they integrate into the fellowship.

It is all too easy for dysfunctional communities to model a judgemental rather than a non-judgemental regard for others. Hence, the way community members treat others will be based on the vision of God living in their own hearts. A community's vision of how God treats them motivates them to behave in the same way towards each other. How we treat others will be the practical outpouring of how we consider God has treated us and therefore how He must also treat others. In other words, a community can talk much of God's unconditional positive regard in theory, but if a vision of grace and unconditional forgiveness does not come across in the behaviour of community members toward others, then that community is not inhabited by the grace of God in practical terms.

ı   For grace to be real in biblical terms it needs to be lived out in the behaviour of community members towards each other. A church is not a good news gospel community if it does not act and behave as one that is based on a vision of the love of the Multicultural Trinity, who has treated them in a thoroughly confirming manner. In others words, people will find it difficult to be followers of Jesus unless they have accepted that they are completely accepted by the Christ of grace. The role of the church's fellowship needs to affirm people through the unconditional positive regard of the Christ of the Multicultural Trinity if people are to learn how to adopt a more positive self-image within a community.

The Christian community forms disciples who follow the Christ who leads them to become healing fellowships, where people know deeply that they are loved sons and daughters of the Trinity's eternal family. The hyper-individualist West needs multi-ethnic breakthrough congregations to be planted that will be a foretaste of this kind of kingdom of God reality.

This may all sound rather heavy and deep. But we believe we really need to allow ourselves to be converted, not only to believe in God's grace in theory, but also to allow all our behaviour to be informed by His all-encompassing grace. It is this grace that affirms others completely because God has deemed them worthy of His love.

During His ministry, Jesus shaped the thinking of His disciples about the kingdom community, based on the way He welcomed lost seekers, healed them and transformed their outlooks about God to see themselves anew as His disciples (John 13:18; 17:9, 12). After Pentecost, the first apostles and disciples helped the believers to shape their community based on a sacrificial approach to community life – one that put others first. The book of Acts records that they shared all things in common (Acts 2:42-47).

Moreover, the famous foot-washing passage in John's gospel has Jesus washing the feet of His disciples, yet they were caught up in their egotism wondering who would have the highest places in the kingdom of God (Matthew 18:1-4; John 13). His call was for them to consider what sort of Lord He was to them. He, the Lord, had washed their feet. He radically deconstructed their vision of Himself as the Son of God in what followed. As their Lord, He had set the example of kingdom behaviour – it was to serve others first. A new picture of God emerges from John's gospel at this point, with the picture of Christ's Father in heaven being that of a parent, giving Himself to His sons and daughters in an act of service and unconditional love, through His one and only special divine Son (John 3:16-17). Jesus iterated soon after this definitive vision-setting event that to know Him is to know what the Father is like (John 14:6-10).

Just as Jesus had washed their feet, so all of them were to serve others based on unconditional positive regard, modelling grace as service just as Father, Son and Holy Spirit do in their inner Trinitarian life together. The quality of their community would be based on the new commandment to love others as Christ had loved them. When people engaged in fellowship with the disciples, they could be encouraged to model this same sort of sacrificial love to each other as well. It would be this kind of love that would provide convincing proof that they were part of God's family and that His presence could be found among them (John 13:34-35).

It will take this kind of gift-love for us to join together in the multicultural missional conversation. Some scholars believe 1 John is a covering letter to John's gospel. This little letter may have accompanied the gospel when it was sent to different congregations in Asia Minor. John writes of the new kingdom communities' outlook, and the basis of its people's fellowship:

> Dear friends, let us love one another, for love comes from God. Everyone who loves has been born of God and knows God. Whoever does not love does not know God, because

God is love. This is how God showed his love among us: He sent his one and only Son into the world that we might live through him. This is love: not that we loved God, but that he loved us and sent his Son as an atoning sacrifice for our sins. Dear friends, since God so loved us, we also ought to love one another. No one has ever seen God: but if we love one another, God lives in us and his love is made complete in us.

This is how we know that we live in him and he in us: he has given us of his Spirit. And we have seen and testify that the Father has sent his Son to be the Saviour of the world. If anyone acknowledges that Jesus is the Son of God, God lives in them and they in God. And so we know and rely on the love God has for us.

God is love. Whoever lives in love lives in God, and God in them. This is how love is made complete among us so that we will have confidence on the day of judgment: in this world we are like Jesus. There is no fear in love. But perfect love drives out fear, because fear has to do with punishment. The one who fears is not made perfect in love.

We love because he first loved us. Whoever claims to love God yet hates a brother of sister is a liar. For whoever does not love their brother and sister, whom they have seen, cannot love God, whom they have not seen. And he has given us this command: anyone who loves God must also love their brother and sister.

1 John 4:7-21 (NIV UK)

John very clearly shared the view that the 'fellowship' of the 'us' (community) he was writing to needed to model the love of the Trinity community to each other. There was to be no fear of judgement in this community by the way people behaved towards each other. In other words, unconditional positive regard and non-judgemental grace needed to define the people's behaviour towards each other. Forgiveness, welcome, support and sacrificial service were to be evident among all of its people. Non-judgemental regard could then become the healing balm that would encourage hurting people to join them for healing. They could open up their petals like flowers in the sunshine of God's grace to let healing love transform them. This is the healing love expressed to us in the metaphor of the all-embracing Multicultural Trinity. It is also what we would call the mission of the Trinity (the *missio Trinitatis*).

We believe it is important to recognise that *missio Trinitatis* is an important way of describing the work of the Multicultural Trinity. At the core of the Trinity's life together is Their all-embracing love that reaches out to all of creation to reconcile it to God's cosmic family.

It could be further suggested that transformation in John's vision of the missional church was based on creating an atmosphere of welcome for people so that they could share their lives together in fellowship without fear of judgement (see 1 John 4:18-19). The net result could be that these same people would then find courage to extend this love towards the hurting multi-ethnic Greco-Roman culture around them. In other words, the picture of God was to motivate this community to model God's grace and welcome to all who experienced its atmosphere. God's Spirit was allowed to inhabit the behaviour of the people of this church so that everyone could share in it.

This kind of missional community was surely magnetic as it welcomed displaced people into a relationship with the gracious Trinitarian family. The questions we can ask ourselves are, 'In what ways can we help our churches to become these kinds of healing communities that welcome cross-cultural diversity?' How can we shape or plant multicultural congregations to become the kinds of environments that can make a variety of peoples from different cultures feel at home?'

Before we seek some answers to these questions, it is important to understand some of the challenges that migrant Christian groups face when they come to live in the West. It is important to understand these challenges based on the rationale of this chapter, because sensitive understanding of the challenges they face when trying to integrate into Western culture must be achieved through multicultural conversations. If we do not understand each other's challenges because of our cultural differences, we certainly won't be able to plant multi-ethnic breakthrough congregations together later.

Reflective exercise

Take a few minutes to reflect on some of the following questions.

- In what ways does your picture of God affect the way you treat others?

- What picture of God is portrayed by your church?

- How do the doctrines of your church help you understand what God is like? How do they help motivate the behaviour of the people in your church?

- What have you learnt from this chapter which might change your view of God?

- How could the picture/s of God discussed in this chapter help your church to rethink how it represents itself to the surrounding secular community?

Comments

Chapter 3
Challenges Faced by Reverse Missionary and Migrant Congregations

Introduction

It is all very well to talk about the need for our various multicultural Christian groups to get involved in the missional conversation together, but first we need to extend our hands to welcome the dialogue. However, we are all part of a Western society that is largely no longer Christian, which makes it hard enough to help our own churches thrive, let alone engage in planting multicultural churches together. We need to think of ways in which we can successfully work more closely together, which means we need to understand the cultural differences that make it hard for us to understand each other's perspectives. The significant differences that exist between Western secular culture and non-Western ones do not make it any easier for non-Western Christians who have come to live in the West.

Our colleague Martin Robinson, a scholar and senior minister in the Fellowship of Churches of Christ, has shown in his book, *Winning Hearts, Changing Minds* that there have been huge changes in Western society as it has moved from a Christian to post-Christian worldview.[61] About 100 years ago, delegates at the 1910 Edinburgh World Missionary Conference felt satisfied that European society was safely Christian.[62] They considered that what was left to do was to convert the rest of the world to Christianity. This would lead, in their view, to the completion of the Great Commission so that Christ would come again to finally establish God's kingdom. Not long after this conference, the 1914–1918 war broke out, and not so many years later the Second World War. The dreadful loss of life, the mass genocide of

---

[61] Martin Robinson, *Winning Hearts, Changing Minds: When the Western World Ignores the Gospel – What Should Christians Do?* (London, Monarch Books, 2001), pp.58-75.
[62] World Missionary Conference, 1910, 'To consider missionary problems in relation to the non-Christian world'. Available at
http://archive.org/details/1936337.0004.001.umich.edu (accessed 25 August 2014).

the Jewish people in the Holocaust and the failure of the modern world that came from promising Christian foundations contributed to people returning from the war to ruined cities with far less faith in a culture of Christendom. Many who returned after the wars had lost their innocence and their Christian conviction of a God of love.

Andy's father was among these soldiers returning from the war. Prior to its outbreak he had received a call to ministry. Instead of pursuing his calling he joined up and fought in the re-conquest of Europe, beginning with participation in the D-Day landings. He lost his faith during the war as he witnessed many young men lose their lives at the hands of other young men, divided by nationality and their convictions.

In 1910, the delegates at the World Missionary Conference lived in a Europe that was culturally and historically Christian. In the years that followed, Christian Europe became secularised, and the formal Christian religion came to be deeply distrusted because Christian nations had sought to overpower each other through the violence of war. Conversations with Andy's father and other war veterans he knew were often tinged with deep suspicion of the church. This is part of what has led to today's post-Christian Europe. For migrant Christians who come to live among us, it is often a great shock that the nations who took the gospel to them during the period of colonialism now need the gospel to be brought back to them. For those of us who were the children of the boomer generation, we can understand some of the social and political trends that have transformed our Western society to become secular and postmodern. The confusion that many of our migrant Christian friends share with us concerns the question, 'How could Christian Europe give up on its Christian foundations so quickly, in just a few decades?'

Answering this kind of question is not easy, especially to people from non-Western nations where rapid Christian growth is bringing about transformation for the better. Their experience of life back home is of people who are hungry for the message of Christ and eager and passionate to follow Him. Their arrival in the West presents them with a dreadful shock – they are faced with a secular, non-Christian society where most people seem to have no faith and little interest in discussing it. This is a great challenge to first-generation migrant

Christians who soon discover that Europe has become largely a dark and godless continent.

This poses huge challenges, particularly to first and second generation migrants, to survive in this godless environment. In this chapter we need to consider these challenges seriously, because they make it difficult for migrants to find the time and energy to do more than survive in their own diaspora churches, faced as they are by a godless, challenging secularism. It is very hard for many first generation migrant Christians to have the confidence to join the multi-ethnic missional conversation because they are experiencing culture shock as well as finding it hard to survive and cope in a godless Western society.

Scholarly literature that discusses the challenges faced by ethnic reverse missionaries when they come from post-colonial nations to share the gospel with Westerners is still very limited. Although this book is not intended to be a scholarly piece of work, it is important to try to understand some of the debate that has begun in recent years about the arrival of so-called 'reverse missionaries' and the challenges they face.

Two broad areas are identifiable in the literature to be discussed in this chapter. Firstly, the challenges are concerned with the great differences that exist between migrant groups from non-Western cultures and secular Western societies.[63] Secondly, they consist of theological differences in outlook between migrants and established Western Christians who largely do not share, for example, the Pentecostal outlook on the spiritual world.[64]

This is a real problem. We have many friends among leaders of Neo-Pentecostal Churches (NPCs), Ethnic Churches (ECs) and Black Majority Churches (BMCs). BMCs and NPCs particularly recognise the real struggles their members have with engaging with Western non-charismatic church cultures, where the work of the Spirit – prophecy, miraculous healings, spiritual warfare, etc – are not part of the way

---

[63] Peter Smith, *Global Warming: The Fire of Pentecost in World Evangelism – An Anecdotal History of the Work of Elim Missions (1919 – 1989)* (Antrim, Antrim Printers, 2007), p.91.
[64] Rochelle, Cathcart, and Mike, Nichols, 'Self Theology, Global Theology, and Missional Theology, in the Writings of Paul. G. Hiebert', *Trinity Journal*, Nov, 2009, Nos. 209-221.

people in these churches think. This makes it very hard for missional conversations to develop cross culturally. Moreover, many English church people frankly find claims that people can be demon-possessed and in need of deliverance to be bizarre and open to abuse. It is true that native white Pentecostal and charismatic churches resonate better with some BMCs, but this does not make the problem less acute in the other instances.

This all adds to the culture shock for migrant Christians, and it also tends to limit the enthusiasm of migrant reverse missionary congregations to engage in missional conversations with native Western Christians. This chapter will consider what some informed scholars have to say to help us understand these challenges more deeply. This is important to consider so that these challenges can be openly addressed as part of the multicultural missional conversation.

Historical–cultural challenges

Reverse missionary Christians who seek to bring the gospel back to Europe is an emergent development that has been given more recognition recently in scholarly literature.[65] The historian Osgood suggests that it most noticeably revealed itself in the 1980s[66] and came from developing nations who were once on the receiving end of European colonialism in the nineteenth and twentieth centuries.[67]

The theologian Ojo suggests that two forces caused this increase in migrant Christians coming to live in Europe with a desire to bring the gospel back. Firstly, economic and political tensions in some of their homelands led to large migrations to Europe of ethnic Christians seeking a better life for their families.[68] These groups shared somewhat nomadic theologies which resonate well with the Abraham narratives in the book of Genesis (see chapter 4 on nomadic disciples).[69] The

---

[65] Catto, in David Goodhew (ed), *Church Growth in Britain 1980 to the Present* (Farnham, Ashgate, 2012), Chapter 6.

[66] Osgood, in Goodhew (ed), *Church Growth in Britain 1980 to the Present*, p.112.

[67] Osgood, in Goodhew (ed), *Church Growth in Britain 1980 to the Present*, p.112.

[68] Ojo, in Bonk, *The Routledge Encyclopedia of Missions and Missionaries*, p.381.

[69] David Phillips, *Peoples on the Move: Introducing the Nomads of the World* (Carlisle, Piquant, 2001), Chapters 5, 6.

people who engaged in this movement to the West often sensed a call to leave their native places and go where God was sending them.

Secondly, the establishment of the Third World Missions Association (1989) has legitimised Christians from other cultures to send missionaries to every part of the globe, including secular Europe, in order to bring the gospel back to its people.[70] Hence mission in reverse, with the rest coming to the West with the gospel to reconvert it to the faith it took to them, is not an unfair description of the current trend.

We will use the term 'reverse mission' in this chapter more than in others in order to give it a distinctive recognition. However, as we noted in the first chapter, we also want to speak more broadly in this book about being missional together by planting some multi-ethnic breakthrough congregations. To the extent that this chapter aims to help us understand the challenges that make it hard for Western Christians to join in multicultural missional conversations with migrant Christians, we will use reverse mission as a distinctive term that needs to be transformed, we believe, to become part of a broader, joined-up missional conversation. If this happens, the term 'multicultural missional conversation' does away with a boundary term that can keep us apart rather than enable us to engage in dialogue.

The birth of AICs and BMCs

Osgood notes that rapid church growth in Nigeria in the 1970s led to 'Deeper Life' and 'New Covenant' church leaders sending some of their experienced ministers to plant new churches in London during the 1980s.[71] These experienced leaders were part of a new movement which began in Nigeria, known as African Initiated Churches (AICs). AIC leaders came to Europe to help their people, who were now part of a Nigerian diaspora, to retain their faith and their African cultural roots. This agenda to help them preserve their identities was, of course, a noble aspiration, and it certainly added to the richness of what Nigerian people can bring to our multicultural society. However,

---

[70] Ojo, in Bonk, *The Routledge Encyclopedia of Missions and Missionaries*, p.381.
[71] Osgood, in Goodhew (ed), *Church Growth in Britain 1980 to the Present*, p.112.

there is a downside, in reverse missionary terms, because it has often meant that Nigerian BMCs have resisted changing their approaches to work cross culturally and to adapt in order for other cultural groups in the West to understand the importance of the gospel in a language they can appreciate.

This trend of growth has led to a continuing 'sent to plant' strategy to Britain (and Europe) by AIC leaders.[72] It is important to understand that the churches planted are encouraged by AIC ideology to retain their homeland culture and their BMC status, made up as they are of the same national members. This is a challenge we need to face together. If we want these kinds of BMCs to be involved in the multicultural missional conversation, when they are trying to maintain their people's originating culture to the detriment of becoming involved in cross-cultural missional endeavours, how can we hope to work together cross culturally?

Osgood focuses attention on two trends related to this AIC strategy:

> the 'sent to plant' pattern has continued in Britain, either with a view to gathering emigrated members or to extending influence through establishing a new work.[73]

He implies that African leaders were sent to plant churches for other peoples in the West, including English native people, as well as migrants from their former home nations. The cultural anthropologist Gittins suggests that it is not easy for them to do this with secular Westerners because of the significant cultural differences that exist between European and non-Western peoples.[74]

The theologian Burgess reckons the majority of church-planting ventures are among BMCs and have been undertaken by leaders from various non-Western diaspora homelands.[75] This also means that the AIC monocultural ideology is a major issue to address in order to help Western and non-Western Christians dialogue together. How can we

---

[72] Osgood, in Goodhew (ed), *Church Growth in Britain 1980 to the Present*, pp.109-110.
[73] Osgood, in Goodhew (ed), *Church Growth in Britain 1980 to the Present*, p.113.
[74] Osgood, in Goodhew (ed), *Church Growth in Britain 1980 to the Present*, pp.113-116.
[75] Burgess, in Goodhew (ed), *Church Growth in Britain 1980 to the Present*, p.141.

get to know each other more intentionally when ideological differences drive a wedge between us?

It is also important to understand the motives that prompt homeland BMCs to send experienced leaders to help African migrants who have come to the UK to seek a better standard of living for their families.[76] BMCs partly function as a means to maintain their homeland Christian culture.[77] Another major motive is to help their people hold fast to their Pentecostal charismatic faith, or the faith of other ethnic churches who are Anglican, Baptist or Methodist. They can also help migrant Christians to maintain an ethnocentric attitude, which can stop them from adapting to the new host culture or wanting to join in missional work together.[78] Extensive numbers of native white converts have not been evidenced as a result of ministry having been offered by reverse missionaries.[79]

There has been a tendency for rapid growth of BMCs in Britain.[80] This has raised interest among national church planting forums because of their great passion for Christ and the successful planting of churches for their own ethnicities.[81] We all need to share in this passion to share the gospel with others – hopefully including those who are not from our own ethnic group.

Ethnic churches with the majority of their members from one nationality tend to find it hard for white people to be invited to join them because of the cultural differences.[82] This may be easier for other cultures – for example, if we were discussing other European experiences of church, such as a Polish church, but often Polish churches use the Polish language in their services. This obviously makes it hard for English speakers to fellowship with them.

A 2012 BBC documentary series entitled *Reverse Missionaries* demonstrated that individuals from Jamaica, Malawi and India who worked with Baptist, Congregational and Presbyterian churches while

---

[76] Burgess, in Goodhew (ed), *Church Growth in Britain 1980 to the Present*, p.130.

[77] Burgess, in Goodhew (ed), *Church Growth in Britain 1980 to the Present*, Chapter 8.

[78] Giddens and Sutton, *Sociology*, p.641.

[79] Burgess, in Goodhew (ed), *Church Growth in Britain 1980 to the Present*, pp.128-130.

[80] Osgood, in Goodhew (ed), *Church Growth in Britain 1980 to the Present*, pp.128-130.

[81] Olofinjana, *Reverse in Ministry & Missions*, pp.3-4.

[82] Burgess, in Goodhew (ed), *Church Growth in Britain 1980 to the Present*, p.127-131.

they were in the UK were able to generate some interest from white people who were interested in joining their congregations.[83] And this must not be missed as a very real benefit for migrant Christians to engage in the multicultural missional conversation with white churches who need to be ignited with this kind of passion. There is a very strong chance that doing so will mean that we can start to work together to bring the passion and experience of migrant missionaries to some Western congregations in order to win a variety of people to Christ. This will obviously mean some real sacrifices, some of which we will discuss in this book.

It was, sadly, impossible to judge from this documentary series whether missionaries who worked with white churches could achieve real long-term converts who would commit to the churches concerned after these missionaries on short-term mission went home. This was because the missionary visits only lasted for about one month, and there was no follow-up later to establish whether there were any enduring results from the good work they had started.

What evidence is there that reverse missionary goals to share the gospel with Westerners are more than aspirations for them? The missiologist Catto has provided some examples of South American and Korean missionaries who have come to the UK.[84] For instance, Melanesian Brothers and Sisters who visited various regions of the UK from May to August 2005 came with a mission that offered gospel messages in song. Their work did not provide measurable results in terms of Caucasian or other ethnic converts.[85] In actuality, it is hard to recognise well-founded evidence from Catto's case studies that they represent more than aspirational forms of short-term mission enterprises, indicating that missionaries from the southern hemisphere want to bring the gospel back to the north.[86] We may conclude that her data cannot properly be termed 'reverse mission' because the people in her case studies did not plan to remain in Britain to see their projects through. Catto was not able to identify good samples of sustainable reverse mission ventures which had led to the establishment of

---

[83] *Reverse Missionaries*, BBC2, 2012.

[84] Catto, in Goodhew (ed), *Church Growth in Britain 1980 to the Present*, Chapter 6.

[85] Catto, in Goodhew (ed), *Church Growth in Britain 1980 to the Present*, pp.93-94.

[86] Catto, in Goodhew (ed), *Church Growth in Britain 1980 to the Present*, Chapter 6.

multicultural churches or other missional ventures.[87] It would seem fair to argue that her case studies demonstrated how little cross-cultural preparation reverse missionaries had been provided with prior to entry to Europe. We believe that reverse mission engagement should aim to lead to the establishment of sustainable longer-term multi-ethnic churches, while at the same time understanding that all new types of church plants often only survive for a few years.

We also need to understand that reverse missionaries will not be able to make a significant impact on the postmodern population of the West when they first arrive because of their need to understand Western culture by living in it for some time first.[88] However, even if this is true, it should not stop migrant Christians starting to engage in the multicultural missional conversation, as doing so will hopefully help them to discover insights from those who have been in the West for a while, and this in turn could help their congregations adapt better to life in the West.

Moreover, first and second generation migrant churches will probably need to make serious attempts to communicate with Western people in idiom and language that will make it possible for them to build meaningful relationships.[89] We need to help them to do this through things like English classes and by spending time and intentionally sharing life together, possibly at events like fellowship days where different churches get together. The ethnographer and missiologist Hanciles informs us that reverse mission and 'its long-term significance and impact remain to be seen', because it takes time for migrant peoples to be accepted in a new host's culture.[90]

We may wonder whether this recent historic trend of non-Western Christians wanting to bring the gospel back to the West is no more than a vain hope for success, with little evidence that it really works.

---

[87] Catto, in Goodhew (ed), *Church Growth in Britain 1980 to the Present*, Chapter 6.

[88] Steve Moon, 'The Recent Korean Missionary Movement: A Record of Growth, and More Growth Needed', *International Bulletin of Missionary Research*, Vol.27, 1 Jan 2003, p.13.

[89] Kraft, *Christianity in Culture: A Study in Dynamic Biblical Theologizing in Cross-Cultural Perspective*, Chapter 4.

[90] Jehu Hanciles, 'Migration and Mission: Some Implications for the Twenty-First-Century Church', *International Bulletin of Missionary Research*, Vol.27 No.4, Nov.2003, p.152.

This is very hard for us to gauge. What we do need to consider helping reverse missionaries to do is to be better prepared to share the gospel cross culturally with Westerners. There is not a well-established period of preparation for many who are sent to bring the gospel back to the West.[91] The missional scholar Moon provides evidence that demonstrates this thesis, most particularly among Korean missionaries. In 1979 they sent workers to 26 countries; by 1990 to 87 and by 2000 to 197.[92]

Moon recognises that this rapid increase could suggest that missionaries who are being sent overseas are exceeding the capacity to properly train them.[93] If this is the case, reverse mission will not make a significant impact on Westerners unless proper training is offered to help them in the process of acculturation so that they can work within the Western secular worldview, which is unlike their own.[94] We need to engage in multicultural missional conversations in order to help

---

[91] Olofinjana, *Reverse in Ministry & Missions*, p.57.

[92] Moon, 'The Recent Korean Missionary Movement', pp.12-13.

[93] Moon, 'The Recent Korean Missionary Movement', pp.12-15.

[94] Olofinjana, *Reverse in Ministry & Missions*, p.57.

each other in the aspiration to communicate cross culturally more effectively.

However, we may hope together that the situation may not be too bleak.[95] If current migration trends continue, it is quite possible that larger numbers of better-trained reverse missionaries will come to Europe in the future, particularly if they learn lessons from earlier efforts to communicate the gospel to Westerners.[96] Once again, it is important that we all overcome our natural inclinations to remain separate from each other. We are brothers and sisters in Christ. In the final analysis, the critical measure for the success of reverse mission will need to be the planting of churches where white converts fellowship in multi-ethnic breakthrough congregations. The question we are challenging everyone to think about is, 'How can we do this together?' These multi-ethnic churches will need to include other non-Christian ethnicities who live in the West as some of the people we want to invite into the family of Christ.[97] However, Moon raises another challenge:

> Indigenous [ethnic] mission agencies tend to be weak in establishing sending structures. In many cases an agency's entire operation revolves around a charismatic leader, with little commitment to developing a structure that will allow it to survive after the passing of the leader.[98]

Missiologist Jaffarian adds:

> In the year 2000 there were more than four times as many Western missionaries as missionaries from the Four-Fifths-World.[99]

---

[95] Hanciles, 'Migration and Mission', pp.145-148.

[96] Hanciles, 'Migration and Mission', pp.148-152.

[97] Garces-Foley, *Crossing the Ethnic Divide*, Chapter 4.

[98] Moon, 'The Recent Korean Missionary Movement', p.13.

[99] Michael Jaffarian, 'Are There More Non-Western Missionaries than Western Missionaries?' *International Bulletin of Missionary Research*, Vol. 28, No. 3, July 2004, p.131.

The sending of lower numbers of non-Western 'missionaries' to the West compared with those sent from the West to non-Western mission fields is indicative of a still emergent trend that will take time to be addressed. Better training and awareness of the need for support structures that can sustain mission enterprises will need to be established to support such efforts.[100] It will also be vital for these missionaries to become involved in the multicultural missional conversation with others who are already engaged in planting multi-ethnic churches in the West, or with those thinking about how to do this.

Having said this, there is more money available from the affluent West to fund work in developing Christianised nations than there is for those coming to the West coming from the poorer south. Hence most of those who come to the UK arrive as poor migrants with no intentions of planting churches, and they face huge challenges – including culture shock – when they first arrive. They first need to establish themselves in their new home.[101]

Jaffarian notes that in the past decade, the 'Four-Fifths-World-Missions-Movement' is growing at a faster rate than that in the West.[102] There is hope that as some of the nations sending reverse missionaries become more affluent, this will help to fund better-trained missionaries, as well as help prepare more effectively those who come to live in the West in order to bring their skills into the job markets here. However, the lack of convincing examples that reverse mission is more than aspirational at first for many of those migrants is a weakness to be witnessed generally among BMCs and NPCs.[103]

The missiologist Kim informs our understanding by suggesting that there is clear substantiation that people are still coming to Europe for the specific purpose of missional endeavours. It is important to understand that many come with the intention of making a real

---

[100] Hanciles, *Migration and Mission: Some Implications for the Twenty-First-Century Church*, pp.150-151.

[101] Hanciles, *Migration and Mission: Some Implications for the Twenty-First-Century Church*, pp.146, 150-151.

[102] Jaffarian, *Are There More Non-Western Missionaries than Western Missionaries*, p.132.

[103] Hirpo, Kumbi, *The Development of Ethiopian and Eritrean Evangelical Churches in the United Kingdom: Missional Movement or Cultural Dead-End* (Birmingham: Springdale College, MA Missional Leadership), Chapter 4.

contribution to our efforts to re-win the West. They do not simply come to find a better life here. They also make sacrifices, leaving their extended families so they can engage in mission in the West.[104] The Anglican Church Mission Society, for example, has been a key player in seconding overseas ethnic missionaries to come to minister in the UK.[105] Experienced ethnic ministers are being brought to the UK to engage in mission in native white churches as well as to encourage the establishment of multicultural churches.[106] We need to feel very encouraged by this wonderful sacrificial desire to join us in our efforts to bring Christ to Western people. Moreover, the Catholic Church impressively has the largest constituent of migrant Christians in Britain, with ethnic and multi-ethnic configurations worshipping together.

A further encouraging trend is the increase in the numbers of BMC congregations planted in the 1990s, growing from a figure of 100 in the 1960s to 1,000 by 1990.[107] The new millennium witnessed the number grow to more than 3,000 in the UK, and similar trends were witnessed in Europe overall and in North America.[108] And this is vital to grasp. Even if it takes time for newly planted ethnic churches to acclimatise to life in the West, it does not need to stop us learning from each other about the challenges we all face in our lives together in the secular West.

It is also important to note that BMCs are only newcomers to the West in terms of their significant numeric increases among us. Hanciles suggests that in the 1950s and 1960s there was substantial growth in the numbers of Afro-Caribbeans entering Britain, and in the 1970s there was a significant influx of Asians.[109] The 1980s saw an important trend in Black African immigration.[110] BMCs brought reverse mission to the foreground as a possible means to bring the

---

104 Kirsteen Kim, *Joining in with the Spirit: Connecting World Church and Local Mission* (London, Epworth, 2009), pp.99-103.

105 Kim, *Joining in with the Spirit*, p.12

106 Kim, *Joining in with the Spirit*, p.12, 13.

107 Ojo, in Bonk, *The Routledge Encyclopedia of Missions and Missionaries*, p.381.

108 Hanciles, 'Migration and Mission', p.150.

109 Hanciles, 'Migration and Mission', pp.146-152.

110 Hans Kung, *The Christian Challenge* (London, Collins, 1979), pp.69-113.

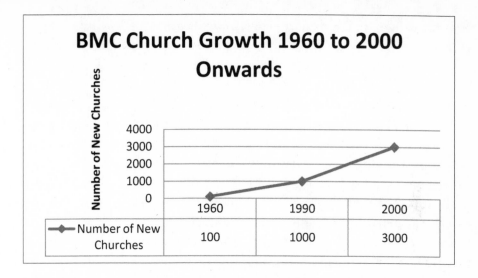

BMC Church Growth 1960 to 2000 Onwards

	1960	1990	2000
Number of New Churches	100	1000	3000

gospel back to Britain, especially beginning in the 1990s.[111] In 2000 *The Sunday Times* reported, 'Missionaries arrive to save heathen Britain.'[112] This may have been a tongue–in-cheek editorial. However, the Afro-Caribbean churches which have been established here since then have become acclimatised to life in the West. A few of these congregations are multi-ethnic and have had some success in bringing the gospel back to the West. One example is a Baptist church in north London which is making some headway toward becoming multi-ethnic. Those attending come from Afro-Caribbean, African, Asian and white English backgrounds.

It seems that the largest challenge we need to overcome as Christian churches made up of different ethnicities is to intentionally join together in sharing our missional challenges, as part of the multicultural missional conversation. In later chapters we will consider practical steps we need to take in order to do this. Having said this, reverse missionary leaders now living in the West can become consumed by work with people from their homelands coming to join them in the West, to such an extent that it takes energy from their leaders to engage in missional endeavours outside their own people group.[113] However, this trend may soon change. It has been

---

[111] Hanciles, 'Migration and Mission', pp.146-148.
[112] *The Sunday Times*, 1st July 2000.
[113] Hanciles, 'Migration and Mission', pp.149-151.

suggested that the UK Border Agency (UKBA) is not allowing as many ethnic clergy into the country,[114] and far fewer migrants may enter in the future if the trend to limit the numbers continues as a political strategy.[115]

This raises the challenging question about the medium- to longer-term viability of ethnic missionary success in the UK among people from their own people groups, even if greater success is theoretically possible. The focus will naturally become how second and third generation offspring from these ethnic churches can integrate into multicultural churches. This is an important discussion for all of us. However, existing migrant churches could be stimulated by this change in immigration policy to focus more attention on planting multi-ethnic congregations in the future, as a matter of practical necessity if nothing else.[116]

If sociological forces subverting reverse missionary numbers coming to the West can be addressed, it may be missionally fruitful to move from homogenous group congregations to heterogeneous multi-ethnic churches, because of changes in migration policies.[117] It seems strange theologically that Christ's call to take the gospel to all nations (Matthew 24:14) should not include efforts to unify diverse heterogeneous peoples living in Britain today (see Galatians 3:28).

We need to define our terms here as well. As we noted earlier, the missiologist McGavran famously came up with the homogenous unit principle in terms of mission theory. It is without much doubt that we find it easier to plant churches for our own people groups. This will remain a continuing challenge to the successful planting of multi-ethnic churches.

Heterogeneous mission thinkers suggest that it is possible to plant multicultural churches. They believe that as people come to understand other peoples better in our multicultural society, it will lead to friendships developing and cultural barriers being broken

---

[114] Rev Julian Mann, 'UK Border Agency obstructs the path of overseas clergy', 3rd October 2012. Available at http://archbishop-cranmer.blogspot.co.uk/2012/10/uk-border-agency-obstructs-path-of.html, (accessed 25th August 2014).

[115] Giddens and Sutton, *Sociology*, pp.654-669.

[116] Hanciles, 'Migration and Mission', p.152.

[117] Moynagh and Harrold, *Church for Every Context*, pp.168-170.

down. This can be seen in the example of the Baptist church we mentioned above. In a church in Oxford, at least five different nationalities regularly worship together.

It seems that cities are the best places to try to plant multi-ethnic churches. Oxford is a special case in point as the university brings students from many nations and cultures to become part of its multicultural tapestry.

As we engage in chaplaincy work with Christians in university colleges, we have engaged in many stimulating multicultural missional conversations. What this experience has taught us is the real possibility of intelligent discussion, which could help Christian students to think about working cross culturally with their peers. It has also proved possible to build cross-cultural bridges of shared understanding in cities like Oxford because of its cosmopolitan atmosphere and its broad range of international students, as well as some of the summer English language schools that are hosted in the city.

Challenges and learning opportunities

Gittins helps us think about theological challenges for mission from a cultural and anthropological point of view. Anthropologists are fascinated with how different people groups experience life. He comments:

> I understand missiology to be concerned with raising up the wisdom of other cultural traditions and with the study of the workings of grace in cross-cultural relationships.[118]

Gittins is quite right to suggest that we can discover the workings of God's grace when we work together 'in cross-cultural relationships'. As we come to understand each other's cultural differences by engaging in multicultural missional conversations, we can discover new ways of sharing the gospel with a variety of ethnicities and cultures to be found in the localities where we live. Engaging together

---

[118] Anthony Gittins, 'Reflections from the Edge: Mission-in-Reverse and Missiological Research', *Missiology: An International Review*, Vol.21, No.1, Jan. 1983, p.26.

in mission helps us to obtain a greater understanding of what other cultures have to offer to our own. Moreover, different people groups have much wisdom to share from the rich tapestry of their 'cultural traditions'.

In what ways have you been enriched and stimulated by interacting with other cultural groups? The best way to experience this richness is to build friendships with people from other ethnic persuasions. Gittins suggests that traditional mission courses taught in colleges have often not tested their theological concepts in the context of working with people from other cultures until after courses have been completed by participants, who then leave with no practical experience of how to apply what they have learnt.

At Springdale College, we believe one of the strengths of our missional ministry courses is that students engage in placements while they are studying. They do 13 hours a week of placement work throughout the academic year. By doing this it is possible for them to reflect on what they are learning as they try out ideas at their placements.

Gittins challenges us to take seriously the observation that 'salvation occurs in the real life situations of human history'.[119] The part we play in human history together is part of the rich tapestry of life. History generally provides us with good witness of the many cultures and nations that make up its wide historical literature, and records the many influences that have helped shape the world of today. This requires us to understand the theological workings of God's grace in history as it has helped shape human societies in explicit and implicit ways.

In order for us to make sense of how God has worked with His people throughout history, we need to understand what Scripture has to teach us about this subject.[120] The Bible is made up of historical faith-documents which explore how God has engaged in His mission to save the nations of the world, covering hundreds of years of Israel's history.

---

[119] Gittins, 'Reflections from the Edge', pp.27-28.
[120] Gittins, 'Reflections from the Edge', p.27.

The theologian Jürgen Moltmann is a significant voice who considers salvation history to be the arena through which the Trinity engages with the various cultures of the world by the work of the universal presence of the Spirit.[121] Theologian Amstutz helps us to understand that salvation history covers the whole world's history and that different people groups and their cultures have formed the tapestry of how God has worked with them to bring them to readiness to receive the gospel.[122] Gittins calls us to an experiential appreciation of theology that views God to be active without partiality among all peoples.[123] By intentionally sharing deep friendships among different people groups, we begin to discover what God is doing in His mission among them.

Different points of view challenge us to reconstruct our theology based on a reflective process of learning and interaction with other cultures living in the multicultural West in order to understand what God is doing with them.[124] This has to happen as Christians in our multicultural society seek to build friendships with non-Christians and Christians alike, who as yet are not engaged in the missional conversation. This kind of friendship-based dialogue requires us to develop rapport with people of different cultures so that learning can happen and meaningful communication can take place and we can learn even more from each other.[125] Gittins argues that the missionary and the recipient of the missionary's work are both challenged to change the way they view the world by the cross-cultural processes of their interactions.[126]

The writers Branson and Martinez make the case for biblical reflection when crossing cultural boundaries.[127] Placing biblical stories

[121] Clark Pinnock, *Flame of Love: A Theology of the Holy Spirit* (Downers Grove, IVP Academic, 1996), pp.10, 25, 26-28, 29, 30-21, 200-202, 232.

[122] Frans Verstraelen, and F. J. Camps (eds), *Missiology: An Ecumenical Introduction, Texts and Contexts of Global Christianity* (Grand Rapids, Eerdmans, 1995), p.449.

[123] Gittins, 'Reflections from the Edge', pp.27-28.

[124] Gittins, 'Reflections from the Edge', p27, 28.

[125] Gittins, 'Reflections from the Edge', p27, 28.

[126] Tite Tienou, and Paul Hiebert, 'Missional Theology', *Missiology and International Review*, Vol.34, No.2, April 2006, p.221.

[127] Mark Branson, and Juan Martinez, *Churches, Cultures and Leadership: A Practical Theology of Congregations and Ethnicities* (Downers Grove, IVP Academic, 2011), p.34.

that exhibit 'boundary crossing' alongside the missionaries' own experiences of crossing cultural boundaries to share their faith can help to stimulate imagination about how God might want to relate to a new culture in a similar way, as He did with a variety of peoples in the biblical narratives.[128] It is vital for us to realise that there are many unreached people in the West with regard to the gospel – the majority of whom are postmodern, secular white people.

It is not just consideration of Scripture as the conveyor of the message of mission that is important when we engage in mission in the multicultural marketplace.[129] The life stories and contexts of non-Christian seekers which they share with us in missional friendships will also help us to understand them. As we compare our stories and experiences with theirs, we can learn about the similarities and differences between their perspectives on life and our own.[130]

When one of us worked with a gypsy community, we were as much influenced by the values of gypsy family life and their deep respect for their kith and kin as we were by the need to consider what Jesus Christ meant to their community and what He had done for them personally. Personal stories were more important to them than Bible studies aimed at converting them to theological ideas. They wanted to hear authentic personal stories of what the real, living Jesus was still doing by His Spirit in our lives as much as about what Jesus did during His earthly ministry. The largest impact occurred when their own prayers began to be answered as they had been inspired by stories we had shared with them of answered prayers. God often shows up, not in the preached word so much as in the lives of people we come to care about as we seek to bring Jesus into their lives.

One of the best things people who come to live in the West can do is to build friendships with Westerners who are seeking to understand what God can do for them. Many of our ethnic Christian friends have amazing stories of how God has answered prayers. This is a great opportunity to share with Western people who are seeking to learn more about spiritual experiences. A simple strategy like this can empower migrant Christians in their attempts to try to understand the

---

128 Branson, and Martinez, *Churches, Cultures and Leadership*, p.34.

129 Gittins, 'Reflections from the Edge', pp.27-28.

130 Gittins, 'Reflections from the Edge', pp.27-30.

new host culture.[131] The psychological factors that cause 'severe reverse-culture-shock'[132] are well known to experts in cultural adaptation theory and praxis.[133] Culture shock is a real problem that can make people feel disempowered, confused and disorientated. It is very hard for first generation ethnic Christians to appreciate their new Western receptor culture.[134] Building friendships can be a great way to get to know some of the customs of those among whom they now live.

Our cultural heritage tends to be deeply programmed into our unconscious minds from a young age, and it tends to predispose us to see the world in terms of our own cultural pre-programming.[135] A sense of being called to bring the gospel back to Europe may be put off for a number of years because of disorientation caused by encountering secular Western culture.[136] And this means that part of the missional conversation in which we engage together needs to be about how we can support and care for first generation migrants who enter the West with a desire to share their faith here.

What makes life even harder is the multicultural melting pot of different ethnic groups in the West today. Each comes with its own cultural perspective, and this can add to confusion for those who come to live here for the first time. Not only is secular society in many ways godless; it is also influenced by the gods of other religious groups. The challenge here has to do with the different theological ideas of these groups and their outlooks on the world. Culture shock can be compounded by this additional complication. First generation migrant religious groups often gather together in their own ethnic groups and seek refuge from this confusing society.

Western society can be a complicated environment for first generation migrants to understand.[137] There is not, as such, a stable core identity that we all share in common. Postmodernism means that

---

[131] Kraft, article in, Scott, Moreau, *Evangelical Dictionary of World Missions* (Carlisle, Paternoster Press, 2000), pp.256-257.

[132] Gittins, *Reflections from the Edge: Mission-in-Reverse and Missiological Research,* p.24.

[133] Kraft, in Moreau *Evangelical Dictionary of World Missions*, (Carlisle, Paternoster Press, 2000), p.256.

[134] Kraft, in Moreau, *Evangelical Dictionary of World Missions*, pp.256-257:

[135] Kraft, in Moreau, *Evangelical Dictionary of World Missions*, pp.256-257

[136] Kraft, in Moreau, *Evangelical Dictionary of World Missions*, pp.256-257

[137] Kraft, *Christianity in Culture*, pp.131-141.

people in our society do not embrace one belief system. Furthermore, most secular people would challenge anyone who claimed to have 'the truth', by replying with something like, 'This may be your truth but I don't believe in one version of truth – there are lots of possible truths.' This postmodern Western outlook also includes peoples from all kinds of differing religious persuasions and outlooks on the world. When we engage in conversations with people from a significantly different cultural outlook it can feel very uncomfortable if we do not agree with some of the things they assume to be true. Some of our most cherished beliefs can be challenged in such circumstances, if we desire to find common ground.[138]

Reverse missionaries who come with a view to bring the gospel back to the West do not just have their interpretations of the host culture affected by their own cultural perspectives.[139] A Western Christian may not meaningfully understand the cultural differences between their own outlook on life and that of a reverse missionary group.[140] The whole question of differences in theological outlook can mean that the same passage in the same Bible can be interpreted in very different ways by readers from different cultural traditions.[141] For example, when reading the parable of the lost sheep, a person from a pastoral culture will attach a very different value to the loss of a sheep to a Westerner living in a town or city. To a person who has come from a poorer pastoral culture, a lost sheep represents a significant loss to the livelihood of a shepherd. Finding it will be a cause for joy to the shepherd in that culture, who may only own four or five sheep, and which is what his personal wealth is measured by.

These kinds of pastoral stories will mean much more to members of migrant churches who come from cultures like this than to Western church people. This kind of cross-cultural difference will potentially make it harder to understand the values we place on key Scriptures

---

138 Kraft, *Christianity in Culture,* p.117.

139 Kraft, *Christianity in Culture,* pp.117, 118.

140 Paul Hiebert, *Transforming Worldviews: An Anthropological Understanding of How People Change* (Grand Rapids, Baker Academic, 2009a), compare and contrast, chapters 6, 9.

141 Anthony Thiselton, *Hermeneutics: An Introduction* (Grand Rapids, Eerdmans, 2009),pp.21, 23, 85-87, 89, 96, 251, 291.

when we meet cross culturally to talk about working in mission together.

It is important to realise that many non-Western Christians now living in the West do not readily appreciate the perspectives of secular people, who define themselves as individuals with absolute rights to live their lives based on their own desires and needs.[142] It can be a shock for migrants to realise that many Westerners do not believe in one overarching metanarrative (big story like the Christian story), but rather they do not believe that there is absolute truth about what to believe about almost anything.[143] Ethnic people often come from cultures where one singular metanarrative is what shapes their society's outlook, and this makes for a higher degree of culture shock when they come to live in the West, because of the relativistic outlooks of Westerners.[144]

Because postmodernity does not accept one overarching metanarrative,[145] it becomes very difficult for reverse missionaries to formulate any strategic approach to communicate a biblical worldview to relativistic Westerners.[146] To exacerbate this problem further, many who come to do mission here have not been properly prepared to understand Western cultural relativity.[147] They probably better understand some of the other religious persuasions that are found among ethnic minority groups, those who are not Christians but who share some similar perspectives on life because of closer cultural ties.[148] The question to ask ourselves might be, 'Are we better off working

---

[142] Paul Hiebert, *The Gospel in Human Contexts: Anthropological Explorations for Contemporary Missions* (Grand Rapids, Baker Academic, 2009b), Chapters 6 to 8.

[143] Hiebert, *Transforming Worldviews,* Chapters 8, 9.

[144] Craig Van Gelder, 'Postmodernism and Evangelicals: A Unique Missiological Challenge at the Beginning of the Twenty-First Century', *Missiology and International Review*, Vol.30, No.4, Oct. 2002, pp.492-494.

[145] Colin Greene, and Martin Robinson, *Metavista: Bible, Church and Mission in an Age of Imagination* (Milton Keynes, Authentic Media, 2008), Chapter 2.

[146] Greene and Robinson, *Metavista*, Chapter 2.

[147] Haralambos and Holborn, *Sociology Themes and Perspectives,*, pp.525-530.

[148] Nazir-ali, in Christopher Partridge, *Dictionary of Contemporary Religion in the Western World* (Leicester, IVP, 2002), pp.44-49. Chris Barker, *Cultural Studies: Theory and Practice* (London, Sage, 2008), pp.31, 48, 197; David Burnett, *Clash of Worlds: What Christians Can Do in a World of Cultures in Conflict* (London, Monarch Books, 2002), p.46; K. P. Yohannan, *Revolution in World Missions* (Carrollton, GFA Books, 2004), pp.199-208.

with people from similar cultures in the multicultural West than those that are significantly different to our own cultures?

Sociologists Pollock and van Reken suggest that missionary children make up what is termed a 'third culture', which we will discuss in greater depth later.[149] It is worth mentioning now that migrant children often find it hard to fit either into the culture of their parents or into that of the host culture. It can lead to psychological and sociological estrangement and maladjustment for these offspring if great care is not taken to help them acculturate to the best bits of Western culture.[150]

If the process of acculturation to life in the West fails, reverse missionary work will be critically undermined in the second generation.[151] And it is unlikely that the missionary zeal of first generation missionaries will ever be realised by their generation, but rather by later generations. It needs to be recognised that before mission to Westerners can be undertaken by first generation migrant parents, significant time must be invested to prepare the second generation to be socialised to Western life.[152]

Migrant parents will also need to think about how they exercise authority over their offspring, particularly if this contradicts Western laws that consider it abusive to use physical violence of any type.[153] The use of physical punishment may even estrange their children from them if their children come to adopt the values of the Western host culture regarding discipline.

It is these very practical kinds of questions that need to be addressed, alongside the bigger-picture issue of how to prepare the second generation to become missionaries to bring the gospel back to the West. If vision is passed on as missional DNA by parents to their

[149] David Pollock and Ruth van Reken, *Third Culture Kids: The Experience of Growing Up Among Worlds* (London, Nicholas Brealey Publishing, 2001), Chapter 2.

[150] Pollock and van Reken, *Third Culture Kids*, Chapters 1, 3, 4; Eddie Gibbs and Ryan Bolger, *Emerging Churches: Creating Christian Communities in Postmodern Cultures* (London, SPCK, 2006), p.23.

[151] Pollock and van Reken, *Third Culture Kids*, Chapters 6, 8.

[152] Mike Cardwell, Liz Clark and Claire Meldrum, *Psychology* (London, Harper Collins, 2004), pp.292, 526, 569, 587, 597.

[153] Richard Hecht and Vincent Biondo, *Religion and Culture: Contemporary Practices and Perspectives* (Minneapolis, Fortress Press, 2010), pp.223, 224.

children, a sustainable process could be fostered towards longer-term successes, bringing Westerners to faith through their offspring in the future.[154]

Theologian Walter Wink classically suggested a significant theological challenge faced by ethnic churches, especially among those who have Pentecostal theologies regarding spiritual warfare as part of their liberation theology.[155] The NPCs coming from the poorer southern hemisphere tend to have an 'Ancient Worldview'.[156] According to Wink, it fits well with the culture of the first-century church which thought of all levels of life and nature to be sustained or threatened by various supernatural forces. Much of what happens in the material world for NPCs is viewed against the theological backdrop of conflict taking place between Christ, Satan and demons behind the scenes. Evil demonic forces are considered to cause most illnesses and diseases – they are thought of as part of demonic oppression or possession.[157]

Many reverse missionaries hold this perspective,[158] and this has led to much criticism of some Pentecostal ethnic minority churches, and native Western white churches, by the Western media when abuses of this kind of power theology lead to spiritual warfare practices that cause deaths and suicides.[159] Abuses have at times been identified by

---

[154] Garces-Foley, *Crossing the Ethnic Divide*, p.146.

[155] Walter Wink, *The Powers that Be: Theology for a New Millennium* (New York, Galilee Doubleday, 1999), Chapter 1; Peter Wagner, *Warfare Prayer: How to Seek God's Power and Protection in the Battle to Build His Kingdom* (Venture, Regal Books, 1992), Chapter 2; Adrian Hastings, *African Catholicism Essays in Discovery* (Philadelphia, Trinity Press, 1989), p.90.

[156] Wink, *The Powers that Be*, p15; Walter Wink, *Engaging the Powers: Discernment and Resistance in a World of Domination* (Minneapolis, Fortress Press, 1992), Chapter 2; Walter, Wink, *Unmasking the Powers: The Invisible Forces that Determine Human Existence* (Philadelphia, Fortress Press, 1986), Chapter 2; Walter Wink, *Naming the Powers: The Language of Power in the New Testament* (Philadelphia, Fortress Press, 1984), Chapter 1.

[157] Wagner, *Warfare Prayer*, Chapter 2.

[158] Vinay Samuel, and Chris Sugden, *Mission as Transformation: A Theology of the Whole Gospel* (California, Regnum, 1999), Chapter 2.

[159] Chris Greenwood, 'Boy, 15, 'tortured to death with hammer and chisels on Christmas Day because relative thought he was a witch', *Mail Online*, 6th January 2012. Available at http://www.dailymail.co.uk/news/article-2082618/Kristy-Bamu-15-tortured-death-witch-claim-Christmas-Day-Newham.html (accessed 30th October 2014).

social services[160] and the media to be the direct result of spiritual practices used to cast out demons, or to enforce a Christian way of life on some believers.[161]

Having made what seems to be a rather pejorative case here, it is important to note that white and black leaders alike are very concerned about abuse of all kinds – including spiritual abuse – in their churches. Key black leaders have spoken out strongly against portrayals of their churches that misrepresent them. An important article was written which highlighted an outspoken rebuke by a BBC documentary that had misrepresented black churches as dangerous places for children. The header of the article began, 'Britain's leading Black Church leaders have released a joint statement rebuking a BBC documentary, saying that the programme portrayed inaccurate stereotypical attitudes towards children among black Christians.'[162] It went on to comment:

> Bishop Dr Joe Aldred, the Secretary of Minority Ethnic Christian Affairs (MECA), which is part of Churches Together in England, and also the Chair of the Council of Black-led Churches in Birmingham, said, 'We are aware that some cases of child abuse have come to light in the UK, which the police are investigating with our full cooperation. But to imply, as this broadcast seemed to do, that abuse of children is widespread amongst black Christians in the UK is misleading and very unhelpful.'[163]

---

[160] Katherine Houreld, 'African Children Denounced as "Witches" by Christian Pastors', *The World Post*, updated 25 May 2011. Available at http://www.huffingtonpost.com/2009/10/18/african-children-denounce_n_324943.html (accessed 26th August 2014).

[161] Jeff Maysh, '"We're not like normal teenagers": Meet the exorcist schoolgirls who spend their time casting out DEMONS around the world, Mail Online, 11th August 2011. Available at http://www.dailymail.co.uk/news/article-2024621/Meet-exorcist-schoolgirls-spend-time-casting-demons-worldwide.html (accessed 30th October 2014).

[162] 'Britain's Black Church Leaders Unite to Speak Out Against BBC Documentary', *Christian Today*, 8th April 2006. Available at http://www.christiantoday.com/article/britains.black.church.leaders.unite.to.speak.out .against.bbc.documentary/5898.htm (accessed 26th August 2014).

[163] 'Britain's Black Church Leaders Unite to Speak Out Against BBC Documentary'.

And we indeed concur with this point of view. It is very unhelpful for any such stereotypes to be assigned to black churches or any other ethnic churches. It only seems to take a few extraordinary isolated cases of spiritual abuse to cause fear and suspicion and to tar some Christian leaders with the label of misuse of their leadership power, which is thought to be exercised to control their congregations.[164] Moreover, white Western congregations have also had more than their fair share of publicity on some notable cases of abuse. Indeed, we have noticed how non-Christian people we speak to from time to time in conversation will share their disquiet about reports of abuse in the media.

Having said this, Westerners have been becoming increasingly interested in the supernatural dimension of their lives as certain television programmes bear testament to. It is vital, however, that reverse missionary ethnic leaders understand that this interest does not mean that postmodern people would welcome exorcism practices as part of a missionary outreach strategy towards them.[165] Most Westerners still tend to view reality more readily through a rational and scientific lens, although there are signs of interest in the spiritual dimension as well.[166] Hence there will be perceptual worldview conflicts of perspectives[167] if reverse missionaries try to communicate with them using this kind of spiritual warfare language. This is equally true of overly fundamentalist charismatic Western Christian congregations.

We do not deny the reality of evil, or its power. We simply want to note the cross-cultural challenges of how we should think about it, Westerners and non-Westerners alike. The outspokenness of those who regularly use power encounter theology and practices may well come across to Westerners as cultic or sectarian. Postmodern people seriously question the motives of people who claim to have power from God to cast out demons, and this can lead them to think of all, or

---

[164] Donal Dorr, *Spirituality of Leadership: Inspiration, Empowerment, Intuition and Discernment* (Blackrock, Columbia Press, 2006), pp.84-86.

[165] Burgess, in Goodhew (ed), *Church Growth in Britain 1980 to the Present*, p.40.

[166] Hiebert, *Transforming Worldviews*, Chapter 8.

[167] Andrew Kirk, *What is Mission? Theological Explorations* (London, Dartman Longman and Todd, 2006), Chapter 6; Haralambos and Holborn, *Sociology*, pp.166-167;

most, good Christian migrant leaders as manipulative and dangerous to Western society.

Paul Hiebert suggests that we need to learn how to incarnate within the context of the people with whom we want to share the gospel. What he means is that as Jesus was born a Jew so that He could be listened to by Jews, we need to provide our rationale to get to know each other more deeply through incarnational cross-cultural conversations. The apostle Paul expressed this incarnational mindset well. He said that to Jews he was a Jew, to Greeks he acted as if he were a Greek; he sought to be all things to all men so that he might win some of them to Christ (1 Corinthians 9:19-23).

If we were to want to build missional friendships with a small community of Mizoram people in Birmingham, for example, we would need to be willing to spend a lot of time joining in community activities with them. Community life is a key value in their culture, and being part of it would make it possible to have influence on them. Moreover, we would need the permission of those considered to be elders/gatekeepers of such a community to join in with them. This means we would need to build friendships with the gatekeepers first of all, and for some time, in order to gain their trust. Hiebert makes his case for this incarnational ministry from an Anabaptist perspective:

> By 'incarnational ministry' we mean that mission is first and foremost the work of God. The incarnation of the missionary, the message, and the church are meaningless if God is not present in the missionary endeavour. We must become incarnate because God himself is already incarnate among people before we arrive, preparing their hearts to hear God's Word, revealing that Word to them by the work of the Holy Spirit, and transforming them through the power of the cross.[168]

Like the Anabaptist missionaries who were among those who followed Carey's call to take the gospel to the 'heathen' in the

---

[168] Paul Hiebert and Eloise Hiebert Meneses, *Incarnational Ministry: Planting Churches in Band, Tribal, Peasant, and Urban Societies* (Grand Rapids, Baker Book House, 1995), p.373.

nineteenth century, reverse missionaries in the West today are starting to recognise the need to be incarnational in their approach to people they want to reach.[169] A Mizo church plant we know of in Birmingham started to meet in a Scout hut near a park with sports facilities. It did this in order to incarnate into the community of young people who played in the park whom they wanted to reach with the gospel. About ten non-Christian youth who played sports in the park came to join them for games and social activities in the Scout hut. This simple missional approach came out of a feeling that God wanted them to reach out to these white, working-class young people. As they started to play sports with them in the park, it became clear that the youth were interested in their motives. They were honest and explained that they enjoyed playing games with them as well as wanting to tell them about their faith. A few of these young people became believers and started meeting together for spiritual activities in this Scout hut. This sort of missional incarnational approach towards people we sense a call to work with is vital to foster and stimulate in our churches.

Hiebert provides a much-needed insight for us to consider as part of our missional conversations:

> Our response to human cultures must be an ongoing process of critical contextualization (Hiebert 1987). In this we critically examine different areas of culture in the light of God's Word to test what is good and can be kept, and what is evil and should be changed. We seek to transform cultures into what God wants them to be.[170]

Hiebert's thinking here may motivate those who have had time to sufficiently settle into Western culture to start to think about how to work contextually in mission with Caucasians. It is becoming a common theme in academic literature to talk about the darkness and perceived evil of much of European culture from the perspective of migrant Christians. Fola-Alade, a missionary from Africa, commenting about the first efforts of his mission work in London, says, 'My first reaction was an inward desire to turn back.' He faced a crisis and

---

[169] Ojo, in Bonk, *The Routledge Encyclopedia of Missions and Missionaries*, p.380, 382.
[170] Hiebert and Hiebert Meneses, *Incarnational Ministry*, p.19.

needed to restructure his approach in order to be able to engage incarnationally in the cultural context in Britain.[171] The culture seemed to be very unwelcoming to his own intuitions for how to share his faith based on his experiences at home. What made the difference for him was his spiritual life and the work of the Spirit in his devotional practices:[172]

> But while I pondered this extremely attractive proposition [to turn back], I heard a clear voice in my spirit saying, 'You have this treasure in earthen vessels.'[173]

Following on from this, he planted a church in London which had a strong social gospel ethos to help deprived ethnic people with the problems they were facing as part of their new lives in Britain.[174] This is yet another vital conversation for all of us engaged in mission in the West to work on together. How can we help migrants who come to the West for the first time, not only to have their basic needs met, but also to become integrated into Christian communities made up of other peoples as well as people from their own homelands?

The late Bishop Lesslie Newbigin, upon returning from India in the 1970s after many years of missionary work, realised that there was a need to apply missionary insights he had obtained to the secular Britain he came back to. He perceived the need to help post-Christian people hear the gospel in culturally sensitive language which would speak to them in their secular situation.[175] He believed that God is a missionary God and that His purpose is to communicate the gospel in a language which people in secular society can understand.

---

[171] Fola-Alade, in Joseph Thompson, *How the Spiritual Explosion Among Nigerians is Impacting the World Out of Africa* (Ventura, Regal Books, 2003), p.124, Chapter 6.

[172] Veli-Matti Karkkainen, *Pneumatology: The Holy Spirit in Ecumenical, International, and Contextual Perspective* (Grand Rapids, Baker Academic, 2002), Chapter 6.

[173] Fola-Alade, in Thompson, *How the Spiritual Explosion Among Nigerians is Impacting the World Out of Africa*, p.124.

[174] Fola-Alade, in Thompson, *How the Spiritual Explosion Among Nigerians is Impacting the World Out of Africa*, pp.125-130.

[175] Geoffrey Wainwright, *Lesslie Newbigin: A Theological Life* (Oxford, Oxford University Press, 2000), p.14.

The book of Acts reflects the multicultural and multi-ethnic world of the Greco-Roman Empire in the first century AD. In Acts 10 and 11 we find a helpful story of cultural boundary crossing, when Peter the Jew took the gospel to the Gentile Cornelius and his household. This signalled the beginning of the early church's mission success with many Gentiles who soon came to embrace the Christian faith.[176] These chapters demonstrate how Peter was able to help his fellow Jewish brethren overcome some of their prejudices towards sharing fellowship with Gentile Christians.

Several important points can be drawn from the narrative. Firstly, Peter engaged in a conversation with his brethren and helped them to understand how God's Spirit had guided him to Cornelius' household for the purposes of his conversion (Acts 11:1-18).[177] Secondly, the response of Cornelius' family to the gospel was confirmed when the Holy Spirit was received by each of them prior to baptism.[178] Thirdly, the importance of the conversations and theological evaluations of Peter and the other leaders in Jerusalem helped them to think through what they should require the Gentiles to observe of the culture and traditions of Israel.[179] Later, in Acts 15, the leaders in Jerusalem decided that the Gentiles should not be circumcised and that the religion and culture of the Jews should not be required of the new converts; this included Torah observances.

Although there were conflicts with Christian Jews over whether Gentiles should be circumcised, keep the Torah or keep the Sabbath, it seems that this conflict did not in the end undermine the work of the gospel with new Gentile believers. Indeed, the Pauline epistles provide much evidence of how Paul tried to help his Gentile converts adapt the gospel message to their own cultures.

The crucial thing to recognise from this passage in Acts is that conversations were a vital part of the way the first leaders and apostles

---

[176] John Stott, *The Message of Acts* (Leicester, IVP, 1991), pp.181-213.

[177] Howard Peskett and Vinoth Ramachandra, *The Message of Mission* (Leicester, IVP, 2003), Chapter 13.

[178] Howard Mellor and Timothy Yates, *Mission and Spirituality: Creative Ways of Being Church* (Sheffield, Cliff College Publishing, 2002), pp.43-66.

[179] The evaluative processes can be recognised in the narrative.

came to make their decisions. And we must not forget that these decisions were made by seeking the Spirit's guidance.

Useful principles can be drawn from this passage to help us work with reverse missionaries and grow together in our understanding of how we might overcome some of our discomfort when working with postmodern people, who inevitably will not find many non-Western cultural practices easy to understand or cope with, or indeed our own white church practices.

Conclusion

Social sciences and theological reflection on our experiences can help theologians and leaders to understand the challenges reverse missionaries may face in this multicultural society, as well as our own indigenous groups.[180] They highlight cultural difficulties with regard to interaction between people groups when efforts are made to share the gospel.[181] This is important to recognise as it can help us to understand together the real challenges of communication of the gospel to Westerners by people from radically different nations and cultures.[182]

Hiebert suggests that dissimilar cultures need to share the gospel based on thorough training and preparation in cross-cultural studies and missional practical theology, in order to be successful as missionaries in any context.[183] The challenges for ethnic churches in the West are by no means insignificant in the light of this review. It is important to understand that whether we are indigenous to the West or if we come from somewhere else in the world, we must unite in the love of Christ to share together our challenges and opportunities for mission in conversations. We will be stronger together than if we seek to sort out our challenges alone.

---

[180] Kraft, *Christianity in Culture*, p. 17.

[181] Hiebert, *Transforming Worldviews*, Chapter 3.

[182] Hiebert, *Transforming Worldviews*, pp.103-104.

[183] Hiebert, *The Gospel in Human Contexts*, pp.11-13.

Reflective exercise

Take a few minutes to reflect on the following questions.

- Which challenges mentioned in this chapter do you identify with and why?

- What are the major challenges your church faces at the moment in terms of working cross culturally with others?

- If you were to rank the key challenges your church faces when it comes to helping members adapt to life in secular postmodern society, what would they be? Start with 1 as the highest priority and then 2 as the next priority to address, and so on.

- What resources can you call on from churches around you to help you work through some of your key challenges?

- What sources of help have you already called on to help you address key challenges, and how effective have they been?

- Which groups around you could you offer to help with challenges you have had some success in addressing so far?

- What strategies can you use to approach other groups to help them?

Comments

Chapter 4
Third Culture Children

Any mature missional conversation that takes place in the multi-ethnic context must surely consider the challenges that children of migrant Christians face when they are raised in the West. Children of first-generation migrant parents often find it hard to cope with the conflicts that happen between their parents' home culture and the Western culture. The culture is still very much alive in their parents' memories, including their expectations for how their children should be raised.

The parents' culture may be termed the first culture. The new Western culture may be termed a second culture. Children of these parents do not fit into the first or second cultures as they are being influenced by both of them, which means they need to adapt their identities so that they can meaningfully relate to both at the same time.

We must be aware that Christians raised in the West also face similar challenges. When white Western children are raised in Christian homes, they, too, face the challenge of the differences that exist between their church's Christian subculture and the main culture of secular society. This means that much of what we write about the challenges facing migrant children is also to some extent true of children born and bred in Western society.

Children become confused about their identities, which leads them to question where they fit in when they are faced with significant differences between their parents' subculture and the main secular culture. Which culture should they embrace – their parent's culture? The new one, or the secular one? A mixture of the two?

These children make up a third culture that is neither their parents' nor that of the new second culture or the secular culture. They develop a third culture which assimilates aspects of both cultures. Sociologists Pollock and van Reken use the term third culture kids (TCKs) when referring to the challenges our children face when confronted by the cultural disparities that exist between their parents' subculture and the predominant secular culture. We prefer the term third culture children (TCC), but the concept is the same. We have found their work on TCKs to be a vital piece of work which we have applied to the tensions migrant children and Western children face as they try to identify which culture they belong to. Pollock and van Reken define TCKs:

> A Third Culture Kid (TCK) is a person who has spent a significant part of his or her developmental years outside the parents' culture. The TCK builds relationships to all of the cultures, while not having full ownership in any. Although elements from each culture are assimilated into the TCK's life experience, the sense of belonging is in relationship to others of similar background.[184]

Those of 'similar background' are other TCC, who come from a variety of migrant ethnic groups. Much of the time TCC will form friendships with other TCC as they will find support and strength from those who are experiencing the same stresses that they are. The largest stress is the feeling that the TCC does not *belong* to their parents' culture or to the new one.

The challenges faced by missionary children is a well-researched area in scholarly literature.[185] Much has been written about the education of missionary children,[186] the psychological challenges of adapting to new cultures, the need to train and prepare missionary families for missionary service,[187] the challenges of the missionary incarnating into a new culture and how this adapts the missionary's self-identity.[188] Such sources have generally informed much of the learning in this chapter. As we have noted, Pollock and van Reken have brought much of the thinking together, and this makes their book a valuable resource for parents and church leaders. The challenges that

---

[184] Pollock and van Reken, *Third Culture Kids*, p.19.

[185] Pollock and van Reken, *Third Culture Kids*, p. 19.

[186] L. W. Sharp, 'How Missionary Children become world Christians: the role of the MK school', *Journal of Psychology and Theology*, 18, no.1, Sept. 1990, pp.66-74.

[187] J. R. Powell, 'Families in missions: a research context', *Journal of Psychology and Theology*, No.2, Summer 1999, pp.98-106.

[188] M. Ralter and M. K. Wilson, 'Culture, human identity, and cross-cultural ministry some biblical reflections', *Journal of Psychology and Theology*, No.2, Summer 1999, pp.121-134.

TCC face is an area of great practical interest to many church leaders and parents we have spoken to.

The reason for such interest is the negative stresses and identity crises that TCC often go through as they grow up in a new culture, or the challenges to their faith that Christian children raised in the West encounter when they go to state schools or meet with non-Christian peers. In research we have conducted into first generation ethnic Christian diaspora churches, we have found that second generation offspring are facing real difficulties.[189] One leader of an ethnic congregation expressed his community's concerns that they would only be a one-generation church, if their children and young people could not integrate their parents' faith into their new TCC identities. Many white churches in the UK face similar problems if their offspring do not keep their faith.

TCC and their parents face the stress of cross-cultural adaptation to life in the West, often with no professional support structures to help them adapt to their new lives. Moreover, Anglo Christian parents often do not receive enough support from their churches to help them and their children to address the challenges that secular education places on their children's faith development. This has been reported to us numerous times during our ministries in a variety of Anglo churches.

In the context of the ethnic congregation just mentioned, some young people have formed their own group and they no longer want to go to church with their parents. They are not seeking to become part of British youth culture as it feels alien to them. They are also finding it hard to fit in with young people of their age at school who do not understand their identity crises. In other words, they have cut themselves off from their parents and peers psychologically, and at the time of the research would only socialise with their select TCC group. The leader's concerns were based on a real desire to help first generation parents and second generation TCC to work out a way ahead, in order to help their offspring to integrate and adapt to the best bits of life in the West. The pastor expressed it well:

---

[189] Andrew Hardy, *A Critical Study of the Challenges Faced by Reverse Missionaries in the West* (MA Dissertation, 2013).

> We want our children to keep their faith now that they live here [the UK]; we also want them to embrace all of the good things of life here, but this does not mean we want them to lose their Christian identities either.

The identity crises TCC face are real, and parents and church leaders of ethnic first generation churches need to be realistic about them. Moreover, Anglo churches need to do much more to identify ways in which their children are struggling to construct their own kind of third culture, which is neither their parents' nor a secular one. It will be important to formulate strategies that will really help TCC to integrate their lives into secular society.

It would be a gross over-simplification to claim that there are easy answers to the TCC challenge. We believe that second and third generation parents whose families migrated to the West have managed to solve some of these challenges. They are now raising a second or third generation of children here. The lessons they have learnt may prove to be useful sources of help to us all. In order for ethnic reverse missionary congregations to be effective in their endeavours to share the gospel with others, they must first be confident that they have effectively shared it with their offspring. Moreover, Anglo churches need to ensure that their evangelistic ministries do not neglect the discipling of their members' children. It is notable that 18–30-year-olds are a largely missing category in Anglo churches today. The children of Anglo clergy and their members are among those who do not share their parents' faith.

In this chapter, whether we write about the challenges facing migrant children or Anglo and Western children, most of what we discuss applies to all categories of people who live in the West today and have children raised by Christian parents. It is important to think through effective discipleship strategies that enable young people to become lifetime followers of Christ. We will return to this later. However, it is first of all important for us to understand some more about the challenges that TCC face.

Challenges faced by TCC and their parents

'Rootlessness'

Firstly, there is the question of 'rootlessness' with the attendant question, 'Where am I from?'[190] We have already raised the question of self-identity in terms of which homeland or culture is 'mine'. Migrant parents of TCC tend to keep their home cultures alive in their own lives long after they come to a new culture. Children will hear stories of what it was like back home. They will also learn about the expectations upon them that come from their parents' originating cultures. As an example, the Western child-rearing philosophy is based on a concept of individuation[191] and the need to empower children at different stages to become responsible for their own self-development. Individuation is the process children go through as they learn to identify themselves as individuals in their own right. Children and young people have the right to be treated as emerging individuals in preparation for adult life, in the Western secular view of child-rearing. And the secular view also strongly suggests that parents give their children alternative choices for what to believe.

This approach has proved to be challenging to Anglo Christian parents who struggle at times with their children being taught about gay marriage, other world faiths, etc. Moreover, part of this ethos includes the right of children not to be punished by the use of physical violence like smacking. The basic philosophical underpinnings to this view are rather complex. One of the views is that adults do not physically abuse peers when they make mistakes, so why should we treat our children in a way that we would never treat our peers. Other aspects of this philosophy are built on complex psychological and sociological theories.

The culture of first generation parents may value the concept of 'spare the rod and spoil the child' (see Proverbs 13:24). Indeed, a number of reformed Christian Anglo groups resisted the new legislation that prohibited smacking when it was introduced in the late 1990s and held on to an outlook which considers some smacking to be

---

190 Pollock and van Reken, *Third Culture Kids*, Chapter 8, p.121.
191 Leonie Sugarman, *Life-Span Development Frameworks, Accounts and Strategies* (Hove, Psychology Press, 2001), pp.70-71.

permissible to reinforce parental authority. Children and young people who come from a migrant ethnic culture will inevitably receive a mixed message here, because their Western peers will mostly not be physically reprimanded. This kind of difference in approach to child-rearing can cause migrant TCC to become confused about the rights and wrongs of punishments. The largest challenge at this point has to do with the question, 'Why should I be physically punished when others are not?'

It must be said that ethnic church leaders we know well seek to help parents in their congregations understand the differences in British law compared to the ways things are done back home. Moreover, picking up on the issue of smacking as an example of a difference in approaches to disciplining children is not intended to indicate that migrant parents are abusing their children. It is an example of a difference of approach illustrating one tension faced by TCC. Of course, it is a matter that first generation parents coming to live in the UK will need to resolve if they disagree with UK children's rights legislation. Having mentioned this, some Anglo parents inevitably still struggle with the prescriptiveness of this legislation as well.

Where is home?

Secondly, both parents and TCC face the question of where home is to be located now they have come to settle in the West. Pollock and van Reken comment:

> For some TCKs, however, 'Where is home?' is the hardest question of all. Home connotes an emotional place – somewhere you truly belong. There simply is no real answer to that question for many TCKs.[192]

It is too easy for ethnic Christian parents to rationalise this question without connecting with the emotional identity crises that their children face. Sadly, Anglo Christian parents are also often unaware of the identity crises their young people struggle with silently, when they are learning things at school or from the TV or the internet which

---

[192] Pollock and van Reken, *Third Culture Kids*, p.124.

challenge their family's faith. What if Anglo young people deny their parents' Christian faith – how will they now fit into their Christian homes?

The families of TCC young people will not have personal insight into the real issues that are raised by Pollock and van Reken. It is also important to remember that all children, whether Anglo or ethnic, face challenges as TCC. They certainly will feel the conflicts that will be raised by the differences between their parents' culture or the Christian subculture as it strikes against secular and postmodern culture. Is the migrant TCC's parents' home their real home? Is their home going to be based on becoming embedded into life in the West? If migrant TCC parents are serious about settling into life in the West, then a natural question will have to do with children wanting to have the same kinds of opportunities and treatment as their Anglo peers.

One of our good friends, a significant leader of a BMC, raised an issue about his ten-year-old son. His son has Anglo Christian friends at school who want him to go to the cinema or a football match with them on Sunday afternoons. It is the tradition of our friend's church to spend the whole of Sunday morning and afternoon at church, so it proves difficult for his son's wishes to be met. The simple challenge faced by our friend and his TCC son is, 'Why is it wrong for my son to go to the cinema on a Sunday when white Christian children do this with their parents?' It may sound like an almost ridiculous question; however, in discussions we have had with adult second generation TCC who are now raising their own children to be Christians in the UK, a very different approach has been taken which allows compromise for their children.

The main reason for this difference in approach is that these second generation parents often rebelled against their parents' cultures during their upbringing because they were overly prescriptive. The question of which culture was to define home for these now adult TCC led them to react against their parents' one as well. They were confused about the rights and wrongs of which culture was their real one. In other words, they had to work it out for themselves as they grew up and became adults in the West. Where did they fit in? What sort of home were they going to make for themselves? Would it be like that of their parents? Would it be like those of their Western friends?

This is exactly what many white Anglo young people go through as well. It must be noted that second generation Anglo parents whose parents were the first generation of Christians in their families also face their own children's rebellion. There is much scope for Anglo and migrant churches to share in the missional conversation about how they can help their TCC to keep their faith. In Andy's experience of having led two multi-ethnic churches, he witnessed second generation parents successfully raising their children to have a Christian faith as well as seeing their children becoming integrated well into Western society. We have both seen probably more Anglo and second generation migrant youth leave their churches than have kept their faith. We believe this is a very worrying trend for all of us.

Restlessness

Thirdly, a key migrant TCC instinct is often expressed by the feeling of restlessness and the desire for something new.[193] This is also often true for Anglo children who have been brought up by parents in ministry. Two of the children in both of the writers' own families have the travel bug. And one of our students at ministry training college told us that he had decided that he and his family would be involved in something else rather than staying for him to prepare for ministry. This 'restlessness' for something new now consumed his outlook, compared to what had been his strong desire just a few months earlier to engage with the course and serve in ministry. At his interview he had convinced the panel that he was committed to completing the programme of study. He was planting a church which already had about 40 people attending. He had also been recommended for the course by a pastor who knew him well. His new plan was to let one of his friends take over the church, and he wanted to do a diploma and become a businessman.

This is not a criticism of the student concerned; it is rather an illustration of restlessness. This man was an adult TCC. Adults who grow up as TCC tend to carry traits like restlessness into adult life. TCC are often faced by major changes in direction because parents struggle with their own identity as they settle into life in a new place

---

[193] Pollock and van Reken, *Third Culture Kids*, p.124.

or culture.[194] TCC therefore often receive mixed messages about what their parents value and what their own values should be. For some reverse missionaries, this restlessness manifests itself because parents never settle into one church but tend to keep moving on, seeking to plant yet another congregation.

This is not only a common challenge for TCC. It is also one that faces pastors' children, who can move from one church to another several times over the course of their childhood.

Our own children faced more than one change in location over their childhoods, and it caused them some challenges in terms of how long they could keep friends before they moved. The largest challenge faced by TCC is not only the change in location, but also the different regional subcultures they encounter as they move from one location to another. The impact on their sense of security and settledness must not be minimised. They often face the double whammy of having to adapt to a new culture they are still struggling to identify with, compared to their parents' home culture which is actively practised in the home environment. The added strain of moving to a number of new locations inevitably means they never really have time to feel secure in one place. Given the choice again, Andy would have refused to be moved from one location to another during his time in church ministry, having witnessed the challenges to his children and family life.

High mobility

This leads us to a fourth major challenge that TCC face. It has to do with high mobility.[195] High mobility is related to restlessness but adds an extra dimension which can seriously affect the psychological well-being of TCC when they become adults.

One adult TCC whom one of us spent some time counselling a few years ago reported the feeling that she never felt settled in one place. She had an incessant desire to move on whenever she had been involved in one place for too long. For her, 'too long' could be

---

[194] This most often is part of culture shock, which has to do with the dissonance that a significantly different culture has with another culture – leading to a person feeling they do not identify easily with the new cultural environment.
[195] Hanciles, 'Migration and Mission', Chapter 8.

anywhere from a few months to one or two years. Hence she had spent her life for the past ten years since leaving home moving from one job to another as well as from one location to another. She never felt settled. The problem as she saw it was that she felt the urge to move on from one thing to another, but it did not actually satisfy her when she did it. She was just left with a desire to keep moving on which overpowered her ability to stay in one location and build friendships there. At first she had conceived of this desire to move on as a sense of God calling her to do so. She thought of it as a mobile ministry. However, it meant that she never settled in one place for long enough to become part of a community. The urge to move on had a debilitating effect on her as it made her feel insecure, which in turn acted as a kind of self-fulfilling prophecy,[196] whereby she projected herself to others as someone who did not welcome friendship.

The consequence was that she had raised an inner psychological wall of resistance to allowing others to get too close to her. In turn this had led to her becoming defensive with those who tried to get to know her better. The result was that she had no close friends, and there was a trail of people who had been hurt by her.

What helped her was the realisation that her compulsion to keep moving on had come from her childhood with missionary parents who moved her around with them. She deeply resented them for this, and felt a lot of anger towards men especially, as it had been her father who had moved them around so much. Her defensiveness had developed as a result of this high mobility and resentment of people. She felt she had to protect herself from the pain of losing friends by blocking the attempts of others to get to know her on a deeper level. The message she had allowed to sink deep into her soul was, 'I cannot let myself form deep friendships with people because I get hurt when I am forced to move on.' Once she realised that she now had control over where she would live and for how long, she started to give herself permission to form deeper friendships. Obviously this was not

---

[196] Self-fulfilling prophecies are set up by the person who has one about themselves. For instance, if I believe that people do not like me, my behaviour will tend to be withdrawn and the net result will be that people will not try to get on with me. My withdrawn behaviour, which may also come over as slightly hostile, will push people away. This is how a self-fulfilling prophecy works.

a quick process for her to go through, but she has now settled in one location and has some good friends.

Alienation

Fifthly, TCC can feel alienated from their parents' culture and that of the new dominant culture. Anglo children can also come to feel alienated from their parents' Christian culture. This feeling of alienation can lead TCC and young adults to become highly conflicted. They might even come to feel that society in general is against them. If they have not done well at school because they have been consumed by negative feelings of alienation, this can come to dominate their whole outlook on life. It is a known problem that this can lead to a life of gang crime, drug addiction and antisocial behaviour.[197] Alternatively, it can cause deep depression, anxiety and stress-related illnesses in later life. Young men and women can also find it hard to form stable families and to remain committed to their partners, because they find it hard to trust others and the normative systems, such as marriage and family structures and the commitments society expects of couples, based on these structures.[198]

Part of Andy's ministry involved supporting Christian single Afro-Caribbean mothers. A predominant reason for their singleness was that they had been expelled from their families because of teenage pregnancies. There were also a number of young Anglo women who had gone through the same experience. The young men with whom they had been involved could not support them because of their immaturity and sense of alienation from society.

These second generation young women had rebelled against their parents' Christian culture by not accepting what they perceived to be rigid views on sex outside of marriage. They had to find refuges or council housing to live in and raise their children. They were often unable to hold down a job because of inadequate childcare arrangements and because they had no qualifications or work experience. They felt highly vulnerable and were often victims of rape and physical abuse.

---

[197] Giddens and Sutton, *Sociology*, p.949.
[198] Giddens and Sutton, *Sociology*, pp.350-358.

This is obviously an extreme example of how badly things can go wrong for teenage and young adult TCC. It is important to note that feelings of alienation can lead to a sense that a person does not fit in anywhere, which in turn leads to inner turmoil and aggressive, self-destructive emotions. It is also important to recognise the power of these feelings of alienation if we are to try to equip first generation ethnic and Anglo parents to adjust well to life in a post-Christian society.

It is important to understand that a short chapter in a book of this sort cannot articulate all of the challenges faced by TCC.[199] Moreover, it is vital to recognise the difficulties TCC parents and their churches face so that these challenges can become a part of the larger missional conversation. A migrant church with first generation parents left to themselves will find it much harder to face TCC challenges than one which seeks insights from others with similar experiences. In other words, joining in with the multicultural missional conversation can help all of us to pool our resources and to do much more together than we have the resources to do alone.

It must not be assumed that all TCC will struggle to the same degree. Experts in developmental psychology recognise that children have an innate ability to cope with challenging situations. In Andy's work with families and young people, he has recognised how resilient children are even when they have been through dreadful experiences of abuse. It is not a foregone conclusion that children will be damaged for life by the challenges they inevitably face as TCC. Indeed, there are advantages to the TCC lifestyle. TCC learn how to relate better to people from different cultures because their exposure to different outlooks expands their social and intellectual horizons for learning, etc. It is too easy for us to focus on what can go wrong, which will lead to too much emphasis on the problems without coming up with solutions.

Pollock and van Reken make some important points about the four classic outcomes that TCC can experience as a result of being raised in the structures of their parents' subculture. When there are significant

[199] We recommend Pollock and van Reken's book for a more in-depth study of the TCC challenge: David Pollock and Ruth van Reken, *Third Culture Kids: The Experience of Growing Up Among Worlds* (London, Nicholas Brealey Publishing, 2001).

differences between a migrant culture and a new culture, the largest challenges become evident in the raising of TCC.

We must not make it sound like the TCC challenge is a bad thing. Many migrant and Anglo church subcultures have strong organisational structures that help their members to feel significant and well defined within their own communities, made up as they are of one ethnic group. Pollock and van Reken comment:

> At the risk of oversimplifying, and recognizing that there are many differences in how each agency [church] may be run, we have identified four basic ways TCKs relate to the system in which they grew up – from the perspective of their own personal makeup, gifts, and personality.[200]

Their observations are based on the question, 'What might make the difference in how or why an organizational system has positive outcomes for one person and negative outcomes for another?'[201] Firstly, it is quite true to observe that TCC can thrive within the organisational structures of their church communities despite the challenges they face.[202] They identify well with their parents' culture and consider themselves to be dual citizens of their homes in the West as much as of their parents' originating homeland. A little later we will consider what factors may help them to identify with their community's subculture.

Secondly, some TCC can spend many years in childhood and young adulthood not really feeling that they fit into their church's subculture, but they try to make themselves conform in order to avoid the larger strain of becoming estranged from it.[203] For instance, they may enjoy more contemporary forms of Western worship music but their church only likes gospel. They may prefer foods other than those appreciated by their cultural group. We could list all sorts of differences which, taken cumulatively, may not be quite enough for them to become part of something different, but at the same time they

---

[200] Pollock and van Reken, *Third Culture Kids*, p.160.
[201] Pollock and van Reken, *Third Culture Kids*, p.160.
[202] Pollock and van Reken, *Third Culture Kids*, p.161.
[203] Pollock and van Reken, *Third Culture Kids*, p.162.

never really feel that they fit in, so they force themselves to conform. This can lead to depression, anxiety and stress – illnesses which essentially derive from this kind of forced conformity. They realise they do not fit their group too well but this self-awareness sits at a preconscious level in their minds, kept in check by fears of alienation.

Thirdly, there are those who don't completely fit into their subculture's organisational systems but they do not yet realise it.[204] An example might be where a young person listens to Christian rap music, unaware that those who make up their organisational system do not like it. People in their community may tolerate some differences but there is an underlying tension which neither the TCC nor the group have as yet fully explored or understood. Because there is not a forced conformity, it can be difficult for the TCC, parents and church people to know what to make of these differences. How can they be helped to explore and understand what is really at stake? This is an example of where becoming involved in the multicultural missional conversation may help them explore commonalities with other groups who are experiencing similar challenges.

Finally, there is the TCC or young adult who does not fit the system and who spends their lives proving it.[205] They remain as part of their church's organisational system, but this is largely to protest against things they want to change about their subculture.

In all four cases we can hopefully identify some of the challenges with which TCC, parents and church leaders need to engage so they can think through ways of addressing them.[206]

Having said all of this, what suggestions can we make to seek to address common TCC challenges as part of the missional conversation?

Before we approach this question the reader may ask, 'What do TCC have to do with the multicultural missional conversation?' We would suggest it has everything to do with it. If we as parents fail to acclimatise and acculturate our children to be able to live Christian lives in an appropriate way in society, we believe we have failed to

---

204 Pollock and van Reken, *Third Culture Kids*, p.162.
205 Pollock and van Reken, *Third Culture Kids*, p.160.
206 Pollock and van Reken, *Third Culture Kids*, pp.160-163.

help them mature and be ready to thrive as adults. Taking the gospel to new people and not taking the time to raise our children to follow Christ for a lifetime would be a sad outcome for any Christian parents who passionately want to bring the gospel to all with whom they engage. We are not claiming that parents deliberately do this but we are just making the point that our families are an important part of any gospel ministry. The discipleship of children, youth, parents and single men and women is a vital one which will be considered in the next chapter.

Overcoming TCC challenges

In this section we will seek to address some of these challenges. They are probably among the most serious ones, but the list is not exhaustive. There is good evidence that there are many experiences common to children and young people in new cultures.

It is important that we consider the need to provide opportunities for TCC to meet other TCC who are learning to engage with cross-cultural living. We believe that part of the missional conversation is for church leaders from different ethnic groups to help others to do this, as well as to help them locate resources that are already available to help TCC and their families adapt to life in the West.

At this stage we also need to recognise that there are no easy solutions. Migrant parents may be going through culture shock and may be resistant to adapting their way of life to fit in to their new host culture. They might can become exhausted by the challenges of adaptation and 'bury themselves' in their expatriate communities. Their children may speak and read English better than they can, and need to communicate on behalf of their parents with social services, schools, benefits agencies, etc.

The resistance of parents to learn a new language can become a defining alienating feature of the way they seek to stay locked in their expatriate church community. People from the new host culture will not be able to understand the preaching, the prayers or the words used in worship. We know of a number of first generation churches like this – it is very hard to feel part of their communities. Perhaps this is the subliminal message that outsiders are intended to grasp.

The very fact that these churches maintain the home language of these groups can be a statement of resistance to building bridges. We know a number of first generation ethnic leaders who want their families and their children to adapt to life in the West, but they encounter strong resistance from some of their members when they try to offer services in English. The overall effect is that TCC are left to deal with the cross-cultural tensions of being, let us say, an Ethiopian who speaks Amharic at home and in church, but has to speak English at school.

In a strange turn of fate, ethnic church leaders who want to bridge cultural limiting factors, and TCC who need to, are joined in some kind of alliance to make change happen. Parental resistance to change because of their need to escape their feelings of culture shock can make this very hard to achieve. We need to exercise a lot of sympathy and empathy with our Christian brothers and sisters who are struggling like this. We must not minimise their very real struggles to live in what feels like an alien land.

Overcoming parental resistance to change

In order to overcome parental resistance to change, it is important to recognise that they have much in common with global nomads.[207] Like Abraham, who was called by God to a new homeland, they can feel they are still on the journey when they suddenly find themselves situated in the West.[208] There are a number of factors behind this which make it very hard for them to take the risk of engaging with their new situation. And these must be understood to help TCC parents adapt to life in the West.

The challenge of an impermanent home
Firstly, first generation migrants arrive in the West to join their families or as refugees who have left their homelands to avoid

---

[207] Norman Long, *Development Sociology Actor Perspectives* (London, Routledge, 2001), p.230.
[208] B. Jentsch and M. Simard, *International Migration and Rural Areas: Cross-National Comparative Perspectives* (Farnham, Ashgate, 2009), p.90.

persecution.[209] There is no guarantee that they will necessarily be granted permanent leave to remain in their new host country. This level of uncertainty means that they live in psychological limbo, being on a journey rather than being settled into their new environments. Secondly, they may be going through a grieving process because they have had to leave loved ones behind and they miss them deeply.[210] Thirdly, they may wish to return home again once persecution or conflict has stopped.[211] Finally, they may feel that their home culture is far better than the new host's secular culture, which is foreign and complex.

Nomadic non-engagement

All of these factors feed a kind of nomadic pathology which inhibits migrants from wanting to engage with either their new host culture or other Christians who live in it. However, children have to go to school, and they have to adapt to life in their new situations. And children and young people often find it much easier to learn new languages than their parents.

Spending six to seven hours at school each day during the week, TCC start to build friendships with children who are not part of their ethnic group. Of course, bullying can sometimes be experienced, which will cause ethnic minority children to feel isolated.[212] Anglo Christian children often experience this at school as well. Having said this, schools are becoming better at identifying this kind of bullying and helping their students to appreciate each other's differences more fully. This can all add to the positive experiences TCC obtain from being part of well-run schools that manage ethnic diversity well.[213] At the same time, however, some TCC have to live with their parents' feelings of displacement and lack of rootedness in their new host culture. From this perspective, TCC can feel unrooted and unable to

---

[209] Rayna Bailey, *Immigration and Migration* (New York, Infobase Publishing, 2008), p.15.

[210] Colin Baker and Sylvia Prys Jones, *Encyclopedia of Bilingualism and Bilingual Education*(Clevedon, Multilingual Matters Ltd, 1998), p.107.

[211] *Congressional Record*, V. 151, Pt. 10, June 20 to June 27, 2005.

[212] Sairah Qureshi, *Bullying and Racist Bullying in Schools: What are we Missing?* (U.S.A, Xlibris Corporation, 2013), p.75.

[213] Qureshi, *Bullying and Racist Bullying in Schools*, Chapter 1.

form close friendships with peers from other ethnicities, because of the emotional atmosphere in their homes. Eidse and Sichel comment:

> Nomadic children are like epiphytes, plants that live on the moisture and nutrients in the air, blown in the wind and propped impermanently in host trees. Lifted from one home and set down in another, these children learn not to attach too deeply. Yet despite their resistance to rooting, these children need a sense of belonging, a way to integrate their many cultural selves and find a place in the world. Like all children, they need a secure sense of self, a stable identity.[214]

It seems logical to assume that it is very hard for nomadic TCC to develop a stable sense of belonging when their parents feel far less than stable with regard to what the future holds for their families and the plans they will make if they have to move quickly again. However, it is vital that they help their children develop a stable sense of self despite their own insecurities. First generation ethnic leaders that we know personally are thinking through some strategies with us and their leadership teams to try to address difficulties like this. Anglo churches must also be careful not to be complacent about the struggles of their own types of TCC.

One way to help many migrant parents to do this will be to develop a practical theology which can enable them to deal with their deeply seated nomadic psychologies if they originally come from pastoralist societies. We will discuss this theology in a later chapter, as it is important not just to ethnic reverse missionaries or expatriate diaspora ethnic churches, but it is also fundamental to missional faith for all believers, even if they are settled Anglo Christians. We would like to suggest seven strategies to help nomadic-style families deal with the challenges of unsettled life in their new homes.

1. Dealing with unsettled life
It is important for ethnic leaders to preach and teach about their migrant people's nomadic journeys. There are plenty of biblical

---

[214] Faith Eidse and Nina Sichel, *Unrooted Childhoods: Memoirs of Growing Up Global* (London, Nichalas Brealey Publishing, 2004), p.1.

predecedents to help them to do this, one of the most obvious being the story of Abraham in Genesis 12. The important thing is to help migrant parents understand that God does not call people without providing for them to continue safely on their journey. In the case of Abraham and his family, it was a journey to a specific destination. However, the New Testament makes it clear that this destination would not be reached until Jesus comes to finally establish the kingdom of God (Acts 1:7-12). The important thing is to help parents understand on a deeper level that they will always be on a kind of journey. And it is also important to point out that Westerners are on their own faith journeys – we are not so unalike in this sense.

Home needs to be a concept based on the God who has called us to build the security of our family's lives on the foundation of God's faithfulness, and His provision for us as we continue on pilgrimage. TCC can be taught that home is based on being part of God's larger international and multicultural family.

This recognition of nomadic movement needs to help parents develop a mentality that God will protect them wherever they find themselves on their journeys. God in Christ is Himself a nomad who is leading us home until the future kingdom is fully and finally established forever. It is important to make this the starting point to help TCC parents engage with their new situations in the West. It will only be once parents and their TCC more deeply recognise that God gives them security and sustenance on their journeys of integration into their new homes in the West that they will find the strength to psychologically step outside their expatriate communities and spend some of their time relating to other people around them.

2. Recognising the opportunities

It is important for church leaders to help parents and TCC to understand what opportunities they have in the West, even if they still face uncertaintities. This is where being engaged in the missional conversation helps. One strategy could be to invite other ethnic church leaders to come and share their experiences of life in the West, or they may be able to offer helpful seminars on how they have adapted. The pooling of ideas will provide a range of views and learning opportunities as each ethnic group will inevitably have come up with their own solutions to manage the differing challenges and circumstances that they face.

It would also be helpful to develop self-help groups, facilitated by church leaders or other significant community leaders, to help parents and TCC discuss their difficulties. As various real-life challenges are brought out through conversations, it will be important for leaders to engage in conversations with other ethnic leaders so that together they can find solutions and resources to help address the challenges. For example, for a time one of the churches Andy led in Oxford sponsored asylum seekers. He stood surety for an asylum seeker with Asylum Welcome, a charity which helps asylum seekers by standing surety for them as well as providing food and somewhere to live. Andy's church was a multi-ethnic, cosmopolitan one made up of at least five different nationalities. His church naturally had an interest in joining in with the missional conversation about how they could help migrants and asylum seekers as they faced numerous challenges.

Another church leader we know met a young Christian woman who had converted from Islam. She had fled for her life from her homeland, leaving her committed Muslim husband and his family. Her dilemma was how she could now support her two sons as well as help them deal with their grief over leaving their father. Over a couple of years she was able to stand on her own feet and see her children settled into life in school. It took quite a lot of networking to help her obtain all the support she needed from other groups who understood her situation.

The point is that there are no quick fixes that suddenly bring everything together in a short time to help parents and TCC go through a process of adaptation to life in the West.

3. The need for insight and support

Parents need to be provided with insightful support from experienced counsellors who can facilitate groups to help them work through the challenges they and their TCC are facing. It would be helpful for them to become more aware of how their own insecurities and culture shock can be transferred to their children, making it hard for their children to feel secure in their home environments.

This may sound like a basic observation to make, but it is surprising how unaware many of us can be about how the things we are struggling with can seriously affect our children. We have observed that, as parents come to understand how their stresses affect their children, they want to address how they can help them to overcome them. Once parents of TCC become more aware of their influence on their children, they can be helped to develop approaches to mitigate the stress.

This can become an important opportunity for leaders to encourage people to seek to engage in some of the customs of the Western world. For instance, the church could host a 'bring and share' meal with another Anglo church, where different ethnic foods could be shared. If it is carefully planned, it may help parents from these congregations to develop confidence to do other things socially together. Moreover, the experience of sharing food and offering hospitality and entertainment can be an important way for people of different cultures to build friendships with others outside their communities.

4. Cross-cultural interaction is vital

Migrant missional leaders can achieve something very important if they make it a policy not just to meet with other ethnic non-Western leaders, but also with white Western leaders. Regional groups of Churches Together encourage their ministers to meet and support one another and discuss their challenges. Such meetings can be important opportunities for ethnic leaders and white leaders to build intentional relationships, which could lead to them sharing their pulpits as well as other resources. We believe it is important for Anglo Christians to find ways of fellowshipping together.

The church constituency we belong to[215] has a range of ethnicities, including Anglos, Asians, Europeans, Africans and Afro-Caribbeans. There is often sharing of resources. Moreover, TCC and native white Christian youth can join together in well-led regional gatherings, where they can form significant friendships. Care needs to be taken here, however: it is also important for parents to get to know each

---

[215] The Fellowship of Churches of Christ in Britain and Ireland.

other or it will only exacerbate the potential for the integration of TCC with white peers.

5. Learning the language

It is important for ethnic parents to learn the new host culture's language well. This is obviously vital as language is the basis of communication. However, learning the language is only part of the answer to help first generation migrant parents adapt to life in the West. About 8% of communication is the words we speak; the rest has to do with body language and the cultural differences that different kinds of body language and customs mean in different cultures.

When Andy started to build a friendship with a Japanese couple he made some basic blunders. For example, when these new friends were invited to their home for a meal, one of dishes offered contained cheese. The Japanese couple graciously ate it. Andy and his family did not understand that eating cheese was a cultural taboo for them. They learnt about this afterwards and apologised to their new friends. They were wonderfully forgiving and gracious, saying, 'When we entered your home we also entered into what hospitality was for you – we really enjoyed our evening with you.'

Communication between cultures will be only partly based on understanding what one another is saying; much more is based on what we deeply value because of our upbringings in our respective cultures. We need to understand more than the actual words uttered.

Cross-cultural communication will take a commitment based on God's sacrificial gift-love to enable each of us to accept differences and diversity among others who are significantly different from ourselves. As we develop deeper relationships with our brothers and sisters who now make up the multicultural tapestry of the West, we will hopefully also be able to understand what it is that we find hard to accept about each other's cultures. The practical theology of the Multicultural Trinity unifies all languages and cultures, and will be needed to help us maintain our unity despite our diversity. And let us be realistic at this stage – there will be times when conflict arises or offence is given, and often these will come from misunderstandings or stresses that develop as we learn to relate to each other on a deeper level. Let us be under no illusion – the kingdom of God welcomes all people with their diverse gifts. This diversity can stimulate our creativity as we share the riches of our cultures.

6. Challenges of class divisions

There is still a strong assumed division in British and other Western societies between different classes of people in society. Anglo Protestant and evangelical churches have often been predominantly made up of white middle-class people. It has historically proven to be very difficult to break into the working-class populace in the UK. Notably the Wesley brothers made important inroads into the working-class masses as they preached to thousands of working men and women, particularly from mining towns.

Dan's earliest ministry experiences were on a white Anglo working-class housing estate, where a real sense of shared community developed. The congregation began to change as a greater number of white-collar workers became part of the church. This led to some of the children of single-parent families moving away from faith into a wider secular culture because they did not so readily relate well to families that had both parents to raise their offspring. The experience of these young people from single-parent families seemed to be based on their sense of alienation from families that were more middle class. Protestant and evangelical churches tend to develop cultures of upward mobility. Parents' aspirations are for their children to excel in education as well as to be employed in professional careers – in business, education, medicine, etc. And this is where it is difficult for migrant and Anglo churches to dialogue meaningfully. There is a kind of intellectual culture among white middle-class Christians which tends to make them move in their own narrow circles. Perhaps one of the best ways to learn the lessons necessary for Anglo and migrant Christians to join in meaningful dialogues will be through the planting of multi-ethnic congregations over the medium to long term.

We believe Anglo and migrant leaders should seek to experiment with multicultural worship services together, to help people worship and fellowship together. It is in the interests of those who want to see the multicultural kingdom of God come, to help TCC and their families to break down the boundaries caused by cultural differences. We believe one of the justice issues Anglo churches must address is the lack of fellowship with ethnic Christian groups, who need their Western brothers and sisters to become their allies and advocates for a place in multicultural society. The social justice tradition is a vital part of our biblical faith, and Westerners must learn to do more than send money to people outside of our rich, overfed society. We need to seek ways to join forces with our ethnic brethren to help them integrate here, as well as find creative ways to share some of our wealth.

7. TCC parents who embrace education

It is important for parents to consider the educational needs of not only their TCC but of themselves as well. This will help them walk alongside their children as they are educated, which will help them to join in with their offspring in some of the lessons they are learning.

Hanciles corrects some wrong perceptions in this respect. In his fascinating research he demonstrates how migrants from places such as Africa, India and China bring with them many needed skills, coming as some do with high levels of education.[216] Yet this does not minimise the observation about the lack of preparation that many migrant missionaries have as they first come to live in the West. When TCC children start school, it can be very difficult for their parents to help them with their learning. This lack of engagement is not intentional on the part of parents, but it is rather inevitable, especially if families have had to leave their homelands quickly because of persecution or war.

This is where the missional conversation can provide opportunities to help TCC and their parents find the best local resources to learn the language and to obtain help with financial difficulties, finding work or housing matters.

Children can be given extra tuition by qualified adults from other ethnic churches, who can help them to overcome some of their learning challenges. This brings opportunities for TCC parents to learn alongside their children. For instance, parents may attend English as a second language classes. They may also sit exams. Several of our colleagues run English language courses for new migrant Christians and non-Christians alike, for example. This will obviously require

---

[216] Hanciles, 'Migration and Mission', Chapters 1, 2.

ethnic church leaders to pool resources, so they can provide homework clubs in their churches for both parents and children.

Much more could be written. It seems clear enough that the education of TCC can rapidly help them to adjust to their new lives in the West in some important ways. The stresses caused by cultural dissonance between their parents' culture and the Western one will remain. What is vital is that parents and TCC seek to solve the challenges they face together. A first step can be achieved simply by parents pooling their ideas and resources in small confederations which act as support groups, which can then become open to others as well. Strength will come from the shared resources that larger groups bring.

Conclusions

This chapter does not even start to really help TCC, parents and church leaders overcome many of the complex challenges they face. We have recognised that the TCC phenomenon is not just limited to migrant Christian families; it is also a useful description of what children of ministers face, as well as what many Anglo children face when they are confused by the dissonance between their parents' faith and the secular outlook they learn about in Western schools. What we have endeavoured to achieve is awareness of the very real challenges TCC are facing every day of their lives, as they try to live among us in the West. This is, we suggest, one of the vital questions to discuss as part of the multicultural missional conversation. We hope we have done enough in this chapter to convince readers that we need to engage in this together.

Reflective exercise

Take a few minutes to reflect on the following questions.

- Who are the TCC in your church and which of the challenges discussed in this chapter are they facing?

- What strategies have you used so far to help parents and children in your church to adapt to secular, postmodern life in the West?

- Who might be able to help you deal with TCC challenges – in your church or in other churches you know of?

- How could you raise the profile of the TCC challenge to parents and other church leaders and members?

- How are you helping your children to form their Christian identities? Be specific about your strategies.

- In what ways are TCC engaging positively in the life of the church?

- How effective is the current ministry to parents and TCC to help them adapt to postmodern secular culture?

Comments

Part 2

Shaping and Training Leaders who can Bring About Change

Chapter 5
Shaping Nomadic Disciples

In this chapter we will consider the need for a practical theology of discipleship that is based on the concept of the nomad. The nomad is a motif strongly implied in Scripture through the ongoing journey of God's people who one day will finally settle in the Promised Land. David Phillips comments about the need for a theology that can help people on the move to understand their relationship to the nomadic God of Scripture:

> The reason for his traveling is the character of God himself. God's freedom over his creation in his transcendence, and yet fulfilling his purpose in his immanence, is expressed in the metaphor of the divine pastoralist. Transcendence means that the nature of God is supremely 'nomadic;' he has no need of creation, and is not limited by any aspect of it. God is free to choose his commitments and make them effective as he wishes, surmounting human and physical boundaries.
>
> As Creator-Shepherd, he has elected to have fellowship with a people traveling with him through time. His freedom is demonstrated, paradoxically, by his involvement in leading the patriarchs and Israel.[217]

The 'Creator-Shepherd' is another way to describe the way God guides His people to follow in His missional footsteps to reconcile the world to Himself. *Missio Trinitatis* has to do with the plan of God to disciple His nomadic people to become like Christ, the prototype nomadic disciple for us to model our lives on.

The recognition that we are to be nomadic disciples will hopefully help our churches to engage in the journeys they need to keep taking, as they learn to disciple others through cross-cultural mission ventures. Nomadic disciples keep on crossing boundaries into new missional regions to take the gospel to people there. Nomadic disciples

---

[217] Phillips, *Peoples on the Move*, p.55.

in the Western multicultural environment cross cultural boundaries regularly because of the diversity of the people we meet in public places. The 'Creator-Shepherd' who precedes us by His Spirit into new territories prepares the ground for new people to be welcomed into His fold. The metaphor of sheep entering the fold is at the heart of Jesus' understanding of His mission, and that of His disciples:

> My sheep hear my voice, and I know them, and they follow me; and I give them eternal life, and they shall never perish, and no one shall snatch them out of my hand. My Father, who has given them to me, is greater than all, and no one is able to snatch them out of the Father's hand. I and the Father are one.
> *John 10:27-30 (RSV)*

The core of this mission is the goal that all of the sheep who belong to the 'Creator-Shepherd' build their sense of calling to make disciples on the reality that they themselves already possess eternal life. We can offer new believers the surety that they are eternal sons and daughters in the Trinity's family (see John 5:24-25; Romans 6:23). It is important to recognise that our Christian brothers and sisters who form all kinds of ethnic churches will particularly find the concept of nomadic discipleship meaningful, because they themselves are on a very real journey, having travelled to live in the West. Even more so, they are still travelling as they seek to integrate here.

There are roughly a million ethnic Christians in the UK today,[218] making up a significant worker force who can join with God in His mission to reconvert the secular West to Christianity. There are also many English, Welsh, Scottish and Irish ethnic congregations who could join with migrant groups in joint mission ventures as opportunities present themselves. The concept of the 'nomad' is a particular way of describing a disciple who follows the missionary God, as God leads a believer to join in His plan to reconcile the whole world to Himself.

---

[218] 'UK Census: religion by age, ethnicity and country of birth' *The Guardian*, 16th May 2013. Available at www.theguardian.com/news/datablog/2013/may/16/uk-census-religion-age-ethnicity-country-of-birth (accessed 31st August 2014).

The idea of following the God who calls us to join Him in mission is also expressed in Scripture in the language of a journey or pilgrimage (Hebrews 11:9-10). The concept of 'journey' is a central theme to the Abraham narratives found in the book of Genesis (Genesis 12:1-3; 13:1). Chris Wright points us to the missional focus of the missionary God that dominates the whole biblical worldview, beginning in a special sense with the story of Abraham:

> Paul tells us in a phrase that comes at the beginning and end of his greatest letter. His calling as an apostle was, he says, 'to bring about the obedience of faith for the sake of his [Christ's] name among all the nations' (Rom. 1:5; repeated at 16:26 ESV).
>
> Now that is an ambition that resonates with strong echoes of Abraham. For Abraham is the Old Testament character par excellence who was the model of faith and obedience – as Paul, James and the author of Hebrews all testify. And the horizon of 'all the nations' goes back to God's promise to Abraham that through him all the nations on earth will be blessed.
>
> So Paul is indicating, by this prominently placed phrase, that his lifetime's service of the gospel was all about producing communities of Abraham look-alikes in all nations, not just in the nation physically descended from Abraham. An ambitious goal, for sure, but profoundly rooted in his reading of God's mission as expressed in his promise to Abraham.[219]

Abraham is called to leave his home and to go to the land that the Lord will lead him to. The Latin word for mission comes from *mitto* which means 'to send,' and is described by another derivative Latin word *missio* (meaning 'mission'). From this we obtain the concept of *missio Dei* ('God's mission') and *missio Trinitatis* ('the Trinity's mission'). In Scripture, the continuous theme is that God sends His

---

[219] Christopher Wright, *The Mission of God's People: A Biblical Theology of the Church's Mission* (Grand Rapids, Zondervan, 2010), p.63.

people out into the world to engage in His mission.[220] The missional Multicultural Trinity sent Abraham as the prototype nomadic man to bless all nations and cultures of the world. Abraham was one of the first great examples of a person sent by God on the mission to lay the foundations for the chosen nation of Israel (Genesis 15:1-8). The Lord called him and Abraham followed Him, looking out for Yahweh's guidance as he went on his journey (Genesis 12:1-3).

This process of travelling meant that Abraham had to proceed through different kingdoms and regions controlled by different peoples (Genesis 12:6, 10; 13:1; 20:1). He crossed boundaries, which meant he had to adapt to the different cultural groups he encountered (Genesis 20:1-7). The peoples he met on his journey came from similar cultural stock to his own; they are known as the Semites by sociologists and cultural anthropologists. Hence there were important points of potential agreement in outlook. Yet there would have been important differences as well. Among these was the tendency for different kingdoms to identify their people by filial relations with a founding father. If a person did not belong to that founding family line, they were not considered to be part of that people. This means that part of the call of the missionary God for Abraham was to engage in cross-cultural interactions with other peoples, who did not consider themselves to be of the same stock as others.

It is important to understand that Abraham, the father of many nations, was to be the means of blessing to all the peoples of the world, including ourselves. We know that Abraham did not always make good decisions when relating to other peoples, but nevertheless, he was called to become the source of global blessing for all peoples of the world. This recognition is important for our practical theology of nomadic discipleship. All the rich varieties of ethnic churches who make up the tapestry of the multicultural West are called on a similar journey – to bless those they encounter on their cross-cultural missional ventures. Blessing will come through acts of practical service and by the communication of the gospel of grace to those with whom we share it. The concept that all Christians share the missional DNA of

---

[220] Craig Altcock, *The Shaping of God's People: One Story of How God is Shaping the North American Church Through Short-term Mission* (USA, Lulu, 2006), p.36.

Abraham, their faith-father, powerfully implies that multi-ethnic breakthrough congregations and/or partnerships between different ethnic groups are a required part of our shared journeys, to bring the gospel back to the centre of the post-Christian Western hemisphere. What we need to do more intentionally as we engage in cross-cultural missional dialogue is to learn how we can help shape each other as nomadic disciples so we can do this more intentionally together.

Nomadic disciples are followers of God. The Christian faith is based on following God and being shaped to become more like Christ,[221] who was the greatest living example of a nomadic disciple. At the heart of His spiritual life was that He only did what he saw His Father doing (John 5:19). He followed the pre-ordained plan which Father, Son and Holy Spirit had agreed for the reconciliation of a lost creation before the world was made (John 17:1-5). During Jesus' pilgrimage in the world, He followed this plan which mapped the journey He eventually took to the cross, the resurrection and then to His ascendant position at the right hand of the Father in heaven. In this exalted position He has all 'authority in heaven and on earth' (Matthew 28:18). He continues His mission through His Spirit whom He sent to His followers to continue to guide them in what He had instructed them to do and teach (Acts 1:8; 16:6-10).

The core mission of the Spirit of Jesus is to empower us as we take the gospel to all people, sharing the good news that Christ has broken down the dividing walls. The nomadic disciple will need to understand the structures that erect these dividing walls, and then help to form new social structures so that people can more easily communicate with one another cross culturally. It is vital that we understand a practical theology of nomadic discipleship, if we are to join hands across cultures in the multicultural West in order to bring the gospel of reconciliation. To do so we need to create networks to enable us to share the stories of our journeys together.

In this chapter we will trace some important lessons from Scripture to help us to understand how cross-cultural nomadic disciples can work together.

---

[221] Dietrich Bonhoeffer, *The Cost of Discipleship* (New York, Touchstone Books, 1995), p.298.

Disciples as nomads and pilgrims

It may sound strange in a Western culture to use the concept of the nomad to describe discipleship. We live in an urbanised society where people live in fixed locations in cities and towns. Culturally we are a million miles away from what is technically termed a nomadic culture, such as we find in pastoral cultures where Bedouin move their sheep and goats from location to location to graze them.

According to Phillips, there are a number of categories of what we might call nomads. Among them he identifies a large variety of Gypsy peoples who have the tendency to move from place to place.[222] The results of an internet search of the term 'nomad' are interesting. Matthewman suggests that one category that crops up are people who spend a lot of time flying around the world on business.[223] Clearly, the concept of a nomadic lifestyle has a range of meanings. The classic definition of a nomad is provided by Phillips:

> Self-sufficient, a law unto himself, a roving warrior ... the nomad may appear both to have an ideal life and to be a threat to civilization. To those unfamiliar with the life of the nomad, it suggests freedom from routine, from restraints and entanglements of civilization. It appears to be a simple life that allows one to be in tune with nature. Such a view is influenced by ideas of the evolution of society that assume that the nomad lives according to humankinds earliest and most primitive lifestyle. We have also been influenced by biblical and classical history to regard the Bedouin as epitomizing the word 'nomad.' With their camels, 'the ships of the desert,' they are thought to roam free from the restrictions of civilized life. The reality, however, is very different.[224]

---

[222] Phillips, *Peoples on the Move*, pp. 11, 13, 28-29, 94, 103-104,236, 254-256, 375, 388-389, 411, 429-445.

[223] Jim Matthewman, *The Rise of the Global Nomad*, (London, Koganpage, 2011), p. 1.

[224] Phillips, *Peoples on the Move*, p.6.

Like all other kinds of human lifestyles, nomads live lives full of routine, with rhythms that define the routes they take to graze their animals or to engage in trade and access goods from other groups. The primary concept of the nomad as a description of a disciple has more to do with following God and engaging on a lifetime journey of faith with Him. It is a great metaphor for following the missional Trinity as They guide nomadic disciple-makers to shape new disciples to become like themselves.

Within the Old Testament writings, the motif of nomadic journey is not only limited to the period in Israel's history when the patriarchs followed God on such a journey; Israel also followed a kind of journey which continued throughout its history. Obviously we see this in the stories of the patriarchs; we find it in the wilderness wanderings of Israel after they left Egypt;[225] we can also call the return to Jerusalem in the time of Ezra after the Babylonian captivity a kind of nomadic journey.[226] Moreover, modern scholars speak of the Jewish people in the time of Jesus awaiting the coming of the kingdom of God.[227] This implies that Abraham's journey to enter the promised inheritance is not fully complete. The concept of pilgrimage or a nomadic journey is particularly emphasised in the book of Hebrews:

> By faith Abraham obeyed when he was called to go out to a place which he was to receive as an inheritance; and he went out, not knowing where he was to go. By faith he sojourned in the land of promise, as in a foreign land, living in tents with Isaac and Jacob, heirs with him of the same promise. For he looked forward to the city which has foundations, whose builder and maker is God ...
>
> These all died in faith not having received what was promised, but having seen it and greeted it from afar, and having acknowledged that they were strangers and exiles on the earth.
>
> *Hebrews 11:8-10, 13 (RSV)*

---

[225] The book of Numbers is a great example of this – although Old Testament experts would tend to think of the life of the people of Israel at that time as more like the life of the Bedouin.

[226] See the books of Ezra and Nehemiah.

[227] Tom Wright, *Jesus and the Victory of God* (London, SPCK, 1996), Chapter 6.

It is important to note that the writer to the Hebrews considered that the journey of the patriarchs did not end in their lifetimes. The Promised Land is a metaphor for the kingdom of God that would be established after the second coming of Christ. Hebrews 11 follows the theme of the Old Testament heroes who did not see the kingdom come in their lifetimes, but they held on to their faith that it would in the future. The writer of Hebrews builds on this concept of an uncompleted faith journey to emphasise the primary quality of a nomadic/pilgrim follower who remains faithful to God's call (Hebrews 11:39). The writer also uses Jesus as the ultimate example of one who 'endured from sinners such hostility against himself, so that you may not grow weary or fainthearted'. He adds, 'It is for discipline that you have to endure. God is treating you as sons; for what son is there whom his father does not discipline?' (Hebrews 12:3, 7, RSV) The Greek word used for discipline here is *paideia* which means 'to chasten, correct or educate'. It comes from the ancient practice where a father would discipline his son with an appropriate form of corrective punishment.

Paideia is not used in the gospels concerning Jesus' disciples. However, the concept of being disciplined by God is a common theme that both the author of Hebrews and Peter in his epistles use to describe believers' experiences of suffering. And the idea of disciples in Paul's letters is that they are sons and daughters of Abraham (Romans 4:16). If they have a faith like his, they will receive the eternal inheritance promised to him as his descendants (Romans 4:13). They also become sons of God, because God has poured the Spirit of His Son into the hearts of those who cry out, 'Abba! Father!' (Romans 8:15). A similar concept is implied in Hebrews as the writer reminds his readers that faith which endures trials leads to the promise of resurrection:

> By faith Abraham, when he was tested, offered up Isaac, and he who had received the promises was ready to offer up his only son, of whom it was said, 'Through Isaac shall your descendants be named.' He considered that God was able to raise men even from the dead; hence, figuratively speaking, he did receive him back.
> *Hebrews 11:17-19 (RSV)*

This promise of resurrection and the eternal inheritance on offer to those who endure to the end means they will inherit the promise given to the father of Israel and his descendants:

> But you have come to Mount Zion and to the city of the living God, the heavenly Jerusalem, and to innumerable angels in festal gathering, and to the assembly of the first-born who are enrolled in heaven, and to a judge who is God of all, and to the spirits of just men made perfect, and to Jesus, the mediator of a new covenant, and to the spirits of just men made perfect, and to Jesus, the mediator of a new covenant, and to the sprinkled blood that speaks more graciously than the blood of Abel.
>
> See that you do not refuse him who is speaking.
> *Hebrews 12:22-25a (RSV)*

The discipline of us as the followers of Christ is to be the same as that received by Abraham the nomad. Abraham's faith was tested when he was commanded to sacrifice his son Isaac. True children of Abraham share a faith that endures like his. Abraham our father is the model follower and disciple on whom missional nomadic disciples need to model their lives. As the father of a multitude of nations, he exercised a faith and discipline which meant he was willing to sacrifice everything in order to complete his part in the mission of God. This missional nomadic discipleship was reiterated by Jesus as part of the so-called Great Commission after His resurrection.

> 'All authority in heaven and on earth has been given to me.
> Go therefore and make disciples of all nations, baptizing them
> in the name of the Father and of the Son and of the Holy
> Spirit, teaching them to observe all that I have commanded
> you; and lo, I am with you always, to the close of the age.'
> *Matthew 28:18- 20 (RSV)*

The command to 'make disciples of all nations' relates directly to the promise to Abraham that through his descendants all nations on earth would be blessed. Immediately it is clear that the disciples are sent out like missionaries. They are also reminded that this will continue to the 'close of the age.' In other words, this missional journey to take the gospel to all peoples is to continue until Christ comes again to finally establish the kingdom of God. We have been sent out to bless all nations and peoples of the earth with the saving knowledge of Jesus the Lord. All who call on His name will be saved. Disciples follow the Jesus who is present with them, leading them on God's mission until the climax of history. The nomadic Spirit of Jesus the disciple-maker will guide His followers to make disciples of all ethnicities. In terms of the multicultural missional conversation, we have opportunities among other things to plant multi-ethnic churches and to work in cross-cultural partnerships to make disciples who will be united by the one Lord who has 'all authority in heaven and on earth.'

In the first letter of Peter, his readers are reminded that they are still on a journey and that their witness to non-believers is an essential part of their journey:

> Beloved, I beseech you as aliens and exiles to abstain from the passions of the flesh that wage war against your soul. Maintain good conduct among the Gentiles, so that in case they speak against you as wrongdoers, they may see your good deeds and glorify God on the day of visitation.
> *1 Peter 2:11-12 (RSV)*

In the current Western secular world this call to missional discipleship remains. There is a need for us to maintain our orthodoxy of beliefs so that these may inform our orthopraxy of good deeds and practices. Those who observe our lives as followers of God will learn the most by how we behave. Postmodern people often object to the church, with statements like, 'Christians are hypocrites'.[228] People are looking carefully at how we behave in our Christian communities. We need to take care not to stop our nomadic discipleship practices that take us on a journey into new places, which may include the house of the neighbour next door. The life of the missional nomad is focused by the continuing call to go out and 'make disciples'.

---

[228] This is a common theme heard by both writers.

It is to this disciple-making theme that we turn our attention next. How can we make disciples who can share the gospel with other ethnic groups in the multicultural society in which we live?

Making missional disciples

Jesus did not invent discipleship or the methods that were used for teaching and training. It was common practice for the majority of ethnic groups in the ancient world to use discipleship as a means to pass on knowledge and skills. Longenecker points out that the term 'disciple' was rarely used in the time of Christ; however, it was common for rabbis to have followers who would learn oral traditions from them:

> The word for 'disciple,' 'pupil,' or 'learner' (whether talmid or limmud or their cognates) have not been found, to date, in the Aramaic or Hebrew texts of the Dead Sea Scrolls, even though great stress was placed on instruction and various degrees of learning in that community.[229]

It is also important to note that disciples were widely known to the culture of the Greco-Roman world:

> 'disciple' (mathetes) was used in many of the Greek philosophical schools of the classical and koine periods for one who learned and became a follower of a particular teacher.[230]

Jesus' practice of having disciples fitted well into the pattern of how teachers passed on knowledge to their students. In this section we will consider some ideas for how we can intentionally shape and form missional disciples who can make other disciples cross culturally. This, too, will require a process of learning from those who already do this well. There are seven matters that will help us to understand the formation of disciples.

---

[229] Richard Longenecker (ed.), *Patterns of Discipleship in the New Testament* (Grand Rapids, Eerdmans, 1996), p.2.
[230] Longenecker, *Patterns of Discipleship in the New Testament*, pp.2, 3.

1. Discipleship as apprenticeship

Ancient discipleship practices were based on what we might call an apprenticeship model. When Jesus called His disciples to follow Him, it also included them accepting Him as their rabbi (teacher). The kind of rabbi that Jesus represented was one who not only taught, but also worked miracles and did good deeds (John 20:16). His followers were to model what He did. Acts records Peter's speech to Cornelius' household in which he shared an important memory of Jesus' ministry, as he recalled:

> 'how God anointed Jesus of Nazareth with the Holy Spirit
> and with power; how he went about doing good and healing
> all that were oppressed by the devil, for God was with him.
> And we are witnesses to all that he did both in the country of
> the Jews and in Jerusalem.'
> *Acts 10:38, 39a (RSV)*

The word 'witnesses' is an important part of the concept of discipleship as it developed after Christ's resurrection. The early disciples witnessed about everything that Jesus did and said, including His crucifixion, resurrection, ascension and the coming of the Spirit. The first disciples learnt how to go about missional ministry by observing how Jesus did it and also by being given opportunities to go out and teach that the kingdom of God was coming as they healed the sick and raised the dead (Matthew 10:1-5). The form of apprenticeship by which they were shaped was based on providing them with fieldwork as they went out in twos (Luke 10), so that they could build their confidence that God was with them as He worked through their ministries. When Jesus sent the 12 apostles out to engage in teaching and healing, He gave them simple but clear instructions of what they needed to do (Matthew 10:1-5). When they returned from their missionary excursions He provided them with feedback and the opportunity to reflect on their experiences so that they could learn from them.

It is important that we apply this to how we engage in the formation of modern cross-cultural disciples. Successful and experienced cross-cultural disciple-makers will need to apprentice

153

trainee disciple-makers to intelligently observe and imitate their practices. We are not talking of a quick win–win situation; it takes time for inexperienced followers to pick up the knowledge and skills required to become effective disciple-makers in their own right. Missional leaders of congregations are not enough on their own to transform their churches to become able to share the gospel with others. It is crucial to have mission teams made up of successful cross-cultural disciple-makers in order to form disciples among other subcultural groups who are part of our multicultural society. The concept of the disciple as a nomad is important here in the sense that the journey alongside an experienced leader helps apprentices to work, over time, in cross-cultural mission settings.

2. Cross-cultural disciple-makers

We come to the need for missional leaders who are experienced cross-cultural disciple-makers who can cultivate congregations of committed disciple-makers like themselves. The apprenticeship model we shared above requires willing apprentices who can be shaped by leaders to become disciple-makers. This brings us to another vital point about the issue of discipleship as the primary mission approach for multicultural missionaries to adopt. If multi-ethnic missional congregations are to be planted, it will take committed leadership teams that can equip their congregations to develop the necessary commitment and skills to disciple others.

The concept of discipleship closest to Jesus' view translates the term 'disciple' as an adherent. Adherents are different to those who show some interest in discipleship among other interests they might have. An adherent as Jesus expressed it is someone who is completely focused on following Christ and sharing their faith in Him in every circumstance of their life. Jesus taught:

> 'He who loves father or mother more than me is not worthy of me; and he who loves son or daughter more than me is not worthy of me; and he who does not take his cross and follow me is not worthy of me. He who finds his life will lose it, and he who loses his life for my sake will find it.'
> Matthew 10:37-39 (RSV)

The radical level of commitment required by Jesus of disciples is well expressed in Matthew 10. The few verses quoted above set out the core of the call and have to do with what human beings build their lives and identities around. It can be around our parents, our families, our work, our friends, acquaintances and so on. Are we focused on building our life around our career or our family, or pursuing personal attainment and the prestige that comes with it? These are some of the huge drivers of secular life. But focusing on these can mean losing our spiritual lives, in the sense that we will not reap the rewards of being shaped by following the missionary Spirit of Jesus if they take our focus off Him.

Are our careers the main passion of our lives, or are they the arena in which we seek to form other disciples? Shaping missional congregations to be committed to disciple-making will require the kind of adherents who put Christ, and the coming kingdom of God, first in everything they plan to do. The important concept here is for each of us to maintain our intimacy with Christ and to be willing to be held accountable to others who can mutually encourage us to grow in our faith and commitment to Christ.

This is where we need to take more time to examine our lives reflectively through prayer and spiritual practices that will keep us close to the living Christ of the Spirit. It is also important to hold ourselves mutually accountable to peers.

Some churches committed to disciple-making encourage their members to form close friendships in groups of four or five people who work hard at encouraging each other to keep growing in their relationship with the Lord. Part of the process in such groups is for participants to mentor and coach each other and to help each other overcome hindrances to their spiritual growth, as well as to reach personal goals to share their faith with others. The overall aim for all of this is to cultivate congregations to become much more than worshippers and spectators. Deep fellowship becomes just as important as worship.

Fellowship takes at least as much time as worship does, but probably more with the goal of participants forming deep friendships with their peers, as well as with those exploring faith for the first time. The type of fellowship implied here is the kind that helps us to share deeper life together. As people become more aware of the deeper challenges facing those they fellowship with, it can cause them to ask pertinent questions. What is challenging us most at the moment? How can members with whom we fellowship perform a ministry to help us with specific needs we have? Does the time spent eating together, praying together and sharing the highs and lows of our lives with each other help us to feel safe to find help from those around us? Do our Christian communities (churches) encourage us to engage in shaping other disciples? In what ways do our communities foster a form of fellowship that is safe for new converts to join?

These types of questions need to be asked, as it will take a careful audit of what level of fellowship and support actually provide for those who need our support. Are our current members ready to take on the responsibility of helping new disciples to overcome the many hurdles that following Christ will challenge them to conquer?

3. A disciple-making culture

We need to say something about the cultivation of a disciple-making culture in a Christian community (church). This has much more to do with the processes that we might use to help form new disciples. Dunn and Senter III discuss one well-thought-through disciple-making process that is used to help shape and form young people.[231] It has to do with, firstly, winning new believers to faith in Christ; secondly, to building them up in their faith so that they learn how to become responsible followers of Christ; thirdly, to equipping them to learn how to make new disciples for themselves as they follow Christ. Finally, this leads to the multiplication of the number of new disciples that join our missional churches. The overall assumption of this model is that it is based on a recycling process, where those who multiply the numbers of new believers help these new believers to become disciple-makers in their own right. In simple terms, this seems like a fair description of how Jesus and the early church went about making new disciples.

---

[231] Richard Dunn and Mark Senter III (eds.), *Reaching a Generation for Christ* (Chicago, Moody Publishers, 1997), Chapter 1.

There is not enough space in this chapter to discuss this model in depth; however, we might consider what each of these steps might need to include.

Step 1 – Winning new disciples

The kinds of things included in this stage will have to be suited to the needs of the target group. If they are secular people, we need to recognise that many do not have a basic cultural memory of what the Christian story is about. During our childhoods in the 1950s, 1960s and 1970s, there were still some assumed cultural values that made it a requirement to teach the Christian faith at school and to tell Christian stories in assemblies. In addition, there were various ideas, words and phrases in popular culture which underpinned a Christian narrative that shaped society. Currently it is more the case that schools represent a multi-faith engagement with different religious points of view. Neither of us were brought up as Christians, but in our late teens we knew enough about the Christian story to assume that it was part of our national culture. Hence, what we needed was a genuine conversion which would lead us to a personal faith in Christ. We assumed that committed Christians went to church regularly and therefore that trustworthy people went to church because they were committed Christians.

However, in our post-Christian, postmodern, secular society, most of those under 35 years of age do not share this kind of cultural memory. Around 40% of people in the UK have never been to church, and figures vary in other Westernised nations. This 40% do not assume that people in churches can be trusted, and they do not generally have influential friendships with committed Christians. Hence, before we can share the gospel with this category of people, we have to build basic friendships with them so that they can learn to trust us. It may take several months or years for them to come to faith – if at all. There is a need for a longer-term investment in secular people because of the time it takes to win their trust. Once they trust us as genuine friends, they might start to take our faith seriously. A big question will regard whether we genuinely believe. Another thing they will look for is evidence that God makes a real difference to the way we live and how we resolve our personal challenges. Postmodern people are looking for genuine experiences that work for others that might be worth trying out for themselves. Winning people to Christ means winning their friendship, not as an ingenuous tactic to convert them, but as a commitment to being real friends despite what they might choose to believe. Winning people to Christ in this postmodern culture calls for them to get to know the Christ who is modelled through our lives. We need to become living human documents whose very lives tell the story of the good news of the living Jesus.

Step 2 – Building confident, convinced followers

Stuart Murray Williams has written much about what the church after Christendom faces.[232] Among other things, it is no longer at the centre of our Western culture. It is not central to politics, economics, business, education, the media, medicine, etc. During Christendom it was far more central to government and the basic social structures of our society. So as we have already noted above, for many postmodern people there is no basic Christian cultural memory for them to draw on. Postmodern society does not, as such, have a defining centre to it, with an assumed belief in the Christian monotheistic faith. Indeed, cultural relativism would be a better description of postmodern culture. There is no one big story (metanarrative) that people assume to be true, telling them where they came from, why they are here or where they are going. Indeed, any number of stories could be true, and the assumption is that it is not possible to prove one story to be any more true than another. The large question is, 'How can we build up new disciples in their faith enough so that they can define their worldview using the Christian story?' In other words, how can we help new believers to become deeply convinced about the Christian story, faced as they are by so many alternative stories which could equally be true, given their cultural predisposition not to accept any one story as absolute?

We believe this will require missional teachers to engage in a process of missional apologetics. It seems this has not been a strong priority of the church for some years, even though there are some very

---

[232] Stuart Murray Williams, *Post-Christendom: Church and Mission in a Strange New World* (Milton Keynes, Paternoster, 2005), Chapter 1.

good ministries that work in this area.[233] Apologetics has to do with a rational defence of the Christian faith. New believers come with many questions which they need help to answer. This is not the place to discuss what kind of apologetics we will need to cover. However, many postmodern people are not just looking to have their intellectual questions addressed, but they also want authentic experiences of the divine to confirm the reality of their beliefs. The whole New Age movement is one thriving expression of this pursuit of meaningful experiences for some Westerners. This is where helping new believers to build a living relationship with the God who speaks by His Spirit will be important in order to help them become committed to the living God.

In a later chapter we will address some of the things that need to be put in place for it to be meaningfully possible for postmodern new believers to discover the living God for themselves. The type of process we are talking about here has to do with a new disciple proceeding on a journey of exploration into Christian spirituality. If we are to engage together in multicultural missional conversations, we must understand the challenge of Western cultural relativism. This ethos of relativity causes postmodern people to have strong doubts about any system of belief which claims absolute certainty as part of its message. We ourselves will have to journey alongside emergent believers, helping them answer their questions, which will in turn challenge our own assumptions. This might mean we will feel uncomfortable when we find our own faith challenged by their questions.

Step 3 – Equipping disciple-makers

The apprenticeship model of disciple-making that Jesus used was to help His disciples learn by watching–copying–reflecting. In order for us to equip new disciples who have attained a level of faith which gives them confidence in their beliefs, they will need to have already learnt much through being shaped as disciples themselves. The equipping phase for disciples who are ready to share their faith with

---

[233] One good example is the Oxford Centre for Christian Apologetics: http://theocca.org (accessed 31st August 2014).

those who do not believe will mean that they need to go through some sort of practical training to reinforce the skills they need to help shape other disciples. We have already discussed that they will need to be mentored by those who have more experience in disciple-making.

One view of post-Christian society is that it is in an in-between-phase, where people are searching for what comes next rather than seeing it as the next thing which has arrived. In this sense, the concept of the nomadic disciple-maker is relevant. Nomadic disciples can walk alongside postmodern people, building relationships with them and helping them to discover what God is bringing about next. None of us, whether we are convinced believers, new believers or seekers, have stopped journeying towards God's future. The nomadic process of disciple-making is a lifelong progression.

What comes next after Christendom? Will it be possible to shape cross-cultural multi-ethnic disciple-makers who can plant multi-ethnic missional churches together? We believe it is vital for our churches to become much more multicultural in their fellowship structures, in order to portray the ability of the Christian faith to help diverse peoples live together in greater harmony in our society. This provides a clear example of what the kingdom of God looks like, and by learning to live it together, we provide a further example to a watching world of the reality of the God who is with us. After all, where else on planet earth can the nations come together under a king who is a servant? The truth is, none of us can be sure what comes after Christendom. One encouraging thought is that the missionary God is a genius at equipping His people to make disciples out of peoples from diverse backgrounds. The apostle Paul expressed his continuing journey as a nomadic disciple in terms which we all need to keep at the heart of our own journeys:

> Not that I have already obtained this or am already perfect; but I press on to make it my own, because Christ Jesus has made me his own. Brethren, I do not consider that I have made it my own; but one thing I do, forgetting what lies behind and straining forward to what lies ahead, I press on toward the goal for the prize of the upward call of God in Christ Jesus. Let those of us who are mature be thus minded and if in anything you are otherwise minded, God will reveal

that also to you. Only let us hold true to what we have attained.

Philippians 3:12-16 (RSV)

Step 4 – Multiplying future disciple-makers

It will never be enough, until the mission of Christ is completed, for us to stop multiplying disciples who themselves become mature and committed to producing other disciple-makers. Nomadic disciple-makers continue on their journeys, praying as Jesus taught them, 'Your kingdom come, your will be done, on earth as it is in heaven' (Matthew 6:10). This is the process of multiplying new disciples who themselves multiply others in the name and power of Christ as He fights alongside us to win the door-to-door battle: to win, build, equip and multiply His followers until He finally comes again and establishes His universal kingdom. Multi-ethnic nomadic disciple-makers need to join together in the missional conversation. We need to realise that the kingdom of God unites all peoples as one in Christ.

4. Reading others

We need to learn how to read those with whom we want to share our faith by considering the context of their own outlooks on the world. The apostle Paul spoke of his approach to doing this:

> To the Jews I became as a Jew, in order to win Jews; to those under the law I became as one under the law – though not being myself under the law – that I might win those under the law. To those outside the law I became as one outside the law – not being without law toward God but under the law of Christ – that I might win those outside the law. To the weak I became weak, that I might win the weak. I have become all things to all men, that I might by all means save some. I do it all for the sake of the gospel, that I may share in its blessings.
> *1 Corinthians 9:20-23 (RSV)*

Missiologists call this approach 'contextualisation'. Contextualisation has to do with studying another person's worldview and then seeking to understand how to communicate the gospel to them using appropriate language. If we can put ourselves in another person's shoes and try to see the world in the way they see it, it will probably help us to form friendships with them. This is essentially what contextualisation helps us to do. Disciple-makers who take the time to put themselves in another person's, or group's, shoes are engaging in a new journey. This kind of journey has to do with walking alongside people so that it is possible to understand how they see the world. It means we need to try to suspend our own ways of looking at the world and rather to start to see the world from another point of view. This process of suspension does not require that we forget our faith, but rather that we try to discover ways and means to convey the gospel message to those to whom we want to communicate it, starting from their perspective.

5. Welcoming diversity

Congregations that welcome people from different cultures will need to be communities that welcome diversity. People who come to faith from a culture that is different from our own will interpret the Bible from the perspective of their own worldview. For example, with regard to Jesus speaking of the need to build our lives on solid rocky foundations rather than on sand (Matthew 7:24-27), most Westerners will not have experienced what many Indian villagers go through, when floods quite literally wash away the soil deposits on which their homes are built. A Westerner may have suffered flood damage, of course, but the total loss of a home with loved ones being washed away and drowned will be a much rarer experience. When a Westerner reads the advice to build on firm foundations it will make logical sense, but it is unlikely to have the same impact as it will on an Indian villager who has suffered the loss of everything. Hence, a first generation migrant from a rural part of India now living in the West would probably take the advice about building their lives on rocky foundations in Christ more seriously.

This potential for diverse interpretations of Scripture will be challenging to negotiate among culturally divergent groups as they try to fellowship together.

6. Following the Spirit of Jesus

Nomadic disciples need to follow the Spirit of Jesus as He guides them to break new ground in new contexts. To be able to be guided by the Spirit, it is vital to be able to discern the voice of God. A classic example of this is to be found in the book of Acts in a passage which finds Paul and his mission team being guided as to where they are next to communicate the gospel:

> And they went through the region of Phrygia and Galatia, having been forbidden by the Holy Spirit to speak the word in Asia. And when they had come opposite Mysia, they attempted to go into Bithynia, but the Spirit of Jesus did not allow them; so, passing by Mysia, they went down to Troas. And a vision appeared to Paul in the night: a man of Macedonia was standing beseeching him and saying, 'Come over to Macedonia and help us.' And when he had seen the vision, immediately we sought to go on into Macedonia, concluding that God had called us to preach the gospel to them.
> *Acts 16:6-10 (RSV)*

It is evident enough that Paul and his team were being guided by the Spirit of Jesus, who was opening up the right doors ahead of the team so that the gospel could be shared in a new region. Of course, at the heart of the story, Paul's nomadic mission team of disciple-makers are following Jesus, because they are dynamically listening to and following the Spirit of Jesus as He guides them on their missionary journeys.

Nomadic disciple-making teams are not a static or stationary category. Missional disciples who keep crossing cultural boundaries to build bridges to share the gospel with new people follow a dynamic Lord who keeps moving ahead of them, preparing the ground for new seeds to be sown.

It is important to understand that the gospel is not simply a good idea to which we give mental assent, but it actually is a person. The resurrected Jesus is the gospel, and He is still calling us to follow Him as He makes disciples of all nations. In a later chapter we will discuss the kinds of spiritual disciplines that missional churches need to develop in order to keep journeying with the dynamic missional Spirit of Jesus. His Spirit must be heard so that we can keep moving ahead.

7. Living in the communities where new disciples dwell

Finally, everything we have said about following the nomadic Spirit of Jesus strongly implies planting new kinds of communities that can enable new disciples to be developed in the places where we have got to know them. This will create some intriguing challenges for us. For example, it is not considered ethical for teachers, doctors, nurses, social workers, etc in the UK system to use their work roles to promote their faith and views. This is probably true to differing extents in other Western nations. Secularism assumes that faith is a private matter for individuals to pursue in their own time. Our private faith and our engagement in church life are, in a strange quirk of secularisation, themselves secularised. What we mean by this is that privatising religion has meant that it has been given its own secular space in the private sphere, which is not easily permitted to invade other secular spaces in society, such as our places of work. Equally, sharing our faith with work colleagues has to be approached carefully, as it will be easy for Christians to sideline themselves with their employers if they abuse these limiting policies.

So how can we make disciples in the secular workplace?

We believe that every Christian has a responsibility to follow Christ into their workplace, and other places of influence, to share their faith. There is not a single part of society that does not belong to Christ. It will at times mean we butt heads with secular powers and authorities. If we are to be sensitive to following His Spirit, it will require each of us to share our faith in the workplace. Leaders need to equip their members to imagine new ways of doing this in contextually appropriate ways. We need to escape from our sacred private zones where we limit our faith to our churches and homes, and instead we need to take our faith into the public zones.

Let us not delude ourselves into thinking it is easy. However, at the same time, work colleagues can become more than acquaintances, and sometimes strong friendships develop. We spend a significant part of our waking lives at work. It may be during a lunchtime, or while having a drink after work or a coffee during a tea break that colleagues will come to know about our faith. It will probably come out in conversation rather than in an intentional, planned way. In larger companies, small groups of Christians may meet to talk about faith issues or to pray. It may be possible to invite seeking colleagues to join us when we pray or have faith conversations during breaks or after work. If colleagues want to explore the Christian faith, small support groups could meet during lunch breaks or after work.

This is very much part of what is known as the emerging church scene. We are having to find new ways to fellowship with those who are exploring faith. For example, we know of Christian groups who hire coffee shops after hours in order to meet people who frequent high streets in the evenings.[234] If disciple-making strategies only include inviting people to become part of our congregations, there will be many thousands of people who will not come. Sundays are for many people a time for visiting family, for sport and leisure, and for work. We need to creatively engage with others who will meet with us in the pub, in a coffee shop, in our homes, in the works canteen, in the hospital chapel – in fact, wherever we can meet. Part of our journey as nomadic disciples requires setting up alternative informal meetings with those whom we are trying to disciple, which will, of course, take time and investment. It is good to be reminded that Jesus, the missional disciple-maker, has invited and called us also to make disciples as we go out into the world (Matthew 28:19-20).

Conclusions

This chapter has set out the case for a discipleship formation strategy that has to do with the need to develop mobile missional communities. By 'mobile', we mean that wherever we find opportunities to make other disciples, we need to create the possibility for support and community to develop around them, in their natural circumstances.

First generation ethnic Christians are on the cusp of being nomadic disciples par excellence. Many in migrant churches have grown up in

---

[234]This approach is called 'Sunday Night Live' which includes live music and testimony. It is a growing opportunity for churches to engage with their communities within a non-church environment. See http://sundaynightlive.org.uk (accessed 2nd September 2014).

their homelands planting new Christian groups on the doorsteps of those who are converted. Having them join in the missional conversation with other groups will help to keep our faith fresh as they challenge us to follow God into new and risky ventures so that we can make new disciples. This will not be a comfortable experience for us, especially if we are settled in the way we do things.

We would suggest that second and third generation ethnic churches tend to assimilate much of Western culture, which means that they can pass on helpful insights to first generation migrant groups. It can mean, too, that they become comfortable and settled in the ways they do things in their own church constituencies and subcultures. We all need help to be liberated from our particular secularised grooves.

In order for us to lead change to develop a culture of disciple-makers, it will be important to become mobile once more – following the nomadic Spirit of Jesus as He calls us to follow Him to break new ground in secular spaces that need reclaiming for the kingdom of God. It is important for us all to include the question of disciple-making in our multicultural missional conversations. Jesus 'made disciples' not as an afterthought or a good idea to add to many other ideas, nor as a plan that had a limited shelf life; rather it was His mission strategy: 'Go therefore and make disciples of all nations, baptizing them in the name of the Father and of the Son and of the Holy Spirit' (Matthew 28:19).

Reflective exercise

Take a few minutes to reflect on the following questions.

- What specific discipleship courses does your church run?

- How effective are these courses at discipling people for the long term?

- How successful have your discipleship strategies been in terms of helping people to become committed to long-term formation into the likeness of Christ?

- What have you learnt from this chapter which will help you to further develop discipleship approaches your church can use?

- What tools already exist which might help you to think about developing discipleship approaches in your church?

Comments

Chapter 6
Shaping Culturally Intelligent Leaders

Leaders who engage in the multicultural missional conversation need to ask themselves, 'What is my motivation for joining in with this conversation?' We have already suggested that a key motivation has to do with the very mission of the Trinity itself. God's plan is nothing less than to bring about the reconciliation and unification of all peoples through Jesus Christ, and indeed the entire cosmos.

Clearly, in a multicultural and multi-ethnic Western society, there are great opportunities to engage in planting new churches which welcome ethnic diversity. If God's mission is to work through Christians to realise the unification of all peoples under one God, then some key motivations for us to embrace in the missional conversation are:

- How can we plant more multi-ethnic missional churches that are led by culturally intelligent leadership teams?

- How can we help members to embrace cultural differences?

- How can we cultivate a coalition of people from different ethnic groups who will be able to fellowship with people from other cultures?

- How can leaders of existing ethnic churches lead their congregations through a change management process towards becoming multicultural churches?

Of course, all of these questions are based on the assumption that it is desirable to work towards at least some multi-ethnic breakthrough congregations. These questions are the subject of this chapter.

The rationale for multi-ethnic churches

Let's deal with the last question first. Part of the rationale of this book is the very fact that Western society is becoming increasingly multicultural and that this raises the aspect of the gospel which calls for all people groups to unite in Christ in order to express the unity of

God's kingdom that is built on equality. Moreover, we have made the case that the Trinity has made mankind in its image, and part of that image is the wide variety of ethnic and cultural diversity that is found in the world. The simple rationale for planting multi-ethnic breakthrough congregations is that God has created the opportunity for different cultural groups to join together in multicultural societies. United multi-ethnic congregations will provide secular society with a new hermeneutic for understanding the power of the love of God that unites diverse peoples.

Lesslie Newbigin famously suggested that the local church is the hermeneutic of the gospel.[235] Simply stated, if a group of believers live in harmony together, overcoming their differences through exercising forgiveness and grace, then society will be provided with a new way of interpreting (ie a new hermeneutic of) what the kingdom of God is all about. United multicultural congregations can provide a practical living parable that narrates the good news of cross-cultural reconciliation in action.

Culturally intelligent leadership teams

Discontinuous change is the defining feature of postmodern Western life.[236] It creates confusion because there is not one simple outlook on life that everyone agrees on and adheres to, in the way Europeans once did with Christendom. This means that Christians can find in the church a refuge from this complex society, with its Christian message of certainty that provides a secure framework to build life around.

The missional leader needs to be very aware of this, as it is one of the driving forces which stop people in churches from wanting to change, even if change is for the better. It can also cause people in congregations to want to keep their churches as safe places which do not welcome the challenge of new people joining them.

Not all congregations share this profile, and some newer charismatic free churches and emerging churches are very open to change. They often desire to find new ways of sharing the gospel with

---

[235] Lesslie Newbigin, *The Gospel in a Pluralist Society* (London, SPCK, 1989), Chapter 18.
[236] David Nadler, Robert Shaw and Elise Walton, *Discontinuous Change Leading Organizational Transformation* (San Francisco, Jossey-Bass, 1995), Chapter 1.

those who do not as yet know Christ. Having said this, some congregations prefer to maintain their own subcultures, which can mean that they resist change. It is hard for them to relate to others who do not share their worldview.

We will be looking at cultural intelligence in this section and how developing it can help congregations to engage in a change management process so that they can more readily engage in cross-cultural mission endeavours with other ethnic groups.

One of the major issues facing churches that want to keep on growing and engaging in God's mission is the need for good leadership. On the courses we are involved in teaching at Springdale College, the primary outcome we seek for our students is the development of missional leaders who know how to lead cross-cultural teams. A missional leader is someone who is able to equip a church to discover God's call for mission to people who do not as yet know Christ. An important part of the educational process on our undergraduate programmes is that participants spend 13 hours a week in a placement where they can put theory into practice. Through this process they engage in action–reflection learning, where they reflect on what they are learning from their placement about working with missional teams. One of the key insights often reported by students is that there is a big difference in churches that are based on maintenance ministry compared to a leadership style that seeks to equip church people to share their faith in broader society.

Maintenance ministry is defined as a type of service that ministers provide to churches which helps them to maintain their way of life, without major changes being encouraged in the ways things are done. The aim is to manage the church's organisational structures and traditions without seeking to change them. Conversely, missional leadership is defined as a ministry that seeks to transform structures and organisational patterns in the church, so that it might equip members to discover and engage in God's mission in their own lives within and outside of the church. Change is something that missional congregations have to deal with creatively with the expectation that it is here to stay. It is vital for us to adopt adaptable and flexible attitudes to change, in order that we can relate to others who do not share the same beliefs and cultural perspectives.

170

The maintenance ministry approach often tends to make people in the church want outsiders to come to them on their own terms. They do not want to adapt their attitudes and behaviours in order to relate to others who see things in different ways. It is about keeping the church the same. Each person knows their place in the structure of the church (and often have their own pew). It is the job of the professional minister to engage in serving the people in the church so that they are not encouraged to change their ways of engaging. Faith is the received faith that their local church's tradition sets in place from its foundations upwards. It is the basis for what they believe and do. Belief has to do with a particular way of interpreting Scripture which creates the rationale and framework which define a church's operation. Maintenance ministers tend to fight hard to protect their congregations from change. Churches of this type may be profiled as inward looking.

Missional leaders endeavour to help members discover their own calling to exercise missional ministry in the contexts of their lives inside and outside the church. Good missional leaders want to help people look in both directions – outwards and inwards. This approach seeks to develop God's people for works of service, not just in the church but also with people outside the church who do not yet know Christ. Missional leaders build teams around them so that different kinds of ministry gifts can be encouraged and then exercised inside and outside of the church. There are not huge boundaries between the inner and outer expressions, but a more fluid interchange of the life of the missional Spirit who does not recognise such categories. The purpose of multicultural missional churches is to engage in discerning God's mission to reconcile all people to Himself. Mission churches operate well when ministry teams look to equip the people in their congregations to care for each other as much as to serve broader society, as God calls each believer to exercise their ministry according to their skill set fluidly throughout the whole of God's created world.

This is obviously a rather idealistic description of team ministry and missional leadership. It assumes that team ministry of the type that seeks to reach all peoples is to be found in Western multicultural society and that it can be achieved. The reality is that birds of a feather tend to flock together. In other words, people of one particular ethnic cultural group tend to attract and focus on people from their own cultural group, as we discussed earlier. The question to ask in this section is, 'How can we lead ministry teams who are cross-culturally intelligent so that it is possible for them to plant or further establish multicultural churches that are not homogenous?'

David Livermore, an expert on cross-cultural leadership, speaks of 'CQ' which he defines as, 'Cultural intelligence (CQ) [which] is the capability to function effectively across national, ethnic, and organizational cultures'.[237]

Livermore suggests a four-step process that continuously recycles itself. Step one considers a leader's drive to engage cross culturally. In step two, they seek to understand those they want to work with cross culturally. In step three they formulate strategies to engage with a new group, so that they can work with them with success. In step four they implement an action plan. He argues that all four steps must be used rigorously and continuously so that they become common practices of effective cross-cultural leaders and their teams.

Livermore's expertise is in the field of business leadership, but his knowledge of cross-cultural leadership is of value for our consideration of leading cross-cultural ministry teams. And 'team ministry' is the operative term. In the vision of team ministry that we think reflects the biblical concept of gifts-based ministry (see 1 Corinthians 12), best practice has to do with every Christian identifying and exercising their ministry gifts to complement the others in the team. Hence, a church of 80 people could have four or five missional ministry teams that meet together intentionally in smaller groups to consider how they can engage in mission in the communities where they live. This may sound rather structuralist, but we think of it as a process, or part of the way of life of God's people. In other words, our concept of team ministry is not hierarchical but rather relational and communitarian in nature.

The role of the main missional leadership team will be to equip these missional cell groups to discover and to exercise their spiritual gifts. In this view of missional team ministry, it is important that these

---

[237] David Livermore, *Leading with Cultural Intelligence* (New York, AMACOM, 2010), p.24.

small groups are made up of people from more than one ethnic and cultural group. Multicultural missional churches need to learn to organise themselves in intentional ways in order to encourage each other to spiritually discern where the Holy Spirit wants to send them to engage in mission in their own neighbourhoods.

Returning to Livermore's definition, it is important for culturally intelligent teams of people to learn to be sensitive to each other's cultural differences, as well as to be able to understand the cultural differences between themselves and the people with whom God has led them to share their faith. It makes sense to help the people of God become aware of how people from other ethnic and cultural backgrounds understand the world they live in, in order to be able to communicate the gospel to them in a language they can relate to. For ethnic churches who define themselves as reverse missionary congregations, it is very important that they learn how to lead missional ministry teams that are cross-culturally intelligent. It is equally important for Christians born and raised in the secular West to become cross-culturally sensitive, if we are to aspire to plant some multi-ethnic missional churches with our ethnic brothers and sisters.

So how can leaders and their teams develop their CQ? Livermore makes some important suggestions as to how we might do this. He sets out a four-part process to help us develop our cross-cultural intelligence so that we can use insights to practically relate to people from other cultures. This four-part process will be adapted in this section to apply it to missional leaders who want to effectively engage with other ethnic groups.

Livermore suggests that effective cross-cultural leaders have to keep working hard at developing their cultural intelligence throughout their lifetimes. So let's consider his four-step approach. It will help leaders in formal positions of influence in the church as much as anyone committed to sharing their faith.

Livermore's four-step process

Step 1 – CQ drive
The leader who wants to develop their ability to work with other leaders cross culturally needs to have high motivation, interest,

confidence and drive to adapt their thinking and behaviours. Livermore offers a sharp profile of such a leader:

> Leaders with high CQ drive are motivated to learn and adapt to new diverse cultural settings. Their confidence in their adaptive abilities is likely to influence the way they perform in multicultural situations.[238]

We are brought to the nub of what it takes for a missional leader to succeed in learning how to work with other leaders within the multicultural marketplace. They start by asking, 'What is my motivation?' If we do not have passion and energy to really want to engage with others cross culturally, we will not succeed. It takes more than a simple urge to work with others who are significantly different to ourselves. It requires drive and stamina. Seasoned leaders will often have learnt how to avoid burnout by developing skills that help them to maintain their stamina so that they can work effectively among their own cultural group, let alone a different one. When it comes to working with others who do not come from the leader's culture, the leader's knowledge and experience will be key to being sustaining in their preferred ministry setting. This experience will also require the leader to transfer these skills to the demanding task of working with people from a different subculture.

At the heart of such a leader's drive will be a passion to actually want to work cross culturally. Leaders with higher levels of CQ drive tend to be energised by working with people from different cultures. This is why it is vital for leaders to ask themselves and their teams, 'Does relating to this new cultural group give me/us energy?' If the answer is yes, it is a good indicator that engaging in missional conversations at a deeper level may be worth exploring with a new group. The same kind of question needs to be asked regarding the congregation's drive to explore ways of relating with another cultural group as well.

A high generalised CQ drive profile for the leader, the leadership team and the congregation will be a strong indicator that it is worth finding ways of getting to know another ethnic group better. We

---

[238] Livermore, *Leading with Cultural Intelligence*, p.41.

would add that the best way to test the level of this drive to work with other groups can be explored most effectively when we engage in missional conversations with leaders from differing ethnic churches. It is vital to explore how leaders from different subcultures understand God's mission for them, as well as to consider their motivation to extend the kingdom of God by seeking to unite with other ethnic churches in mission.

If a missional leader with a high CQ drive is to help their congregation go through a change management process so that they can work cross culturally with other groups, it is important to judge the level of drive and energy that is available in the congregation. The leader's drive will be what motivates them to do more than simply recognise that it might be a good idea in principle. If the leader and the leadership team discern a desire to explore how to work cross culturally in shared multi-ethnic mission ventures, Livermore's next step relating to CQ needs to be considered.

We would add here that linear processes are not tasks or programmes, but they are fluid in nature. In other words, people tend to take time to form attitudes and desires to go through processes of change – especially when they are not imposed by outside forces that cannot be avoided, leading to inevitable change. Leaders with high CQ drive will need to be aware that their congregations are locked into their own cultural norms and values. It will take a process of time and education to enable them to attain the motivational energy to work cross culturally when, and if, they understand and accept the leadership's passion to work with other ethnic missional churches.

Livermore suggests that leaders can develop their CQ drive:

> The first step toward leading with cultural intelligence is addressing the motivational issues for ourselves and others. We can increase our CQ drive. Researchers Linn Van Dyne and Soon Ang describe three subdimensions of CQ drive: intrinsic motivation, extrinsic motivation, and self-efficacy. Their work strongly informs the following strategies for

growing in CQ drive: honesty, self-confidence, eating and socializing, counting the perks, and the triple bottom line.[239]

Livermore's suggestions as to how we can develop our CQ motivation are highly applicable to our discussion of working more intentionally together cross culturally. First of all, our congregations will need to be very honest about their desires and motivations for wanting to join in the missional conversation with another church. For example, key questions have to be, 'Is there a real drive coming from spiritual discernment that God wants us to join with others in shared mission projects?' and, 'Is there a high enough confidence level that our particular church is ready to be challenged by engaging with others whose outlooks on faith and the world will be different to our own?' These questions need to be faced openly and honestly before taking further steps to get to know others better.

Secondly, a good way to develop motivation is to eat and socialise with people from a different church background, in order to test the waters. This will obviously require intentionality on the part of two groups. In our experience, when we eat with others, the very act of hospitality and sharing produces opportunities to want to get to know others better. Certainly, sharing time together over a meal provides plenty of opportunities to see how people get on together.

Thirdly, counting the perks of getting to know another group will help us to realise that there is value in learning from them about challenges they have faced and how they have overcome them. It may sound rather selfish to count the perks; however, we believe God takes delight in blessing us, and the very act of sharing time with others can bring new motivation and resources that we did not anticipate. For example, one of the churches where one of us ministered took the step of getting to know an ageing congregation a short distance away. The ageing congregation was in need of support from experienced preachers at our church, which we were glad to provide. They, in turn, had had a strong desire for a number of years to help support youth ministry, a dream they now felt they could not achieve in their own congregation. They had saved funds for the day when they could launch such a ministry. Because we had a growing work in this area,

---

[239] Livermore, *Leading with Cultural Intelligence*, p.45.

they helped to provide us with much-needed funds. A genuine joint sense of shared ministry grew between the churches as a result.

Finally, we come to what Livermore calls the triple bottom line. It has to do with fiscal, humanitarian and environmental advantages.[240] We live in a world that operates in these three arenas. When the people of God start to join together intentionally, it can provide more finance to fund mission. It can also bring more people together with gifts and skills which can help others, and it can provide new venues and arenas in which to meet and have a positive influence on others. These sub-dimensions will prove to be valuable motivations for people to join together in the multicultural missional conversation. The example we shared above is testament to this advantage. It is hoped that it will also help more multi-ethnic mission churches to be planted, when people start to realise that pooling resources can lead to better ways of carrying out mission ventures together.

In order for multi-ethnic mission churches to be planted, or for culturally different ethnic churches to work more closely together, it is very important that we study each other's cultural similarities and differences. This leads us to Livermore's second step.

Step 2 – CQ knowledge

This simply has to do with a leader's ability to understand issues and differences that exist between their culture and a culture they want to work with. Livermore offers this profile of a leader who is developing CQ knowledge:

> Leaders high in CQ knowledge have rich, well-organized understanding of culture and how it affects the way people think and behave. They possess a repertoire of knowledge in knowing how cultures are alike and different. They understand how culture shapes behavior.[241]

Leaders who want to work with another cultural group need to ask themselves, 'What do I need to know in order to understand the *norms* and *values* of this new group?' *Norms* have to do with the things that

---

[240] Livermore, *Leading with Cultural Intelligence*, pp.45-48.
[241] Livermore, *Leading with Cultural Intelligence*, p.63.

are taken for granted by another ethnic group which are part of their homeland subculture, and outlooks on how they are to live and behave in society. We can discover *norms* by asking ourselves some basic questions:

- How do family members relate to each other?

- Is the father the head of the family?

- Does the wife have a subordinate role, where she defers to her husband when decisions are made?

- Are children treated as mini versions of adults with the right to choose how they behave, or are they expected to accept what their parents tell them to do and to conform to their demands?

- Is the leader of a church considered to be the authority figure who makes decisions for his congregation to follow, or is power distributed so that the congregation makes decisions which the leader needs to heed and follow?

Next we come to *values*. *Values* have to do with such things as individualism, where each member of a church has the perceived right to express their own spirituality and their own faith journey, with less regard for what others have to contribute to their preferred approaches. This 'less regard' needs to be compared to congregations where the community's defined doctrines enforce what should be believed and practised if a person is to remain part of that church. Knowledge of fundamental issues like this will be very important indicators of how well people from differing cultural traditions will adapt to fellowship with each other. This is a complex area of cultural study which this book will not consider deeply.

Having said this, it is important to understand in what ways we are *similar* to another group in order that we can build on the *strengths* of our *similarities* so that we can be enabled to form missional coalitions. It is also vital to understand where we are significantly *different* in our beliefs, practices and outlooks on the world. It is these significant *differences* which will help us to predict the possible *conflicts* we might have with others if we were to join in missional endeavours together. There are some resources suggested in the bibliography for those who want to dig deeper into this important area of cultural studies.

At a basic level, you might want to do a simple audit to look at the *similarities* and *differences* between your church and another church you might want to join together with in some missional activities. Use the table below to help you do this.

Similarity–dissimilarity audit for two churches that might want to consider partnering together in mission[242]

Norms and Values (outlooks on the world that an ethnic group grew up with or assume)	*Similar* (tick if similar)	*Dissimilar* (tick if dissimilar)
1a. Kinship families: the family finds its identity in passed-down family traditions remembered as a family history, and more than one generation lives within a family. Marriage is often by arrangement.		
1b. Nuclear families: based on two generations where parents marry based on free choice of who to marry, and they have children.		
2a. Western rational religious systems: rational religious systems are reason based and rely on scientific answers that are non-supernatural. There is a strong, rationally based work ethic which people adopt to work hard together. They keep well-defined promises made to employers, especially as part of religious duty for Protestant and evangelical believers.		
2b. Non-Western supernatural religious systems: the emphasis is on discerning the work of hidden supernatural forces of good or evil which affect every aspect of life. There is less of a work ethic in these cultures where keeping promises to employers is deemed necessary. In other words, these systems have not been affected by the Protestant work ethic.		

[242] This table has been constructed based on a collation of a number of different profile tools we use when we teach cross-cultural studies.

3a. Non-Western high power distance cultures: leaders and parents exercise power and are treated with great respect for their status. Those with less power know their place in the hierarchy and how to behave towards those higher up.		
3b. Western low power distance cultures: leaders and the people are considered to be on a similar level, with power being exercised by permission and limited to a role rather than to a status.		
4a. Non-Western event-time cultures: time is measured by social relationships where time-keeping can be affected by social obligations that crop up – spontaneity is more important than being on time.		
4b. Western clock-time cultures: the emphasis is on being punctual – being late is considered to be rude or a sign of poor commitment.		
5a. Non-Western collectivist cultures: the person's individual rights are less important than his or her duty to serve the community or family, and to sacrifice themselves for needs of others or the greater good deemed to be this good by the whole community.		
5b. Western individualist cultures: the individual has the right to self-determination and to choose their own destiny rather than others having the right to choose for them.		
6a. Non-Western honour–shame cultures: a person's honour is more important to protect than the person's need to be accountable for mistakes. Hence you would not challenge a person for being late.		
6b. Western accountability cultures: a person is held accountable for their actions based on what they do, or do not do, irrespective of how they feel about being held to account.		

The way to use this list of six predictors for how one church might be significantly different to another church is to discern where your similarities and differences are by putting ticks in the appropriate columns. If one church is a white Anglo-Saxon church and another is a Eritrean church, they would be dissimilar in all cases, from 1a to 1b to 6a to 6b, because, for example, the Anglo-Saxon church would be based on an accountability culture whereas the Ethiopian church would be built on a honour–shame culture. Hence, a cause of tension between two congregations like this, if they were to work together, is likely to have to do with accountability versus the need to keep face. People from an honour–shame culture help each other keep face so they will not be publicly shamed, so if people from an Eritrean church were consistently late to a shared missional project in the community, it would be considered offensive to publicly call them to account for their continual lateness. If a white Anglo visited an Ethiopian church to preach, it would be considered offensive if he did not stay for a large part of the day to join in the fellowship of the church as well. Of course, this is a terrible generalisation and it would only be true if the preacher were to leave immediately after the service finished without engaging in fellowship. It is the general expectation of a collectivist (community-focused) culture which is in view in this case.

It is suggested that the number of similarities shared is a good predictor for the likelihood of conflicts to occur. The more differences scored means there is a higher chance of conflict if the two congregations work together. It is very important to consider the differences, particularly as these will be the areas where conflict is most likely to develop. We would suggest that it is essential to work through differences together, realistically, aiming to come to some agreements on how you will handle them if you are to work together in mission.

We could, of course, spend a lot of time considering the importance of leading missional teams based on in-depth knowledge of cross-cultural similarities and differences. At this stage, enough has been done to provide some insights into the importance of developing Step 2, CQ knowledge.

Next we move on to stage 3 of Livermore's CQ leadership model:

Step 3 – CQ strategy

This step relates to how we make sense of our knowledge of cross-cultural differences, which will help us to formulate effective strategies to be able to work with a new group. Livermore offers this profile of a leader who is developing CQ strategy:

> Leaders with high CQ strategy develop ways to use cultural understanding to develop a plan for new cross-cultural situations. These leaders are better able to monitor, analyze, and adjust their behaviors in different cultural settings. They are conscious of what they need to know about an unfamiliar culture.[243]

Missional leaders need to develop the ability to shape their behaviours and responses to another cultural group so that they can show respect and understanding. It is not simply something we need to manufacture in order to do the right thing; it will have to become a key value or it will come across as inauthentic and superficial.

We have obtained much richness from working among different ethnic churches, including our own ethnicity as Caucasian Westerners. We tend to take on values when we understand what they mean to others from the perspective of their cultural outlooks. For example, when we go out to dinner with Nigerian leaders in London, we let them choose food for us at a local Nigerian restaurant. Andy remembers the first time he had fish-head soup – he loved the taste, and even ate some of the fish heads, but the sharp bones cut his mouth as he was not used to using the potato dough balls to wrap them in as he ate. Since then, he has learned his lesson. What we and our Nigerian friends enjoy doing when we go out to eat together is to go to different restaurants so that we can try dishes from each other's food cultures. Part of our CQ strategy for relating to our Nigerian friends has been to learn the importance of expressing a willingness to embrace their culture by sharing their foods. They have graciously done the same for us.

A key question that a missional leader needs to ask when strategising engagement in missional conversations with other ethnic

---

[243] Livermore, *Leading with Cultural Intelligence*, p.113.

church leaders is, 'How should I plan?' There are three steps that may be helpful. Firstly, make sure you become aware of what is going on internally and externally as you interact with leaders from another culture. What are the formal behaviours of those you greet? How do they greet you? How do others greet them? How should you greet them? What do the forms of greeting they use tell you about what they value? For example, when we meet our Nigerian friends, they personally come to greet us when we arrive at their premises, and when we leave they go with us to the door to wish us a safe journey. They make sure that hospitality is offered. They wait for us to start to eat before they do. This has shown us that respect and honour of a visitor is a high value for our friends. It also needs to be a high value for us when they visit us. At a deeper level, it also demonstrates that hospitality offered well is very important to them, as not to do it would express shame on and disregard for guests.

Obviously, what we have just considered reveals not just external behaviours but also internal values and meanings. It is important to become more aware of both of these factors by carefully observing those with whom we want to work more closely so that we can learn what gestures mean to them.

Secondly, Livermore reminds us that it is important to plan our cross-cultural interactions.[244] How will we best obtain permission from the gatekeepers of a new ethnic church to get to know them and their people better? What are the customs and values of the group? Who are the key people who will want to vet us before they assent to us getting to know their members better? We could keep suggesting questions. It is important to plan interactions with another cultural group and to pay careful attention to what they expect of the person approaching them. Moreover, it is important to find a good reason for approaching a new group. This is where engagement in conversations with leaders from a variety of multicultural backgrounds can help us to strategise about those with whom God may be calling us to work more closely.

Thirdly, let us say we have now approached another church leadership team after having got to know them a little at a ministers' meeting. Let us also assume that in our meeting with them we

---

[244] Livermore, *Leading with Cultural Intelligence*, p.116.

intentionally discussed how we could run a soup kitchen together for young homeless men and women. There is a shared vision to take the gospel to those who are poor as well as to meet their basic needs. The meeting has gone well and the elders from the church want to meet with some of our team as a next step. The next step is to check whether the assumptions and plans we had formulated for our interaction with them were appropriate. If they were, what made them successful? If some things seemed awkward or strained, what caused this? The key point is how we can learn from our experiences so we can relate more effectively with another group next time. And the lessons we learn from this process need to be passed on to those from our own church or organisation so that they too can relate effectively in partnership with such a group in the future. Missional leaders need to help their people engage in change which will help them to join in the missional conversation with those they want to share in God's mission with together.

The fourth step in Livermore's cross-cultural leadership model has to do with the implementation processes entailed in leadership CQ.

Step 4 – CQ action

The action phase of any leadership planning process has to do with the hoped-for outcomes from an interaction with a target group. In the case of CQ action, it has to do with the changing of verbal and non-verbal actions so that we can appropriately interact cross culturally with another group of people. Livermore offers this profile of a leader who is developing CQ action abilities:

> Leaders with high CQ action can draw on the other three dimensions of CQ to translate their enhanced motivation, understanding, and planning into action. They possess a broad repertoire of behaviors, which they can use depending on the context.[245]

A key question that engagement in the action–reflection process of CQ leadership has to deal with is, 'What behaviours do I need to adjust in order to work cross culturally with this new group or

---

[245] Livermore, *Leading with Cultural Intelligence*, p.133.

person?' Action-reflection models of learning are increasingly being used to enhance how we can engage in learning in all sorts of life situations. In the case of CQ action, leaders need to reflect on how their behaviours will be perceived by leaders from different ethnicities and cultures with whom they want to explore joining in missional partnership. Livermore suggests that leaders with high CQ action abilities will 'possess a broad repertoire of behaviors, which they can use depending on the context.' 'Context' is everything, especially when we seek to work with others from different cultural backgrounds.

We have already given some examples of behaviours we want to observe, adopt and then put into practice when we work cross culturally. We mentioned the need to observe how people greet each other. We also mentioned some of the meaning-rich formalities to do with welcoming friends, how we say goodbye to friends and how we engage in eating together. All of these are encoded with deep values held by most cultures.

Another example has to do with high power distance cultures. Often, leaders of African churches come from such cultures, where leaders are treated with deference and respect. Therefore, it is vital for an Anglo leader approaching an African church leader to make sure that mutual deference and respect is paid. For example, allow them to lead the conversation and do not contradict them, especially when juniors are in the meeting, as this would be perceived to be offensive. The rule does not always follow that all African leaders will be treated on the basis of high power distance cultural values, but it is important to take note of what type of power is assumed by a leader's congregation.

In our experience, missional leaders who are flexible enough to adapt their behaviours when they work with other leaders most often win their respect and often are able to establish partnerships with them. Much more could be added to the discussion to help us work better cross culturally in joint mission ventures, or in our attempts to plan for and plant multi-ethnic breakthrough congregations. The bibliography suggests some resources to help readers think through the issues that interest them. Like any four-step process, whether it be based on the Pastoral Cycle[246] or, as in this case, Livermore's CQ model, it is important to understand that they are based on action–reflection learning.

We need to use these tools consistently in order to maximise our ability to lead cross culturally. In order to learn how to lead cross culturally using Livermore's approach, we will need to keep recycling his four-step process. As we experiment with action plans that utilise culturally relevant behaviours in order to help us interact with other ethnic churches, we will need to reflect on how well our interactions went and how we can keep improving in our efforts. We would suggest it is a good idea to keep a journal of specific cross-cultural interactions. Such a journal will need to include dated entries and a description of the group we have been working with – what they are like, what sort of cultural norms and values they have, and how well our interactions with them have gone. These need to be reflected upon critically with an eye towards improving our interactions. We might ask questions like:

- What is driving my desire to work in mission with this group?

- What are the key beliefs, practices, norms and values that I need in order to understand this group better?

- What strategies do I need to implement in order to obtain permission to work with their leaders and their people as appropriate to the task?

- What behaviours do I need to implement or change in order to effectively work with them and to win their respect and cooperation?

Cultivating culturally intelligent congregations

The question of how to cultivate culturally intelligent congregations is a complex one. We will provide some suggestions as to how we might start cultivating people's interest in getting to know other cultural

---

[246] Helen Cameron, John Slater and Victoria Slater, *Theological Reflection for Human Flourishing* (London, SCM Press, 2012), p.xii.

groups. Andy Crouch provides a useful reflection on the concept of cultivating cultural intelligence:

> Cultivation in the world of culture is not so different from cultivation in the world of nature. One who cultivates tries to create the most fertile conditions for good things to survive and thrive. Cultivating also requires weeding – sorting out what does and does not belong, what will bear fruit and what will choke it out. Cultivating natural things requires long and practical familiarity with plants and their place; cultivating cultural things requires careful attention to the history of our culture and to the current threats and opportunities that surround it. Cultivation is conservation – ensuring that the world we leave behind, whether natural or cultural, contains as least as many possibilities and at least as much excellence as the one we inherited.[247]

There are five main guidelines which will prove useful to help missional leaders prepare their congregations to develop their cultural intelligence.

1. Time

Firstly, cultivation takes time. It is particularly hard for first-generation migrant churches to extend their missional work beyond their own ethnic monocultures. An Ethiopian–Eritrean church of about 250 members that we know has achieved something which many first-generation migrant churches cannot: they have the distinction of being the only mixed ethnicity Ethiopian–Eritrean church organisation in the UK that has members now worshipping together. Generally speaking, Ethiopian and Eritrean congregations are separate entities in the UK. This particular congregation is even more remarkable given that there are members in the church who fought each other in their nation's armies when there was conflict between Ethiopia and Eritrea. There are high numbers of both Ethiopian and Eritrean members, and they represent a multi-ethnic breakthrough congregation where two different peoples are learning to worship together.

---

[247] Andy Crouch, *Culture Making: Recovering our Creative Calling* (Downers Grove, IVP Books, 2008), pp.75, 76.

187

Some of the leaders of this church are on Springdale College degree courses and they are very interested in further developing their multicultural missiology. Their church is relatively new – it was planted about eight years ago – and in this short time they have been able to plant a multi-ethnic missional congregation. They recognise, however, that before they can try to include other ethnicities, including people from the majority English population, they will have to cultivate and develop the cross-cultural intelligence of their emerging leaders. In other words, in order for them to establish their congregation for future second-, third- and fourth-generation members, they will need to train their children to keep their faith and also to become cross-cultural missionaries to the West in their own right in the future. It will almost certainly be a number of years before they are able to plant multi-ethnic churches which will include white people or those of other ethnicities. As the congregation is in a major UK city, there are significant opportunities to reach other ethnicities, but at present their efforts need to remain limited to their multi-ethnic Ethiopian–Eritrean congregation. What is very good about their mission planning strategy is that they can see they need to work hard at understanding how to acculturate their children to life in the West before they start to target their efforts to share the gospel more intentionally with other ethnic groups.

The leaders are recognising the need to allow plenty of time for their members to acclimatise to life in the West. They realise that it will take time to cultivate the missional imagination of members to extend their efforts to reach other ethnic groups with the gospel. What is very encouraging is that, at the time of writing, they have planted other congregations in Britain, and they are open to the idea of planting more multi-ethnic breakthrough congregations in the future.

2. Appropriate conditions

It is important to consider Crouch's incisive observation that cultivation requires 'the most fertile conditions for good things to survive and thrive'. This is a creative process which leadership teams need to help their congregations to maintain and develop.

In the first place, a community of believers needs to form a strong identity based on properly understood beliefs and practices. The core of the Christian faith requires us to have well-grounded beliefs which not only tell us who Jesus was, but also who He is for us today. In other words, a living faith that connects with the still active Jesus is vital to missional church life. Without a clear identity founded on who Christ is to us, we will soon lose the compass of our faith when we meet with others who do not have a clear faith. Conversely, sharing our faith with others will expose the deficiencies and can propel us to define it much more sharply.

Engaging in spiritual practices that ground us in the God who still speaks to us today by His Spirit is a primary 'condition' for the 'good things' of God to 'survive and thrive' among us. In the second place, this God who speaks needs to be listened to and understood, as He leads us outward to share in His mission among others who are not part of our churches.

The largest challenge that many first- and second-generation ethnic churches face is the challenge of Western culture to their deep culture. Deep culture has to do with the way our worldviews are imported with us from our homelands and subcultural backgrounds, and we then mix our cultural maps with our Christian faith. This means we allow our culture to colour our Christian understanding. The danger is when we make our particular interpretation of our faith absolute and do not allow for other views which are equally authentic and suited to another cultural group and their situations. This issue is well known to missiologists and cultural anthropologists.

The challenge comes when members start to share their faith beyond their monocultural congregations with secular people. In order to convey our beliefs to Westerners, we need to change the kind of language we use in order to help those who do not share our particular kind of deep culture to make sense of the gospel. Missional ministers from ethnic churches (including white ones) have to understand the post-Christian secular worldview to some extent. The problem occurs when ethnic churches try to integrate people into their missional congregations without realising they do not resonate with the way they worship. A postmodern person will not readily relate to most ethnic expressions of Christian worship services. The presence of someone who does not share anything of the Christian heritage can also challenge the subculture to change, when its people do not want to change. Church people will inevitably begin to realise that change to their Christian subculture will challenge some of their deep cultural assumptions, which might mean they will resist changing how they engage with unchurched people who do not resonate with the way they worship and fellowship together.

This simple illustration has been played out in a number of African diaspora churches we know of, as well as more traditional white churches. BMC leaders and some of their members aspire to reach secular people, but other key players in their congregations fear that this will require a different kind of soil to be cultivated that will harm their faith and commitment to each other and to God. This is, of course, generally true for many monocultural churches, white or black.

What we have recognised here is that it is very important to carefully identify what a congregation is willing to change in the way it operates, so that it can welcome people from other subcultural perspectives. It is also important to identify what they are not willing to change with regard to how they structure their communities. Joining in the missional conversation can help people to explore their similarities and differences and can also help them to think about how they relate in a culturally sensitive manner to those with no faith.

At first, congregations need to be given opportunities to conduct small experiments. The initial step will probably need to be to work with a group who hold similar cultural values to their own, to help them to build up their confidence in possibilities for the future. This may lead to them deciding to try more risky missional partnerships where there are more significant differences. The aim in the end is not to destroy fellowship structures just for the sake of trying to engage in mission with anyone with whom they might have some limited success in working.

3. Removing weeds

This brings us to Crouch's suggestion that cultivating missionally intelligent congregations requires us to identify weeds that need to be removed, as well as to provide optimum conditions for good plants to thrive. At the heart of this principle is the need to listen carefully to what God is telling us by paying careful attention to the kinds of fruit that new opportunities for mission offer and produce.

We have already suggested that a poor form of missional leadership is to just engage with any missional group, without paying attention to what it does to the health of a congregation when they work together. Moreover, if numerous new people coming to church has the effect of stopping members from fellowshipping with new people, this represents a certain kind of weed. It may not be a bad weed, as such, but it may be the wrong time to have too many new faces if the church is not ready for this.

An Anglo church in the Midlands has about 120 members. They are seeing large numbers of homeless people turning up every Sunday to their fellowship lunches. They are genuinely excited by this prospect. However, having so many turn up has meant that many families with children have stopped attending, as they are concerned that the visitors are not known to them and represent a potential risk to their vulnerable children. In this case, the visitors are not being treated as weeds, but the weeding process in this case might mean providing a separate opportunity for young families to fellowship together so that the perceived risk is not an issue. Among other things, the children of these families need to be nurtured to develop their own faith in a safe kind of soil. The visitors also need a soil that is suited to them. Weeding in this case means providing different soils to nourish the different kinds of people.

4. Knowing the history

Crouch articulates the importance of knowing the history of our particular church's subculture. We need to be aware of the threats and opportunities.

A church in East Anglia was an ageing congregation of people from 50 to 80 years of age. No children or young people came to the church. The congregation was hoping for a new mission venture where a new congregation could be planted alongside the old one. In the early days of the church, it had had a very active children's and youth ministry, which helped it to become established as a church. There were still strong memories of this among the established members. They were concerned about the imminent threat of closure as they were now finding it hard to fund the church because most of the members were pensioners. Moreover, several previous ministers had been unable to help turn the church from decline to growth and to encourage younger families to join. Part of the problem, which had undermined previous efforts to bring new families in, was the perceived threat of younger adults taking influence away from the established leaders. The established members also found that they did not have the same tolerance level for the noise and distractions that children brought with them into church services. Neither did they have the energy and stamina to get involved in leading children's and youth work. The question was how to find a solution to turn this situation around.

After a season of fervent prayer with some key members, it became evident that a different type of church needed to be planted – one that would be family orientated and which existing members did not need to attend. It would also require some volunteer support from other local churches who had a surplus of people who could help launch the project. The net result was that existing members accepted the need for a different approach which meant, in essence, planting a kind of seeker-sensitive family church that met in the same building on a different day of the week. The interesting blessing that came from this prayerful enterprise was that about 20 unchurched families began to attend the new services. They also sent their children and young people to the ministries that had been developed for them.

The existing church members had a desire to see new growth occur. The threat was the lack of tolerance and energy to achieve this goal. Hence they graciously accepted that a new church needed to be planted alongside the existing one.

Here was a definite cross-cultural challenge which required new soil to be cultivated. Although the new families who came to faith during this period were genuinely seeking to follow Christ, the way they were raising their children did not fit with the cultural memory of the ageing membership who had a far less tolerant view of what children should and should not be allowed to do in church. The creative solution to plant this different kind of congregation was accepted by the existing members and made it possible to do something contextually suited to the needs of modern families who lived near the church. This kind of approach will only work well if we discern whether it is God's will for this kind of project to be implemented.

5. Keeping the good things

Finally, managing cross-cultural change requires us to consider the good things our present subculture already offers to our churches, as well as to ensure that any change processes we go through to transition our congregations to work in a new missional situation offers things of equal or greater value and excellence to the present and future generations. People in our congregations already have strong values which we need to evaluate to make sure we do not force them to go into new territory which would threaten what is a healthy community.

Of course, not all values and the attitudes that drive them necessarily help us to engage in a mission God wants us to join with Him in doing. A church led by a friend of ours had developed a value that only those who were trusted and established members of the church could use the kitchen facilities or function room. This may sound rather trivial, but it caused some real problems, as it meant that the facilities could not be let out to other users, including other Christian groups who approached the church from time to time. The church was of an excellent design and size, but it restricted use for the local community. This cultural value was not helping the church to share its faith because it was giving the message to the local community that it was not interested in them. This was not a cultural value that needed to be embraced and passed on.

When we seek to help our congregations through a missional change management process, we need to pay careful attention to deeply held values. It is the deeply held values that can cause the greatest potential harm to cross-cultural mission work, especially if these values mean that participants form attitudes that impede their engagement in God's mission. It is vital to help people think through their deep values and to ask 'What if ...' questions: 'What if young men come into the sanctuary wearing caps?' 'What if drug addicts or alcoholics join our church?'

Our cultural values often predispose us to make judgements about people within the first few minutes of meeting them. Long-term attitudes can be formed based on short-term exposure to a new person or situation. What drives us to make judgements will be our deeply held cultural values, such as, 'We are middle-class people and we enjoy meeting other people who are like us professionally and intellectually,' or, 'English people are reserved and cold-hearted; I find it too hard to build friendships with them.'

We could mention many such reservations that form attitudes, expectations and values. What these attitudes tend to produce is our own kind of cultural reserve, which can drive us to try to retain our own cultural values as the best ones and to resist embracing others who do not fit well with our own value systems. It returns us to the question of what people want to leave to future generations. Will what is passed on consist of the things they value the most about their subcultures? Will new values that are formed become embedded enough in order for real cross-cultural multi-ethnic congregations or partnerships to last in the longer term?

Conclusions

This chapter has gone a little way towards addressing the question of how leaders can help their congregations and organisations to go through a cross-cultural change management process. It has suggested challenges and some possible broad solutions to addressing the challenges faced by leaders who seek to engage in cross-cultural ministry. In order for positive missional change management to succeed, the approaches leaders use will need to be appropriate to resolving the hard questions that change will trawl up, for which members will want answers.

It is vital for missional leaders to form coalitions with other missionally gifted team ministers in their church in order to help congregations undergo a change management process, which has the support of those who have the most influence with the people they serve.

We have noted that it is vital not only for a leadership team to embrace the idea of sharing faith cross culturally, and for such a team to consider planting multi-ethnic churches or working in partnership with other ethnic churches; it also requires church people to embrace the vision and drive for change before real change can happen.

There are complex factors that could mean it will take years for meaningful relationships to happen between people from different Christian subcultures living in the multicultural West. The motivation for wanting to join in the missional conversation is based on the kingdom of God, and on the Multicultural Trinity's embrace of all peoples in the one Lord. We must not forget that this vision of final unification needs to start to be realised in our multicultural Western society. Hopefully when some more multi-ethnic breakthrough congregations are planted, they will become the convincing hermeneutic of the power of the gospel to transform our subcultural isolationism into a multicultural fellowship festival, to be witnessed by segregated groups in Western society.

Church exercise

Use the audit exercise earlier in this chapter to think about a church that you may want to consider working with, or alternatively to think about one you are currently working with. Ask yourself three questions:

- What do the similarities between the two churches reveal about the opportunities you may have to work together well?

- What do the dissimilarities between the two churches reveal about the potential challenges you will face if you work together?

- Having weighed up the similarities and differences between the cultures of the two churches, does it seem possible that you could work on a mission project together in some other way?

Comments

Reflective exercise

Take a few minutes to reflect on the following questions:

* Who are the leaders or people in your church who have CQ?

* How can some of the people in the church be helped to increase their CQ?

* What evidence can you point to that would suggest your church is good at working cross culturally with other groups?

* What aspects of Livermore's CQ processes can you see people using already in your church?

* What steps can you take to develop your CQ?

* What cultural legacy can you identify that would be beneficial for developing new initiatives? Also, what legacy can you identity that you might not wish to pass on?

NB: Why not keep a journal for the next three months of your cultural encounters and see if you can map how you use the CQ model, in order to consider how you can improve in areas where you are weak. (See the appendix for a sample journal.)

Comments

Chapter 7
Training Cross-cultural Leaders

The training of missional leaders who can learn how to work cross culturally is absolutely essential in the context of Western society. Christians who want to engage in mission in multicultural society need to develop special skills. Postmodern society's plurality of potential beliefs and unbeliefs will require us to be good cross-cultural missionaries in order to share the gospel with its people. Denominational Bible schools need to do much more today to prepare pastors for church leadership, which they often miss the opportunity to do. It is not enough to simply produce good Bible students who can preach as well as counsel their members. The church of Christ in the pluralistic West needs leaders who have a missional mindset. The Western world is a mission field, not a Christian society. Not only do we need to train leaders who can effectively share the gospel cross culturally; we also need leaders who can equip their members to do this as well. This requires that they learn a new skill set, which many of the denominational Bible colleges may be failing to offer. We sincerely hope that we all may improve our courses to enable students to become equippers and trainers of others to engage in mission.

The undergraduate and postgraduate courses that our college offers aim to achieve these outcomes. We would not claim that what we offer is perfect, as any good missional higher education programme should always seek to stay on the cutting edge of developments in the field of scholarly literature and professional praxis. The students on our programmes are from diverse ethnic and cultural backgrounds, which is essential to the aims of our programmes to equip missional leaders who can share the gospel within the multicultural Western situation.

It needs to be understood that an essential component of Christian missiology needs to begin with the recognition of the incarnation of the Son of God. Just as the Son of God took up residence among ordinary men and women (John 1:14) when He became a human being, so also His followers are called to incarnate their faith in Christ among the people with whom they lived. The ethos of incarnational ministry sharing in the lives of those with whom we want to share the gospel has to be at the heart of a training course that educates missional ministers how to witness to people in the multicultural environment. The writer to the Hebrews puts the benefits of the incarnation of the Son of God for lost human beings succinctly:

> For surely it is not with angels that [Jesus] is concerned but with the descendants of Abraham. Therefore he had to be made like his brethren in every respect, so that he might become a merciful and faithful high priest in the service of God, to make expiation for the sins of the people. For because he himself has suffered and been tempted, he is able to help those who are tempted.
> *Hebrews 2:16-18 (RSV)*

The qualification for Christ's successful representation of mankind to God is that He went through the same experiences that human beings go through. According to the writer to the Hebrews, this bridges the gap between mankind and God and provides people with confidence that Christ sympathises with them so that they can approach Him with confidence. This confidence comes through recognising that Christ has entrusted His people with responsibilities to engage in His mission not because they are the best people to do it, but because He has confidence that they can overcome hurdles in order to continually improve the way they do things. Moreover, Christ modelled excellence in leadership based on the fact that He did not use His divine right to get His own way by force, but rather He went through the same trials that His followers experience, in humility. In other words, He modelled a leadership style which was not superior to the abilities of weaker followers, but rather He walks alongside them through their troubles, thus giving them confidence that He is with them in times of need.

> Since then we have a great high priest who has passed through the heavens, Jesus, the Son of God, let us hold fast our confession. For we have not a high priest who is unable to sympathize with our weakness, but one who in every respect has been tempted as we are, yet without sin. Let us then with

confidence draw near to the throne of grace, that we may receive mercy and find grace to help in time of need.

Hebrews 4:14-16 (RSV)

Because the Son of God understands what it is to be weak like we humans are, it is possible for God to build a bridge between Himself and mankind. This bridge potentially offers to all people the confidence that God really understands the struggles and temptations of humanity. This is why incarnational theology is at the heart of the mission of God to effectively reconcile humanity with Himself. It also helps us develop our own practical missional theology as we seek to help people to get to know Jesus as we live out our faith among them, and to help them to see what Christ is doing for us and can do for them.

God did not come to humanity in His radiant glory, setting Himself at a distance above us so that we could not relate to Him. Rather the Father sent the Son with the mission to relate to people in their own cultural context so that they could understand what God is like. He sent His Son to offer eternal life to all who would believe because He loves His whole creation. The best way He could convey that gift of love to the world was to translate His love into a person by becoming a human being, to whom people could relate on their own terms. Jesus incarnated among human beings as the divine man. He was a living divine–human document whose whole life was open for people to interact with in order to understand what God is like. His disciples were also sent into the world to become living human documents whose lives could be read by all people so that they could understand what God is like.

The incarnation, and the way it made God's nature of grace and love known to humanity, is central to how we need to shape missional leaders and God's people to engage with God's mission as they model Christ to the world through their life examples. We must ask ourselves the hard questions: 'Do our ministry preparation courses equip participants to work incarnationally with people suited to their own cultural contexts?' 'Do our courses teach participants to become trainers in their own right so that the people they lead can be equipped to do the same thing?' This chapter can only offer a modest contribution to this debate. A future volume will need to address the question of educating missional leaders to become trainers.

Training cross-cultural missional leaders

How does a practical incarnational theology help to equip missional leaders if they feel called to mission in the multicultural marketplace? Michael Moynagh makes a vital contribution regarding Jesus' approach to missional ministry as part of His incarnation:

> Jesus did not withdraw his disciples from the world, teach and pray with them, and then send them out in mission as individuals. Jesus identified himself with a visible community, he ministered in everyday settings with this community, he sent his followers to ordinary villages in small communities, and he reveals his presence when the church, in continuity with his original community, multiplies into different cultures.[248]

The learning process that Jesus used to identify Himself with people in the Jewish culture had to do with Him sharing deeply in the lives of those people, in their daily rounds of life experiences. He also trained His disciples on the mission coalface as He modelled His approaches in the 'ordinary villages and small communities' among which He worked. This is vital to any missional training course. As we mentioned earlier, students on the courses we are involved with are required to do 13 hours a week of placement work. The days where students are educated for ministry over three years and then after graduating begin their ministries as raw recruits must certainly come to an end. The concept we need to adopt has to do with the approach suggested by Jesus' own equipping of His disciples. Missional courses need to provide students with more than theory.[249] They need to provide weekly placement opportunities where they can apply it.

In order for missional students to learn how to incarnate alongside people at their placement churches or organisations, they need to

---

[248] Moynagh and Harrold, *Church for Every Context*, p.184.
[249] An influential text towards this development is Banks (1999).

engage in action–reflection learning. This action–reflection learning needs to provide them with the necessary tools to reflect on the life experiences of those they want to reach with the gospel. The action–reflection approach focuses attention on understanding people in their specific life situations. Moynagh adds a contribution which helps us to think through how placement experiences can enable students to become more deeply embedded in the communities they seek to reach:

> The church continues the ministry of Jesus when it 'breaks off' pieces of the body [the church body] and 'distributes' them, as new communities, in the fragments of society. Just as Jesus was present in his culture with a community, he seeks to be present in the details of all cultures with church communities. This should not be understood as the church being present in an indirect way through its prayers, for example, or by resourcing members for individual witness (important though these are).[250]

Placement students can become part of the process of Jesus' continuing ministry through the church. They become a part of Christian communities which are broken off as 'pieces of the body' and are themselves distributed to incarnate Christ 'in the fragments of society'. The important point that Moynagh makes that speaks to a more correct practice for mission trainers and educators to use is that students are not sent out on their own as 'individual witnesses'. Rather they need to learn how to become part of mobile missional communities that share the values of togetherness as they are distributed 'as new communities' among 'the fragments of society'. These mobile missional communities may be defined as small groups of people who gather in more than one location to share the gospel where the Spirit has gone before them. Mobile missional communities of this type are mobile in the sense that they seek to keep up with the movement of the Spirit as new people are revealed to them by the discernment of the Spirit's work ahead of the church as He prepares the ground for new endeavours. Placement students can learn much from this decentralised form of ministry which takes the focus away

---

[250] Moynagh and Harrold, *Church for Every Context*, p.184.

from carrying out tasks in churches to following the Spirit out into the local communities around churches. One way this can be done is to have two or three placement students work alongside an experienced church planter to help plant a new church.

In order for incarnational mission churches to work effectively, members will need to sacrifice the comfort of being less participative and letting leaders do things for them. Students who are being equipped to work as missional leaders in these kinds of team-orientated missional communities need to reflect on how theories learnt in the classroom will work in practice in the mission field. Another question will be, 'How can they help equip church members to develop a missional mindset of this type as well?' Just like missionaries who went from the West to the rest to take the gospel to peoples in non-European lands, there is a need for a new type of missional leader who can take the gospel into local Western housing estates, outside of the normal defined boundaries of churches. The West as the new mission field requires new kinds of leaders who are not trained to lead established churches, but rather who will be prepared to lead fresh expressions of missional communities that will not look like churches.

Action–reflection model

This section will provide us with the opportunity to try out an action–reflection model that is useful for missional leaders to adopt when they are engaged in general ministry or cross-cultural mission projects. We provide some reflection exercises in this chapter so that readers can assess their usefulness for themselves. For some of our students, the idea that practical and academic theology can co-exist is a challenge. What has day-to-day spiritual engagement with God to do with the academy of learning? How can examining leadership practices relate to theological study? These and many other questions are often raised by the thinking students who see less value for the applied, and pragmatic students who feel obliged to engage in theological thinking but hope it will not take away from the activity of ministry.

What is the essence of practical theology? What real purpose does it serve? The practical theologian Schilderman notes the following elements:

> Practical theology as a discipline within the humanities may be said to serve three functions. First, it has a symbolic function that concerns the keeping, caring for, and examining of the historical, cultural, and religious heritage, while taking account of the prevailing interests and networks that maintain and develop the tradition. Second, it has an instrumental function that refers to the relevance of religious heritage for current issues and problems that arise in culture and social institutions. Third, it serves a moral function that appeals to the formation of judgment with regard to this religious heritage, as religion demonstrates normative relevance for the processes of exploring meaning, finding identity, and judging core values of mind and society. These functions are also enacted in religious practices that emphasize the 'human element' in life and that specify the spiritual opportunities to bestow life with a transcendent meaning.[251]

While this is a good description of the essential process, practical theologians Swinton and Mowat add the important observation of criticality and theological input:

> The fundamental aim of Practical Theology is to enable the church to perform faithfully as it participates in God's ongoing mission in, to and for the world. As such it seeks to reflect critically and theologically on situations to provide insights and strategies which will enable the movement towards faithful change.[252]

It is this combination of essential activity and critical and theological reflection that forms the essence of this approach to

---

[251] Hans Schilderman, 'Quantitative Method' in *The Wiley-Blackwell Companion to Theology* (Chichester, Blackwell Publishing Ltd, 2012), p.124.
[252] John Swinton and Harriet Mowat, *Practical Theology and Qualitative Research* (London, SCM Press, 2006), p.25.

reflective learning for missional leaders who want to engage in cross-cultural mission activities.

Approaches to practical theological reflection

One of the most helpful tools that enable us as leaders to engage in reflective analysis is the pastoral cycle. The pastoral cycle is a tool used by a variety of practitioners in ministry and other socially related fields. It is a pastoral theology method developed by Joe Holland and Peter Henriot and is essentially a socio-psychological action–reflection tool which is useful to facilitate reflection on pastoral responses to social and cultural challenges that people in real-life situations face every day. It has been widely used by social justice workers around the world since the booklet *Social Analysis* was published by the Centre of Concern in 1980.

This approach helps us to successfully and effectively think about social issues we face. It offers us a simple but effective model to facilitate intervention in new situations. It is also very useful to help mission teams think through how to share the gospel on an incarnational level with other groups who look at the world in a different way.

It provides a flexible framework that can be utilised for pastoral, missional or community action purposes. This flexibility makes it a very useful tool for all kinds of settings. It would seem evident that this kind of tool will be very useful to help us engage in cross-cultural mission – the benefits that the insights it introduces will help us to better understand those we want to reach with the gospel.

The basic theory of the cycle conceives of opportunities, or 'moments', in which it is possible to engage various challenges, issues or cross-cultural learning opportunities as part of real-life and missional ministry situations. These moments are known as:

- *Experience or contact* – contact may come about through various media and situations which lead to an experience of engagement.

- *Social analysis or simply analysis* – social analysis comes about as a result of the experiences of making contact with varying social needs, challenges and difficulties that might be faced by a community or individuals.

- *Theological reflection* – the pastoral theologian may then reflect on what he or she is analysing to see what Christian theology, biblical sources or a particular traditions dogma or doctrine might do to respond to a given situation.

- *Pastoral and missional planning or response* – the response, or moment of response, comes about after the first three elements have taken place.

Having set out a simple explanation of how this approach might work, it is important to understand that it is not a closed circle: action may lead to new realities and responses because of interventions a ministry team may make in a situation, or mission opportunity, which in turn may call for the new experience to be examined in the light of this circle. For these reasons, the pastoral cycle may go through various cycles and recycling phases in any given contact situation or developing pastoral or missional relationship within a community, or with individuals.

Four key questions raised by the pastoral cycle

The four key questions of the cycle are illustrated in this diagram.

1. New experience

'What is happening in this particular circumstance?' The key issue in this first part of the process is to establish the facts, obtain background information and understand the present frame of reference of those involved in the process of analysis. A frame of reference relates to the way an individual or group understands their present situation, or how they relate to what is happening because of the cultural lens through which they view the world. This is important to grasp as it will help us to contextualise a response later in terms they will understand, using language that describes their present frame of reference in order to help them understand what has been learnt on their own terms. Also, by mapping out their present frame of reference by describing it, or as you map out your own frame of reference in the light of a new missional experience, it will be possible to make sure a good presenting picture is painted and documented. It is important to have a clear picture of the presenting issue, or the way people view their situation from their perspective, with its background elements being carefully considered, in order to map out the experience so that better analysis may be facilitated in order to plan a contextually relevant intervention.

2. Analysis

'What is happening in this situation; what are the causes of the present problems, and the challenges that need to be addressed in order to effectively relate to those concerned?' The next step is to analyse your interpretation of what has led to the present problem, as well as the interpretations and causes which others may have identified from their own perspectives that contribute to the overall picture. This analysis aims to set out the various stages, steps and contributing factors which have led to the challenge being faced. Moreover, the causes of the challenge need to be ferreted out, analysed and understood. Clear statements of what the causes seem to be and what led to them may be analysed and evaluated, leading to a clear statement of causative factors, as well as possible solutions to reflect on in the next phase of the cycle.

3. Practical theological reflection

'What does this mean to the affected parties and what does it mean in the light of Christian beliefs and values? What new ways might be considered to address the situation? What changes need to happen, and what will they mean for the way things are dealt with in the future in relation to a difficulty, challenge or missional intervention suitable for the group being worked with?' The answers to questions like these need to be informed by a theological paradigm that seeks what God's method might be for approaching issues in a specific context in the future. Scripture can be a useful conversation partner, where stories that may parallel a present situation could be reflected on to discern a Christian response.

4. Response

'How shall we respond to this challenge or difficulty?' Once the original frame of reference has been analysed, understood and considered in the light of a Christian way of addressing or understanding it, then a proper response may be formulated. Make sure that responses are carefully weighed in light of the data and that they are pursued in a way that will make sense to a community or individual in the light of their context. It will be of little use to try to encourage an inexperienced single mum from a poorly educated working-class background to join a middle-class mother and toddlers group for social interaction and support, for example. It would be more helpful to point her towards a group that could offer support that would relate to her social needs. Middle-class mums are unlikely to understand the financial worries, the sense of isolation and disempowerment that such a single mum might feel.

The four simple parts of this cycle can become a powerful ally that will help us to think through how we are engaging with a person, persons or a group that we are trying to work with cross culturally. Next we will consider a case study to help us to appreciate the benefits of the cycle.

Case study

In this section we want to share a case study to help us to think through how we can use the pastoral cycle when we try to work with other non-Western Christians living in the West. If we intend to plant multi-ethnic breakthrough congregations who can form the basis for multicultural missional groups, we will first of all need a group of existing Christians from different ethnicities to lay the foundations for such churches to be effective in their outreach strategies. The case study is a conflation of more than one situation where we have needed to use the pastoral cycle to help a church think through how to respond to cross-cultural missional challenges. Identifying factors have been removed so that it is not possible to identify the group concerned.

We will use a hypothetical church profile called West Aston Free Church. This profile fits more than one situation we have known. West Aston Free Church is a multi-ethnic church with members of Afro-Caribbean, Anglo and Indian ethnic backgrounds. About 40% of the 150 members are white Anglos, 30% are second generation Africans and 30% second generation Indians. The church came to have this mix of peoples through intentional connections that the pre-existing Anglo church had formed earlier. Two different ethnic groups rented their church hall to worship at different times about ten years previously. As a result of changes in the leadership of all three groups, discussions had taken place about three years earlier where it was suggested that it would be a good idea to try to bring all three worshipping groups together to fellowship from time to time. What followed were some trial joint worship meetings that then led to all three groups worshipping together every second Sunday of each month, and on the other Sundays worshipping in their three different groups. This has been happening for the last six months, but some challenges have arisen which are causing the leaders some difficulties in working together. The root of these challenges has to do with the different ways their cultures cause them to exercise leadership in the context of worship.

The African group is led by pastor Edward Kwarteng. His parents moved from Nigeria to the UK in the 1970s to work in education. Edward is 33 years old with a wife and children. He has retained many of the cultural norms and values of his parents' culture. He has made some extended trips back to Lagos in Nigeria, which he views as his cultural heritage. Edward shares many of the opinions of AIC church leaders who consider that Africans need to keep their culture alive now that they live in the West. Edward is a Pentecostal leader who set out to plant a church that aspires to help members to share their faith more broadly than just with the Nigerian diaspora. Members of his small group come to church in Nigerian traditional dress. They would like to keep their traditions and also share in fellowship with the other two groups.

Next we move to Pastor Steven Hlawando. Steven is not his real name but a nickname that is used by his numerous Anglo and Indian friends. His parents migrated from India to the UK in the 1970s as well. Steven has gone a long way towards adopting Western culture. He and his wife did not marry by arrangement: they made their own choice. His wife is also a second generation Indian who became Steven's girlfriend at secondary school, and soon after leaving school they were married. Steven's members also want to find ways of helping white Anglo people to come to a Christian faith. Steven's group may be best described as Pentecostal charismatic.

Finally we come to the English pastor, John Adams. John has ministry and mission in his blood. As a child he spent seven years with his missionary parents in India. When they returned to the UK in his early teens, John initially struggled to settle into UK secondary school life. However, when his parents moved with him to a London suburb he went to a mixed-race secondary school where white English, Indian and African young people were in attendance. John found that he was more able to connect with peers in this more cosmopolitan environment. When he left school he worked in IT for a few years before training for ministry. Now in his early thirties, he leads his white English church members who are themselves of a charismatic orientation. Because of John's missionary childhood, he considers the opportunity of the three congregations joining together to be a dream come true.

The challenges regarding differences in leadership style between the three pastors is proving to be the cause of some conflict between them and of concern to members of each group. This section will set out to show how the pastoral cycle can be used in a minimalist way to address these differences in leadership styles. We will not go into great detail, but will set out a description of the main findings that helped the three leaders to understand their differences better. We hope that this minimalist approach will prove the most efficient way to help us understand the cycle's usefulness and benefits when applied to similar real-life challenges.

Analysis

It is worthwhile at this point to remind ourselves of the four key analytical questions of the cycle. They are: What is happening? Why is it happening? What does it mean? How shall we respond?

Let's begin with the first question:

1. What is happening?

As we have noted already, the three leaders are experiencing difficulties over differences in their leadership styles. Here are some notes which describe what is happening:

- *Edward* has a leadership style which is best described as hierarchical. He expects his members to respect his position, opinions and decisions. His congregation has two elders – one male and the other female. His group may be termed as semi-congregational to the extent that big decisions are voted on at a members meeting. However, in reality there is an assumed subculture where members and the elders defer to Edward's opinion when important decisions are made. Edward's leadership style leans toward autocratic when it comes to big decisions. Having said this, his group are happy and fellowship well together, as well as with the members of the other two groups with whom they now meet periodically.

- *Steven* has a leadership style which is best described as a flat-level leadership structure. He and his wife work as partners in ministry and value the sense of community. They want members to base decision making on relationships and how decisions will affect the whole group. Relational leadership is therefore their preferred style. Decisions that affect the congregation are generally made at less formal meetings of members where everyone's points of view are taken into account. Steven's leadership style may be said to lean towards being more *laissez-faire* because changes are made to decisions which do not work for his members without pressure to maintain decisions that the group has made. This group are very easy to get on with and welcome the fellowship they are having with the other two groups.

- *John* has a leadership style which is best described as hierarchical, but it is based on a democratic way of helping his group make decisions on the basis of a vote. He has deacons who are part of a smaller leadership team and to whom authority is delegated to make decisions about the day-to-day operations of the church. In this sense, John's group may be best described as congregational in nature. His members, similar to the other two groups, are enjoying fellowshipping with the other groups.

The differences in leadership style have caused some tensions between the three leaders. For the most part they get on quite well together and continue to be strong in a joint desire for their congregations to worship and fellowship together twice a month. The areas of potential conflict have to do with the way the pastors present themselves to all three groups when they worship together. Edward's style of preaching is perceived to be quite dogmatic and loud. Moreover, it has more of a feeling of demand and command when he draws matters to the congregation's attention. Steven's congregation have mentioned to the three leaders, through a representative, that they have welcomed some of the challenging things Edward has preached about but they prefer more of a suggestive approach to preaching to a prescriptive style.

The three leaders have discussed together the challenges of their differing assumptions about preaching and how they use it to inform and lead their groups. Edward feels strongly that more challenge needs to be communicated to believers than both John's and Steven's preaching styles communicate. John feels that there is room for him to learn from Edward's style, whereas Steven has said he would prefer that Scripture be allowed to challenge listeners rather than what he feels is a more forced preaching style that aims to make this occur. All three leaders agree that a mixed approach to preaching can be experimented with; however, Edward is far less persuaded that a less authoritative style would be a good thing to adopt.

It is particularly the preaching style that is the most challenging area of disagreement compared to other matters such as worship style – interestingly enough. The three leaders as yet have not discussed how they might best work together should they go further than this experimental phase in joint worship services. They feel they need to let things become evident as they progress.

The worship leaders from each group actually get on well together and are enjoying trying out different styles of worship. When the three congregations worship together they enjoy the wider variety of styles. Moreover, once a month they have been having an afternoon musical worship time for about an hour – which members from each group attend after they have shared a fellowship lunch. What concerns members from each group are the differences in preaching styles, particularly as some members from John's and Steven's groups have recently not gone to church when Edward has been preaching. The three leaders have discussed this, but Edward feels strongly that he should still adopt his present preaching style, and is encouraging John and Steven to adopt some aspects of the style themselves. He feels that if they support him in this way it will give a message to the congregations when they worship together that they are united as brothers in leadership.

There are obviously issues raised by this situation that could be looked into in more detail, but we will limit our case study to this one matter regarding differences in preaching styles.

2. Why is it happening?

This part of the process of the pastoral cycle has to do with analysis. A few points will be detailed to help us consider what can be learnt from the descriptive phase of the cycle's process.

- The three pastors have a relationship based on a desire that their groups spend at least half of their time each month worshipping together. They feel this models a strong kingdom value, to do with God's people uniting as brothers and sisters.

- John and Steven have challenged Edward in a sensitive manner about his views on what preaching should include. For instance, they have asked him to think about different styles of preaching in other churches around them to help him think about his style, and to help them to learn from other styles as well. Edward has not been to non-Pentecostal churches very often, or to Anglo charismatic churches, to experience their worship and preaching styles. He agrees in principle that it could be good for the three of them to go to some other groups to experience some different preaching styles.

- The sticking point for Edward seems to be his AIC background, which makes him feel that a more confrontational style of preaching fits best with his tradition.

The three pastors have made use of the cycle themselves to help them think this issue through. The largest opportunity they have to resolve this matter is their joint commitment to reflect on some resolutions that are supported by Scripture.

It needs to be noted once more that this brief analysis is somewhat limited and that much more could be added to fill out other related issues. At this stage we are once more fulfilling our minimalist agenda to keep the discussion within a realistic scope.

3. What does it mean?

At this point some theological reflection will be useful. Broadly speaking, the last part of the process reveals a joint willingness by the leaders to reflect on their views of preaching on a Scriptural level. Here are some findings that were made.

- A study of the gospels highlighted that Jesus used more than one style of communication, including pithy sayings and parables. Jesus also seemed to engage in a form of declarative preaching from time to time. Edward made the point that Jesus' teaching was most often, in his view, delivered and received as authoritative and commanding. John and Steven accepted this point but also wanted Edward to take into account that Jesus' parables did not seem to have this same ring of authority or command about them. Edward was open to this suggestion but

214

still felt that too much narrative preaching was not the best way to challenge the church towards change and holy living.

- The three leaders recognised that in the challenge they faced, the most important value would be to maintain unity even if some compromises needed to be accommodated. They also reflected on the first letter of John with his call for fellowship motivated by unifying love. From this theological perspective they all wanted to avoid making their differences on preaching a point of division. Edward communicated that he felt that he had his back against the wall a bit over this debate, with John and Steven taking one view and himself taking another. Their reflections on 1 John 4 helped them to make fellowship the important thing to protect between them, with a desire to separate the issue of different preaching styles from themselves as persons.

- John brought in some of his childhood memories of how his parents had at times struggled to get on with native Indian leaders because of some of the cultural differences. He suggested that each of them and their congregations had their own subcultures and that these would inevitably cause them to interpret and perceive issues like preaching styles in different ways from time to time. Steven and Edward did not find this insight to be new to them. However, John reminded them of this and they all agreed to try to separate out some of the cultural differences which might be affecting their views.

4. How shall we respond?

- The three leaders agreed that in order for them to continue to honour each other and their congregations when they met together for worship and fellowship, they would have to include different preaching styles to provide a varied diet to which all could relate.

- They agreed that it would be valuable for them to visit some different churches to experience different preaching styles and to consider the strengths and weaknesses of each type they encountered.

215

- They agreed that they would seek to help the members in each of their groups to discuss with the three leaders together the need for a variety of preaching styles. In the first instance, each leader would speak to the members of their own congregation about this matter, and then all three of them would meet together to obtain feedback.

- They decided that they wanted to encourage their joint worship and fellowship meetings and their participants and to give themselves time to get used to different preaching styles, as this was a high value for them to experiment with, in order for them to get used to different aspects of each other's cultures.

Conclusions

This chapter has raised the whole question of reflective practice at the foundation of cross-cultural ministry in an especially important way. The tensions that are caused through matters like preaching styles are crucial to think through. The pastoral cycle offers an important tool to missional leaders to help them engage with the difficulties that arise from planting multicultural missional congregations.

The main points that we have wanted to convey in this chapter are:

- leaders need to be trained to engage in action–reflection learning that is informed by biblical theology

- a tool such as the pastoral cycle is a vital piece of kit that needs to be used regularly by leaders and their teams so that they can keep improving the way they work together cross culturally.

We would encourage everyone who is serious about cross-cultural mission to develop a high proficiency in action–reflection learning which is built around a good biblical theology of mission. We believe it is vital for new forms of training to run alongside theological ministry courses to help emerging leaders to become effective practitioners in missional ministry and leadership.

Reflective exercise

Take a short time to reflect on the following.

- How might you apply the pastoral cycle to your own missional ministry context? It will probably be useful in many different contexts. As it is very flexible, you could use it to sort out:

  ➢ Personal conflicts with team members.

  ➢ Problems faced by those to whom you minister.

  ➢ Your personal challenges as you try to sort out the many and varied demands on your time and in your personal life outside these, etc.

  ➢ How you can overcome communication barriers with a new group you are trying to work with cross culturally.

It is suggested that you consider using the pastoral cycle as a method for dealing with challenges in at least the three of the areas above for the next three months. Take the opportunity to keep a journal about how this approach helps you to resolve various issues. (See Appendix for an example of a journal template.)

Comments:

Chapter 8
Bridging Cross-cultural Barriers: The Missional Contribution of Luke–Acts

Scripture is an important starting point for informing our experiences of developing new missional communities that reflect the diversity of cultures. In recent years scholars have begun to reconsider the writings of the New Testament as indicators of the ongoing missional engagement of the growing Christian community in the first century. Howard Marshall notes:

> It may, however, be more helpful to recognise them more specifically as the documents of a mission. The subject matter is not, as it were, Jesus in himself or God in himself but Jesus in his role as Saviour and Lord. New Testament theology is essentially missionary theology. By this I mean that the documents came into being as the result of a two-part mission, first, the mission of Jesus sent by God to inaugurate his kingdom with the blessings that it brings to people and to call people to respond to it, and then the mission of his followers called to continue his work by proclaiming him as Lord and Saviour, and calling people to faith and ongoing commitment to him, as a result of which his church grows. The theology springs out of this movement and is shaped by it, and in turn the theology shapes the continuing mission of the church.[253]

Two of the greatest missional contributions in the New Testament are the writings of Luke – the gospel and the book of Acts.[254] Unlike the other gospel writers, Luke writes from a unique missiological vantage point. He has most likely been a travelling companion of the

---

[253] Howard Marshall, *New Testament Theology* (Nottingham, IVP, 2004), pp.34-35; See also Christopher Wright, *The Mission of God: Unlocking the Bible's Grand Narrative* (Nottingham, IVP, 2006), Chapter 1.

[254] Marshall, *New Testament Theology*. Most modern Lucan scholarship is indebted to the seminal writings of Conzelmann, (1960).

apostle Paul in the pioneering work among the Gentiles,[255] and he may also provide the first attempt at an expression of authentic cross-cultural mission.[256] In addition, he may provide a 'Christian' history,[257] even though it is important to remember that it is not like reading modern history.

Acts is essentially a continuation work and, not unlike other ancient writers,[258] Luke indicates in the preface that his previous work was about what Jesus *began* to do and teach (Acts 1:1), thereby paving the way for his new volume. Luke brings his action–reflection experience and his own theological framework to his work. This may be why, especially in relation to the book of Acts, it has become such a pivotal text for the ongoing renewal of Christian mission throughout Christianity's 2,000-year history. We would do well to take careful note of this possibility and to listen with fresh ears to its important contributions as to how we might engage in cross-cultural missional endeavours.

Before we focus on his contribution in the book of Acts, including what we can learn from the way the earliest followers of Jesus expressed their own engagement with mission within the ever-changing ethnic context in which they found themselves, it is important to note the unique contribution that Luke brings to these writings, thereby indicating some of his contextualising of the gospel for his own audience and purposes. As an editor, theologian and missional practitioner, Luke expresses his understanding of the story of the gospel with some unique insights.[259] These include:

---

[255] This is especially noteworthy in the 'we' sections of Acts. See Jacob, Jervell, *The Theology of the Acts of the Apostles* (Cambridge, Cambridge Press, 1996), pp.6-8 as well as the general commentaries.

[256] See the important discussion in Charles Barrett, *The Acts of the Apostles,* Vol. 2 15-12, T&T Clark, 1998) pp.xxv-xxx.

[257] Loveday, 'What Patterns of Church and Mission are Found in the Acts of the Apostles' in Steven Croft, *Mission-shaped Questions,* (London, Chichester House Publishing, 2008), pp. 133-145.

[258] Talbert Charles, *Reading Acts: A Literary and Theological Commentary* (Revised Ed., Macon, Smyth and Helwys, 2004), p.1.

[259] A good summary can be found in Edward Adams, *Parallel Lives of Jesus* (London, SPCK, 2011).

1. Passion for the poor and marginalised and prophetic denouncement of the abuses of the rich in Luke–Acts

Of the three synoptic authors, only Luke contains certain understandings about the importance of the poor and their seemingly unique place within the confines of the good news.[260] From liberationist theologians concerned for justice for the vulnerable to recent evangelical commentators, Luke's recognition and empowerment of the poor is a significant and noteworthy theological contribution to the rich tapestry of what the kingdom of God aims to do to transform unjust human systems. This is paralleled by his reversal motif of a prophetic denunciation of the rich.

Within the gospel, Luke's contribution could be summarised within three broad strands:

- Firstly, Luke draws on the prophetic traditions of the Hebrew Scriptures of the Old Testament, where the poor are identified primarily as those who are economic misfits with no hope or security outside of Yahweh. This leads to them receiving the compassionate attention of Yahweh, administered by the community of His people. It also brings the prophetic denouncement presented to the rich when this compassion is lacking. Noteworthy are the contributions of the pre-exilic prophets Amos and Micah, although this compassion is found throughout biblical literature more generally as well.

- Secondly, Luke's chosen vocabulary highlights the importance of this concern. He uses the Greek word for the poor and other key words twice as often as the other synoptic authors. In addition, he uses the Greek word *plousiov* ('rich') in a similar vein. This seems to indicate an importance in terms of Luke's outlook on what the gospel of Christ offers to a society in which the rich too often neglect the needs of the poor.

- Thirdly, Luke includes in his gospel key stories that support this concern. These include his own version of the beatitudes which

---

[260] A concise and thoughtful contribution is found in David Bosch, *Transforming Mission* (London, Orbis, 1991), pp.98-104.

highly contrast the plight of the poor compared to the rich (Luke 6:20-24), the parable of the rich fool (Luke 12:16-21), and the parables of chapter 16, most noteworthy of which is the story of the rich man and Lazarus (Luke 16:19-31).

Paramount in Luke's gospel is the first public expression of the ministry of Jesus in His home town of Nazareth (Luke 4:16-30). Jesus begins to reflect His mission in reference to the scroll of Isaiah that has been handed to Him. This manifesto has at its heart the preaching of good news to the poor, which enables the compassion and care of Yahweh to be expressed afresh and thereby become a key aspect of Christian witness and mission.

In Acts, the focus continues within the life and contribution of the emerging Christian community through the care of widows, healings, exorcisms and communal table fellowship which welcomes all classes and races of people. Those who are marginalised and in need are thereby included, demonstrating the compassion of Yahweh. This is especially noted within the two summary statements of the early Christian church's community living (Acts 2:44-45; 4:32-35). The theme in these revealing passages is the believers sharing all things for all to use as the need arises. This is clearly of high value in terms of conceiving how we might today form the fellowships of multicultural missional communities around the common sharing of resources.

2. A universal understanding of the importance of Jesus and His mission in Luke–Acts[261]

Luke's intentional focus on missional engagement with the Gentiles (*eqnhnations*) brings much to bear on our understanding of how a relatively small Palestinian sect of Judaism rapidly expanded to become a world-focused faith. This trajectory of transformation in ethnic diversity[262] is quite a feat and indicates that, at least for Luke, the good news of Jesus cannot remain contained within the confines of

---

[261] Glenn Rogers, *Holistic Ministry and Cross-cultural Mission in Luke–Acts* (Mission and Ministry Resources), pp.17-57. This seems to be one of the more significant contributions by Luke which then informs the ongoing mission of the church in Acts.
[262] The following key texts in Acts support this diversity of engagement: 8:27; 10:1-3, 11:18, 20; 13:46-48; 14:11; 18:6; 28:4, 28.

one small part of the Roman Empire or limit itself to one people group. Rather it is a cross-cultural boundary-breaking ministry in which the Spirit of Jesus continues to guide His church.

Within the gospel, there are very specific examples of this development. Phillip Esler notes the following examples:[263]

- Simeon's speech. Here he depicts the salvation to be found in Jesus for both Israel and the Gentiles (Luke 2:31-32).

- The quotation from Isaiah 40 follows the LXX (the Greek version of the Old Testament) rather than the Hebrew Masoretic Text to include the phrase, 'And all people will see God's salvation' (Luke 3:6, NIV).

- Luke's genealogy goes back further than Matthew's, to Adam (Luke 3:23-38).

- Jesus' reference to the activity of Elijah and Elisha among the Gentiles adds a further indication of a missional engagement of God's great prophets in ministry to non-Jews (Luke 4:25-27).

- Luke's reference to a feast includes people who will come from all directions (Luke 13:29), not just from East and West as is the case with Matthew's version of the story (Matthew 8:11).

- Luke's version of the great banquet (Luke 14:15-24) is highly inclusive.

All of this seems to indicate openness to a wider understanding of mission which will require the new covenant people of Christ to cross cultural boundaries. This is further evidenced in the outworking of the book of Acts which illustrates the wider nature of Jesus being the Saviour of the world, not just of Israel. The question is how this wider missional agenda is to be accomplished. Several important points may be raised to help us think about this.

A. Luke's intentional focus
Luke records, at the beginning of both of his volumes, that he is in fact researching and writing his work for the most excellent Theophilus.

---

[263] Phillip Esler, *Community and Gospel in Luke–Acts* (Cambridge, Cambridge University Press, 1987), pp.33-34.

Whoever he may have been, his Greek name indicates something of Luke's intended audience. The name means 'God lover'. From the very beginning, then, this is not just a gospel for a growing Jewish sect, but it has a more universal appeal to engaging in mission and making disciples out of all nations and peoples who will come to love God. So we find in the framing of the writing a potential focus for wider multicultural mission. It is important to recognise this as it provides the rationale for helping our missional churches to think about what needs to motivate their continuing missional activities in their localities.

B. Luke's engagement with key Scriptural texts

Luke's use of key Old Testament texts illustrates how this has informed and influenced his own missional thinking. We have already noted the use of Isaiah 40 and the LXX (Greek translation of the Hebrew Bible) as a means to bring a wider reading to the passages in Luke's writings. The LXX seems to have been his preferred translation. Other essential texts in developing his theology of mission include Deuteronomy and Psalms, especially in the book of Acts. This hermeneutical approach challenges the then ethnocentric reading of certain texts which ultimately prohibited the inclusion of Gentiles in the purpose of God and in His salvation, which the early Messianic Jewish believers struggled to come to terms with.

C. Luke's reflections on key experiences

To fully engage with Acts, we need to recall how much it is shaped by key experiences: the departure of Jesus, the coming of the Holy Spirit at Pentecost, the ensuing church growth and persecution, the martyrdom of Stephen, the conversion of Paul, the encounters with religious leaders and angels, the conversion and acceptance of Cornelius and his household as the first recognised Gentile converts in Acts, the Jerusalem council, the missionary journeys, the imprisonments and the final coming to Rome. These all help to shape and engage our understanding of mission. Each is important to the overall development of the missional engagement of the early church. It is clear enough that God's mission for Luke was a boundary-breaking exercise which was to include all people groups in its compass. This recognition is vital to our own thinking about what our mission is in a multicultural society.

3. Prayer and praise in Luke–Acts

For Luke, every major movement that he records seems to usher in a sense of worship and praise as a demonstration that God is behind the continuing mission of Jesus to take the gospel to all peoples. Within the gospel we find such expressions to the coming of Jesus and His birth within the infancy narratives (Luke 1:39-56; 2:1-21), within the context of various healings (for example, Luke 5:17-26; 13:11-17; 17:11-19) and through revelations of the divine nature of Jesus (Luke 10:20-23; 19:37-38; 24:41-53). This experience is also firmly expressed within the writings of Acts. While including much of the above, the conversions of various Gentiles through both Peter (Acts 10:45-46; 11:2-18) and Paul (Acts 13:46-48; 27:35; 28:15) are especially noteworthy mentions, adding to the perspective of the missional nature of the work which includes a rich diversity of new followers of the living Christ who guides His apostles and disciples to cross cultural boundaries.[264]

4. Hospitality in Luke–Acts[265]

Central to the engagement with the marginalised (as well as the rich) is the importance for Luke of hospitality and generosity. This focus on 'welcome', especially in his gospel, becomes significant as it indicates something of the nature of the God who is sending workers out into the harvest, which includes new opportunities for missional engagement (Luke 10:2). Part of this new opportunity is for believers to embrace those on the margins, including women, children, the poor, tax-collectors and outcasts. All who are open to faith are embraced, including two Samaritans (Luke 10:30-37; 17:11-19), two centurions

---

[264] For an important treatment of this, see Kindalee Pfremmer de Long, *Surprised by God: Praise Responses in the Narrative of Luke–Acts* (Berlin/New York, Walter de Gruyter, 2009).

[265] Joel Green, *Practicing Theological Interpretation: Engaging Biblical Texts for Faith and Formation* (Grand Rapids, Baker, 2012), pp.55-70.

(Luke 7:1-10; 23:47) as well as two followers who discover that Jesus is revealed in the meal and breaking of bread (Luke 24:13-35).

Recent authors[266] have noted that in the sending of the 72 we can find an important focus for our own missional engagement. We find it helps to make use of the Ignatian practice of 'dwelling in the word'. Participants are invited to reflect personally and individually on this passage which is found in Luke 10, and then to share together what they believe God is saying to them about His continuing mission for them and His people today. Often when we have been involved in this practice, the importance of welcome is firmly noted as an expression of the Father heart of God in mission (see Chapter 9 for further consideration of hearing the voice of God).

5. The role of the Holy Spirit in Luke–Acts[267]

Of all the themes found within the writings of Luke, perhaps none have brought more focus, discussion and engagement as the importance of the Holy Spirit. Some have even suggested calling the second Lucan volume the Acts of the Holy Spirit, so prominent is this focus. Max Turner notes:

> Luke devotes particular attention to the topic, with some twenty references to the Spirit in the Gospel (compare with just six in Mark; twelve in Matthew), and a further sixty in Acts. The Spirit is a major uniting theme within his double-volumed work, indeed nothing less than the driving force of the 'salvation history' and mission that Luke describes.[268]

One consideration is how the earliest members of the new Christian community would have understood the Holy Spirit. Clearly, the Pentecost experience set the stage for the remainder of the various experiences of Acts, partly as a continuation of the ministry of Jesus,

---

[266] Roxburgh, *Missional Joining God in the Neighbourhood*, pp.115-31; Greene and Robinson, *Metavista*, pp.110-12.

[267] There are numerous studies on the importance of the Holy Spirit within Luke–Acts. See commentaries for these.

[268] Max, Turner, 'The Work of the Holy Spirit in Luke–Acts', *Word and World* (Vol. 23, No.2, 2003), p.146.

and partly to break new ground in mission. In addition, through various expressions of power for healing, deliverance from demons and prison, as well as the grace to face persecution, imprisonment and death, the Spirit is often at the forefront engaging with the new challenges that are being faced by the marginalised church. This is important for us to recognise in our own efforts to work together across cultures as we seek to plant multicultural missional congregations.

All of what has been written so far demonstrates the broad appeal of the Luke–Acts material in helping us to think about what is involved in God's mission to reach all peoples of the earth. This naturally leads us to focus on specific issues related to cross-cultural mission in Acts.

Expressions of cross-cultural mission in Acts

Understanding some of the intentionality of Luke in what he included in his writings brings a needed perspective on our own engagement with it as a source for mission. In Acts 1:8, the final words of Jesus are set out as a way for the disciples to intentionally engage with the world around them. Some missiologists[269] have identified a centrifugal movement within the structure of Acts that has been identified in the following way:

1. E0 – Jerusalem

2. E1 – Hellenists

3. E2 – Samaria

4. E3 – ends of the earth

---

[269] The first occurrence of this framework is to be found in Winter, 'The Highest Priority: Cross-Cultural Evangelism', in James Douglas (ed.), *Let the Earth Hear His Voice: International Congress on World Evangelization, Lausanne, Switzerland* (Minneapolis, World Wide Publications, 1975), pp.213-22. A slightly modified version applied to the Book of Acts can be found in Peter Wagner, *Spreading the Fire Vol. 1* (Ventura, Regal Books, 1994), Chapter 1.

If we look at each of these settings, we can discover some important lessons and potential approaches to consider within our own understanding and engagement of cross-cultural church planting.

E0 – Jerusalem

In missiological terms, E0 indicates the most similar culture to the ones who are engaging and expressing that mission. In the history of Western mission, this would most often mean male, white Anglo, European and Western peoples. This was the most traditional paradigm used within the nineteenth and twentieth centuries, although there are good examples of women and people from other ethnicities who also engaged in smaller missional ventures, but, sadly, these were more the exception than the norm. This means that the easiest people group to engage with would be those 'just like us' – those with all the cultural, sociological and psychological moorings in place that shape our worldviews and theirs.

One of the earliest proponents of this approach was the missionary and missiologist Donald McGavran. While a missionary in India, he took note that the missiological approaches that were normal in his day indicated that the easiest and quickest conversions occurred within the same culture, class and ethnicity. He called this the homogenous unit principle (mentioned earlier in this work).[270] Essentially, for him, the quickest way to plant and grow a church, or to do effective mission, was to focus key energies and resources on people who were most like the missionary initiators. This was developed more fully into Church Growth Theory, and especially within North America became a leading agent of change during the 1980s and 1990s. Within Britain and Europe, this had a slightly different flavour, as there were some theological concerns that just 'attracting people just like us' didn't fully engage with an understanding of the kingdom.

That said, we can glean some important insights for our own potential development of missional multicultural churches, as like tends to attract like.

---

[270] See page 27.

For the earliest Christians, we discover that the first disciples were those who were most like Jesus: northerners (Galileans), Jews, tradesmen (assuming Jesus was a carpenter), etc. The early chapters of Acts indicate that these are the first people group who responded to the expressions of the gospel. The first level of engagement within the writings of Luke–Acts indicates a clear beginning point for mission to include those most like us.

E1 – Hellenists

Hellenisation was for all practical purposes a form of globalisation in the first-century situation in which Christianity took shape. Developed from the beginning of the Persian Wars, and intentionally moved forward by Alexander the Great, it formed a significant cultural and religious upheaval for the conquered nations. Palestine was not exempt, and much of its development happened within the inter-testamental period where a number of key cultural conflicts arose between Jews and Gentiles due to the deliberate policy of seeking to Hellenise the Hebrew people.

Kostas Vlassopoulos notes that while scholars have rarely and clearly defined Hellenisation,

> in most cases it describes the process through which non-Greek communities adopted Greek material culture, language and literature, styles and iconography, cults and myths, cultural practices like athletics, and even Greek identity.[271]

We find this development in the sixth chapter of Acts where a potential divisive issue arose around the lack of supportive care for Hellenist widows. The appointment of the seven leaders is noteworthy of how the apostles sought to address these cross-cultural challenges, especially since they all have Greek names which means they were most likely from the wider diaspora of Hellenised Jews who lived around the Mediterranean basin, rather than Palestinian Jews, who seemed to have been the earliest core substrate of the church.

---

[271] Kostas Vlassopoulos, *Greeks and Barbarians* (Cambridge, Cambridge University Press, 2013), p.9.

This is the second focus in Acts, and the main consideration is that there are some small but significant differences. Here we begin to see the first stratification of those who are a little different from the E0 set, which means, among others things, that we can see how they responded to the good news and became part of the E0 set. This was not primarily about language differences between the two sets (Hellenists speaking Greek and Hebrews speaking Aramaic), but it was a step towards the fulfilment of the church eventually learning to engage cross culturally with those who had no Jewish stock as part of their ethnic and cultural heritage.

E2 – Samaria

Some new issues arose as the good news was expressed within a new cultural framework. This moved the boundaries both sociologically and religiously for the nascent missionary church. Witherington explains that while they were still part of Israel, Samaritans were viewed and treated as if they were on the fringe, much like the Ethiopian eunuch in chapter 8 of Acts.[272] Marshall adds that they were considered schismatics – still part of the house of Israel in keeping the Law and showing great piety, but hated and often treated as heretical.[273]

This is not to be seen as a logical step towards engaging with the Gentiles, tempting as that may be. There was a larger issue of reconciliation that needed to take place before the Gentile mission could be undertaken.[274] A major racial and cultural divide had been crossed, which gave credence to the gospel message with its appeal to bring all people into the kingdom of God.

---

[272] See the relevant discussion in Ben Witherington III, *The Acts of the Apostles: A Social-Rhetorical Commentary* (Grand Rapids/Cambridge, Eerdmans, 1998). His earlier work is also of value: Ben Witherington III, *Women in the Ministry of Jesus* (Cambridge, Cambridge University Press, 1984), pp.57-63.

[273] Howard Marshall, *The Acts of the Apostles* (Tyndale Commentaries, Eerdmans, 1980), pp.152-53.

[274] John Proctor, *Acts of God: The Message and Meaning of the Book of Acts* (Grove Booklets B49, Cambridge, Grove Books Ltd, 2008), p.8.

E3 – Gentiles (ends of the earth)

Here we begin to see much of the overall theological fulfilment of Luke's focus: that Jesus is not just the Messiah of the Jews, but is in fact the Saviour of the world. This brings some significant challenges and upheaval to the mostly sectarian understanding of the gospel that is represented within the first nine chapters of Acts. How would the church really learn to engage with those who were generally outside of the ministry of Jesus?

The conversion of Saul of Tarsus is the significant event that begins to develop and fulfil this approach to global cross-cultural mission. His own unique background, education, understanding and experience enabled him to finally reach the city of Rome. Thereby, for Luke, the Gentile mission reaches not so much a conclusion as a normal part of mission, which is to take the gospel to the centre of the Greco-Roman world, and to true cross-cultural Gentile mission beyond the ethnic cultural boundaries of Israel. Here, then, is the real cross-cultural expression of the Luke–Acts missiological message for us to consider and apply to our own cross-cultural and multicultural missional situations.

Forming multicultural partnerships

While not wishing to diminish the importance of Paul's contribution as a missional leader in Acts, in chapter 10 we find a significant watershed moment of re-forming an understanding of the gospel. In the narrative account of Peter's vision on the rooftop, we see a number of challenges which create a new paradigm of understanding and therefore engagement for the mission of the early church. It is important to briefly reflect on some key learning points from this boundary-breaking moment in the missional framework of Acts.

1. Peter's 'conversion'

Peter would have had enough education in his faith to realise that the vision he received would at first have been considered to be without credibility to an early Christian Jew. Why would God command him to do that which the Law had forbidden? It is no wonder it took three requests before he began to act upon the real meaning of the vision –

calling for the early church to accept Gentiles, formerly considered unclean by his compatriots, to become an accepted part of the kingdom community. In many ways, this was a conversion for Peter regarding how he would later come to interpret his theology to fit the new missional situation, which the Spirit of Christ was guiding the early church to understand and embrace for the future of God's mission to the nations.

2. Cornelius' household conversion

The coming of the Holy Spirit upon Cornelius and his household was also a watershed event. Here, as at Pentecost, charismatic experiences are noted, and Peter's conclusion is that this is the same as what he had encountered on the day of Pentecost. Once again, new theological thinking must ensue (they are not Jews, not circumcised, but they are God-fearers). Peter's only conclusion is to baptise them.

3. The Jerusalem council and missional decisions

Dan, while not a great fan of lots of ecclesial meetings, recognises that the one in Jerusalem was another watershed event. The combined wisdom and spiritual insights at this early church council demonstrate the fine balance between not accepting everything and not forbidding everything. It is a mission moment that demands a new response, and Luke records a very good way of considering how to develop missional thinking when boundary-breaking moments lead to the need for new radical points of view.

Something similar may have occurred within the book of Daniel. In an exilic situation, the four young Jewish men were willing to adapt and adopt new cultural statuses without compromising their core faith. Their names were changed (not an easy thing for a young Jewish male) and they adopted new clothing, but their spirituality and food hygiene practices remained intact. It was costly, as they all faced persecution as a consequence of their new missional situation.

4. The releasing of Paul for mission

The development of this new situation demanded a new kind of missional response. Here entered Paul and his missionary journeys. These journeys were full of adventure, teamwork, challenges and difficulties both without (through misunderstandings, beatings, persecution and imprisonment) and within (as can be witnessed in his falling out with Barnabas, his loss of key team members like Demas and his conflict with Christian Jews who wanted the Gentiles to keep the Torah).

5. Coming to Rome as a fulfilment

The capital was the ultimate place for the good news to be heard, seen and experienced. If the gospel could influence people here at the centre of Gentile power, even as it did in a subversive way, then the newly formed missional churches could find peace in the context of the *Pax Romana* (the peace that Rome offered to the kingdoms it conquered or brought under its protection and rule).

What value does this have for our own missionary context?

In order to embrace the book of Acts for mission, we need to realise that Luke's descriptive account has much to teach us about flexibility, change, taking risks and working out what is essential to God's mission and what is fluid. This is a real missional challenge, especially as we work towards modelling forms of multicultural churches that look, sound and feel like the all-inclusive kingdom of God.

It means trusting in the Holy Spirit to lead us, but not being dismissive of education, learning, culture or other expressions that may not be our preference but may still be legitimate forms of the gospel. It also means allowing mission to shape our churches rather than church trying to make its maintenance and function the largest concern of its mission, to the neglect of God's mission to save people where we live. This is a core DNA issue, and the church in Acts seems to model this kind of approach to what is important. It may mean embracing new expressions and forms of spirituality to fully engage with other cultural communities. This will take great love and patience for each of us, as well as understanding and determination filled with grace to enable this to happen. It will not be easy, but it will be fulfilling.

One of our favourite verses in the book of Acts is in chapter 8, located between the revival that took place in Samaria where the kingdom is present, and the relocating of Philip to meet the Ethiopian eunuch in the desert. The verse concerned is verse 8, and it simply says, 'So there was great joy in that city.' We often try to imagine what our city would look like if it was filled with joy. How would the church express itself? Might some intentional multicultural communities that are committed to being an expression of the kingdom be part of the answer? Could we take our learning from Acts and find new ways of expressing this in our Western contexts? Could London, Birmingham, Manchester or Leeds become places where God loves to dwell? A city of joy is something to dream of, to live for, to aspire to and to work towards. All of these questions can raise our hopes, our dreams, our visions to see the multicultural kingdom come on earth as it is, and finally will be, in heaven.

Reflective exercise

Take a few minutes to reflect on the following questions:

- In what ways does the cross-cultural narrative of Acts help your church understand how to engage in cross-cultural mission?

- How might the centrifugal mission strategy spoken of in this chapter help your church to engage in mission enterprises locally and more broadly?

- What would your city or town look like if it was full of joy? How might this dream of bringing joy help to motivate your congregation to engage in the *missio Dei*?

Comments

Part 3

Overcoming Obstacles to Engaging in the Conversation

Chapter 9
Discerning God's Mission

Lesslie Newbigin highlighted somewhat prophetically a number of years ago the importance of reinvesting our missiology with the third person of the Godhead. The prophetic voice is very much a part of this reinvestment, and we all need to consider how we can come to discover the Trinity's mission.

Pentecostal Christians arriving in the West since the early 1980s have brought their spirituality for us to share and are adding to the prophetic dimension within the missional conversation. The Welsh revival early in the twentieth century was a great precursor to later movements of the Spirit which came to the UK in the 1980s with John Wimber and the development of the Vineyard charismatic churches. To a large extent, the work of Holy Trinity Brompton and the development of the now famous Alpha Course was stimulated by the so-called third wave movement of the Spirit. Some of our readers may have experienced the excitement and challenges that occurred at the time of the third wave.

Newbigin became interested in the charismatic contribution to the missional conversation towards the end of his life. It is not widely known that he consulted with Holy Trinity Brompton, which is well known for its emphasis on the living presence of God's Spirit in the Christian life through the Alpha Course teaching material. Many of us may still be using the Alpha Course as part of our outreach strategies.

The arrival of Pentecostalism has further stimulated churches which are part of the charismatic movement to seek the missionary God's guidance even more intentionally. It helps us to consider the good aspects of the spiritual awakening now that it has been around for some time, as well as some of the more troubling abuses that put many Christians off the movement.

We need to be careful to understand that we all come with differing levels of openness to explore more overt spiritual practices such as glossolalia (speaking in tongues) or prophecy. And those whose faith has been enriched by charismatic spirituality must be very careful not to over-emphasise gifts like tongues. It is just one gift which we may choose to exercise or not. The bigger issue has to do with our faith and continued commitment to serve God faithfully. It is troubling when someone strongly argues that people should exercise supernatural gifts but their lives do not measure up to the likeness of Christ's example. One of the primary roles of the Spirit is to guide the church to discover God's mission for the world. The starting point of joining Christ in His mission to redeem mankind needs to begin with His people becoming more like Him. Those who know how to discern God's voice will inevitably be challenged to follow Christ as He continues His ministry to reconcile the whole world to God.

Newbigin pointed out that the work of the Spirit is to lead the church so that it can discern God's mission to reach those who need to hear the gospel. In his insightful and trend-setting book *The Open Secret: An Introduction to the Theology of Mission*[275] he conceived of a practical theology of mission based on a Trinitarian model. This model vitally recognised that the mission of the church (the community of Christ) fundamentally derived its authority from the persons of the Trinity. God, in the name of 'the Father and of the Son and of the Holy Spirit' (Matthew 28:19), may be said to have commissioned the church to preach the gospel to every nation in the name of the Trinity.[276] Newbigin contended that our authority to engage in mission is based on the Trinitarian gospel of the kingdom:

> Here the important point is that we be clear about the authority. Every proposal to seek authorization elsewhere than in the gospel itself must lead us astray. The only proper response to the question 'By what authority?' is the announcement of the gospel itself.[277]

This 'authority' takes as its starting point that the church's mission is based on the Trinity's mission. It is the Father of Christ who sends disciples to proclaim the gospel by the guidance of the Holy Spirit, in contextually appropriate ways. The church does not send out disciple-

---

[275] Newbigin, *The Open Secret*, p.55.
[276] Newbigin, *The Open Secret*, p.56.
[277] Newbigin, *The Open Secret*, p.18.

makers; the Trinity sends them out, guiding them by the presence of the missional Spirit. The multicultural missional church founds its drive for mission on sharing in the Trinity's work. *Missio Trinitatis* needs to shape the way we approach mission: it needs to be shaped with theological reference to the three persons of the Godhead. Newbigin conceived of this threefold aspect with reference to each person of the Trinity related to their particular roles in the economy of salvation.

Father

Firstly, Newbigin spoke of the part of the Father in the economy:

> Mission [is] the proclaiming of God's kingship over all human history and over the whole cosmos. Mission is concerned with nothing less than the completion of all that God has begun to do in the creation of the world and of humankind. Its concern is not sectional but total and universal.[278]

We need to note that 'kingship' expresses the reign of God in terms of the theology of the kingdom of God. God is not just Lord of the sphere of the church but He is Lord of the 'cosmos', which needs to be reunited with Him. God is not involved in the salvation of just the church but of the whole cosmos. 'Mission' therefore entails the 'completion' of the whole of God's cosmic plan to reunite all nations and peoples in Christ. Newbigin developed this theme with reference to Ephesians 1, which declares God's plan to unite all things in heaven and earth under His kingdom reign. This is to come to fruition through the body of Christ (the church), with Christ as its head (Ephesians 1:9, 10).

Our local congregations are to be a representation of the unification of diverse peoples under the headship of Christ, just as the kingdom is to be realised throughout the church worldwide. Hence the Trinitarian dogma provides the rationale for us to plant multi-ethnic breakthrough congregations who can share in the life of the Trinitarian family, who are eternally united by their love. Equality rather than

---

[278] Newbigin, *The Open Secret*, p.56.

segregation is the goal of the Trinity's mission. Church growth experts Gibbs and Bolger argue that the reign of God needs to be understood to extend outwards to reclaim every space for God, which at present have been possessed by the forces of secularism.[279] Robinson and Smith make a similar point.[280] The Mission of God is not just to be limited to within the walls of our local church, or to the circumscribed spheres of Christian institutions, but rather God's people need to go out into their local communities with the authority of the Father, Son and Holy Spirit. Secular spaces need to be reclaimed from the dominion of the spirit of secularity itself.

Newbigin worked as a missionary in India for some years before he returned to the UK in the 1970s to find it had significantly changed from a Christian to a developing post-Christian society. He was shocked by the decline in church attendance and the diminished influence of the Christian worldview on important segments of people in society. He spent the rest of his life seeking to help others re-engage the West with the gospel.[281] Important to his thinking was that lessons needed to be learnt from the experiences of missionaries returning to the West with regard to methods they had successfully used to communicate the gospel.

As we have noted, the authority for bringing the gospel back to postmodern Westerners has to be based on a deep conviction about the reign of God as the only solution to redeem human society from its dividedness. If we are to engage in the multicultural missional conversation together, it is important that we align our convictions around the authority of the Father of the kingdom, who commissions us through Christ to form welcoming and open Christian communities for those who are seeking to re-engage with God.

---

[279] Gibbs and Bolger, *Emerging Churches*, Chapter 4.

[280] Martin Robinson and Dwight Smith, *Invading Secular Space* (London, Monarch Books, 2009), Chapter 6.

[281] A good summary of Newbigin's concerns can be found in the essay 'Can the West be Converted?' Available at www.newbigin.net/assets/pdf/85cwbc.pdf (accessed 30th October 2014).

Son

Secondly, Newbigin addressed the importance of the person of Christ to the practical theology of mission for the church to follow:

> I have spoken, secondly, of mission as the presence of God and kingship in Jesus and in the church. In this aspect mission is concerned with the limited, the particular, the contingent.[282]

The locus of salvation is located in the person of Jesus. A discussion that mission scholars have had over the years relates to the means of salvation. If the Holy Spirit after Pentecost was sent out into the world to empower the mission of God to save the world, then might not this universalism of the Spirit imply that He would save people even if they did not fully accept Christ? Newbigin powerfully denied this idea. His words remind us that Jesus is God's particular means of reconciling mankind to Himself. He made the point that salvation is contingent on people putting their faith in Jesus as their personal saviour. A universalist theology of mission that takes Christ out of the equation would not be Christian, in Newbigin's view. Hence the work of the Spirit who is sent to empower the mission of God's people needs to be viewed as the work of the Spirit of Jesus, which is identified in Paul's writings and the book of Acts to be the guiding Spirit for us to follow as He takes the message of Christ to the nations. Not any old spirit would save mankind without reference to the sole agency of Jesus Christ the Saviour of the world. This particular recognition is paramount to a Trinitarian missiology and it is why the Trinitarian dogma is vital to help us keep the focus of salvation on the nature of the persons of the one God, the primary community to whom all peoples need to be reconciled.

Moreover, for Newbigin, the expression of the 'kingship' of God found its locus in the person of Jesus the Messiah (Acts 4:11-12). Christ the anointed one is the prototype for all Spirit-anointed followers of Christ. The apostle Paul's concept of Jesus the representative man would have us model our lives on Jesus the Son of God, so that we too may become images (impressions) of God, stamped with the seal of

---

[282] Newbigin, *The Open Secret*, p.56.

His likeness. This will also help our communities to be the hermeneutic of the gospel, because we look like the Christ of the Trinitarian community. At the heart of the mission of Jesus in Luke's gospel is the theology that the Spirit of God motivated and empowered His teaching and deeds so that the whole world could be reconciled to the kingdom community.

Luke begins the book of Acts by reminding Theophilus of the words and works of Jesus, followed by the theology that the followers of Christ are to continue the mission of Jesus as they are guided by His Spirit to unite all peoples as one family in the kingdom. This kingdom community will help us to share intimately with God and the people of God who live as real brothers and sisters rather than as mere acquaintances. Acts 2 portrays the first believers as thoroughly committed to deep fellowship, gathering around Jesus and having all things in common. We need to reform our churches to become families that share deeper fellowship with God and each other, rather than as business-like networks that work like limited companies with the CEO pastor being the professional and expert Christian. We need to develop all members to exercise their gifts based on the needs for ministry in our churches and local communities, which are theologically built on every believer being priests of Christ, representing His ministry to the whole world to reconcile people to God's family.

The classic passage in Acts which articulates this theology is 16:6-10. It is so important to our understanding of a Trinitarian theology of the whole community consisting of missional disciples making other disciples that the Spirit of God guides them to apprentice:

> And they went through the region of Phrygia and Galatia, having been forbidden by the Holy Spirit to speak the word in Asia. And when they had come opposite Mysia, they attempted to go into Bithynia, but the Spirit of Jesus did not allow them; so, passing by Mysia, they went down to Troas. And a vision appeared to Paul in the night: a man of Macedonia was standing beseeching him and saying, 'Come over to Macedonia and help us.' And when he had seen the vision, immediately we sought to go on into Macedonia,

241

concluding that God had called us to preach the gospel to them.

Acts 16:6-10 (RSV)

It is enough to point out that it was not any old spirit that guided Paul's mission team; it was the 'Spirit of Jesus'. This is the theological language of the New Testament, that the multicultural church is being led by Jesus Himself to continue His mission to reconcile the world to the Trinitarian family. Our churches need to be families that share life deeply together in order to become these new kinds of multicultural missional communities that they need to be. This type of church family welcomes diverse peoples and cultures into its community and to participate in its life.

It is also important to note that for Newbigin, the extension of God's ownership of the cosmos was to be through the person of His Son, and that we as Christ's followers are to share in shaping the coming kingdom of God (Colossians 1:14-15). The community of believers are subjects of the Son. The Son is God's particular medium of salvation for the reunification of all things to God's ownership and rule. This salvation is contingent on lost people groups finding in Jesus Christ alone the way to make them part of the kingdom's unifying reality.

Spirit

Thirdly, Newbigin focused on the theology of the Spirit and the Spirit's vital role in helping to lead the mission of the multicultural church:

It is essential to add a third affirmation, without which the first two would be misleading. I have affirmed that God's kingship is present in the church; but it must be insisted that it is not the property of the church. It is not domesticated within the church. Mission is not simply the self-propagation of the church by putting forth of the power that inheres in its life. To accept that picture would be to sanction an appalling distortion of mission. On the contrary, the active agent of mission is a power that rules, guides, and goes before the church: the free, sovereign, living power of the Spirit of God. Mission is not just something that the church does; it is something that is done by the Spirit, who is himself the witness, who changes both the world and the Church, who always goes before the Church in its missionary journey ... From the very beginning of the New Testament, the coming of Jesus, his words and works are connected directly with the power of the Spirit.[283]

Newbigin considered the work of the Holy Spirit to be sovereign in leading the church on God's mission. The Spirit of Jesus is to lead the church rather than the church leading the Spirit (John 3:8). Our churches need to ask God to develop their powers of spiritual discernment. It is no mistake that Newbigin found the first chapter of Ephesians to be so informative to some of his theology of mission. Paul prayed that the believers in Ephesus would be provided with:

> a spirit of wisdom and of revelation in the knowledge of him, having the eyes of your hearts enlightened, that you may know what is the hope to which he has called you, what are the riches of his glorious inheritance in the saints, and what is the immeasurable greatness of his power in us who believe, according to the working of his great might which he accomplished in Christ when he raised him from the dead and made him sit at his right hand in the heavenly places, far above all rule and authority and power and dominion, and above every name that is named, not only in this age but also in that which is to come; and he has put all things under his feet and has made him the head over all things for the church, which is his body, the fulness of him who fills all in all.
> *Ephesians 1:17-23 (RSV)*

Paul's prayer is that God would renew the hearts of the Ephesians by giving them a spiritual ability to understand the Holy Spirit's guidance regarding the purpose for their community. The multicultural missional church needs to ask the Father in heaven for

---

[283] Newbigin, *The Open Secret*, pp.56,57.

the ability to hear the voice of God, and to have our hearts tuned into the Spirit's frequency.

Moreover, the Holy Spirit may not be 'domesticated' within our churches. He is to lead our churches. The church is to follow the signs that the Spirit offers to see where it is to follow God next to engage in His mission. It might be suggested that Christ's nomadic modern disciples follow the lead of the Spirit of Jesus as they renew their powers to do God's will (Acts 16:6-10).

We recently attended a conference where Alan Roxburgh was speaking. He suggested that we need to become the sort of missional leaders who are divine detectives, seeking to discern the fingerprints of the Spirit in the world around us, and learning to discern where He wants us to engage in mission next. The Spirit of God is the leading agent that our churches need to follow, looking for signs of His work among our local lost communities.[284] When He opens new opportunities, the people of God need to cooperate in His work, which entails establishing the reign of God in other lives, as much as the reclamation of secular spaces from the powers that presently need redeeming back to the lordship of Christ. By following the guidance of the Spirit of Jesus into these 'spaces', we will bring the Christian faith back into them, reclaiming them and helping to inform political debate about the role of faith in the public square.

At the heart of the debate about the role of religion and its influence on policymaking that affects people in the public square is a political tension which makes it hard for politicians to translate secular laws and policies into the right forms to protect religious rights. Brunner Verlag comments:

> The nexus (or collusion) of secular law and religious society happens in the political realm. Where there are strict restrictions to creating laws that favor or prohibit religion or giving a political candidate a religious test, there are no hard and fast rules for the role of religion in political life. As a result, the political realm has and continues to present a very

---

[284] Acts 16:10 – notice Luke use of the word 'concluding' to indicate that the Pauline team reasoned about what the Spirit's derived vision of the man of Macedonia might mean.

vibrant discourse on religion. A religious and religiously diverse citizenry seeks to reconcile issues that may be religiously inspired but must be translated into non-religious laws. This is the arena where politicians debate the role of religion in the nation's identity and strength. This is the arena where law makers challenge the relationship between religion, morality, and law. This is the arena where religious majorities and religious minorities struggle for power and protection. Religiously inspired issues like abortion, gay marriage, and prayer in schools powerfully divide the ... electorate in what has become known as the culture wars.[285]

Verlag's concept of the 'culture wars' is a metaphor for the challenges posed by religion in the public square. It is the territory where minority groups fight for laws and policies that will protect their rights to determine how adherents to their faith should be allowed to exercise this faith in the way they deem most fit. The issues he raises, such as gay marriage, are generally hot potatoes for Christians, and particularly for many migrant Christian groups.

Leaving that aside, political decision making in the West includes the consideration of the religious views of minority groups. If we all seek to more extensively and regularly join together in missional conversations, we can create important coalitions that could inform political decision-making. The power of organised think tanks developed out of coalitions could make important representations to politicians which could influence policymaking on a political level.

Of course, there are great opportunities today to speak out on major social and theological issues. The Archbishop of Canterbury Justin Welby has spoken out about the need to address issues of inequality, asylum matters, and so on. In the areas we live in, as well as nationally, major Christian forces for change are at work in areas such as food banks, credit unions, street pastoring, debt counselling, soup kitchens, places for the homeless to sleep and to obtain clothing and food. Care for the Family is an important organisation which helps families in need, as are voices providing advocacy for the poor, the under-privileged and low-waged.

---

[285] Verlag, *Religion in the Public Sphere I*, p.137.

We could mention many ways that Christians are involved in major social issues. Another great example is the Exposed Campaign which is part of the Micah Challenge. Their mission statement says:

> Micah Challenge is a global movement of Christian agencies, churches, groups and individuals which aims to deepen people's engagement with the poor and to help reduce poverty as an integral part of our Christian faith.[286]

It is very important that we all become much more aware of major issues within our society and then engage in making a difference to the needs of people in the public square. We have done woefully little in this chapter to express the wide range of Christian works and voices that are making serious contributions to the debate about the role of faith in the public square. What we hope we have done is to have whetted appetites to look more closely into the missional contributions that are needed, as well as at key organisations that are working for the good of the under-privileged in secular society.

Further analysis and synthesis

What we have been discussing so far is the nature of mission, and suggesting that it is the Trinity's mission. God may be thought of as the one who leads that mission rather than the church trying to lead it for Him. There are some passages in the Bible where this point of God needing to lead His mission to save the world is clearly articulated. As mentioned earlier, in Acts 16:6-10 we read about Paul's vision of the Macedonian man who called Paul and his team to take the gospel to Macedonia, and shortly thereafter to Greece. Paul and his team understood the vision to mean that God's Spirit was guiding them to take the gospel into Europe. This is one very good example that demonstrates that it is God who ultimately needs to lead His people to the right places at the right times to share the gospel with those who are ready to hear it.

---

[286] Micah Challenge. Available at http://www.micahchallenge.org.au/about-us (accessed 17th September 2014).

It is vital that we are able to hear the Spirit's voice so that we can discern where God is leading us to take the gospel next as we fight the battle to reclaim secular space for God. This is suggestive of a new paradigm of how mission can be carried forward in the Western hemisphere. It distinguishes itself by viewing mission as following God and seeking signs of His activity among the secular places of Western society. This view will almost certainly call for a new type of discipleship formation process to be adopted by churches, to enable followers to hear God's voice.[287] The nomadic disciple is one who, like Abraham, needs to be guided by the living Spirit of God.

This new type of missiology is not:

1. Unitarian (belief in one God – with Son and Spirit as less than God – Modalism). Unitarianism emphasises the ownership of the world by God and the need for all human beings to accept that rule as a matter of necessity. It neglects to do more than recognise this. A Unitarian missiology focuses on God's ownership of everything but fails to recognise God's agent of salvation and the establishment of His rule through Christ.

2. Binatarian (belief in the Father and the Son only; the Spirit has a more subordinate role). Binatarianism may emphasise the importance of sharing the gospel of Christ, but it lacks emphasis on the power of the Holy Spirit to guide people in the process of sharing Christ. It seeks to domesticate Christ to the church without the sovereign power of the Holy Spirit to ignite and guide the *missio Dei*. It could be said that it endeavours to lead God by defining what God asks of His people and limiting the guidance of God to its particular interpretation of Scripture, suited to its own traditions. In this scheme, Christ is locked away in a holy Scripture world which becomes the interpretative intellectual property of the church, to disseminate information to those with whom it sees fit to share the gospel. The church somehow may assume it owns this intellectual, information-based Christ.

---

[287] See Acts 10. Notice how the Holy Spirit guided Peter to go to Cornelius – He led the mission.

However, **Trinitarian** theology brings the living Christ to the foreground as the sovereign Spirit is brought into the guidance of the missional church. Christian missiology needs to be Trinitarian:

- It needs to recognise the Father as owner and originator of the cosmos.

- It needs to acknowledge the gospel of Christ and His lordship over the whole cosmos for the Father's sake.

- It needs to allow God's Spirit to be sovereign and to lead its mission. This makes missional disciples followers of the Spirit's discernible actions as He continues to guide their endeavours. The people of Christ need to cooperate in sharing in the mission of the Trinity as they are motivated to share in reconciling new brothers and sisters into the family of God.

- This leading of the Spirit means that the real living Christ, not the Christ of printed page alone, can more readily propel His mission through His spiritually discerning people to reach those God identifies for them to engage with. This may be thought of as evidence of the continuing sovereign action of the Spirit of Jesus.

Trinitarian missional theology needs to be theistic rather than deistic in its orientation on the basis of Newbigin's thesis.

Deistic theology

We need to understand the difference between deistic and theistic theology. A deistic theology assumes that God created the universe in the beginning but subsequently left it to its own devices. God is considered remote and uninterested in His creation. He is transcendent but not imminent. He is impersonal rather than relational. In effect, He is not involved in the daily affairs of the creatures of the cosmos or in any of its other facets of existence. This view of God makes *missio Trinitatis* impossible because a non-relational God cannot seek to reconcile people to Himself.[288]

Theistic theology

A theistic theology of mission which holds that God both created and sustains the universe is naturally going to fit more readily with a Trinitarian missiology. In this view, God is both transcendent and imminent. He is God the owner–creator and sustainer of all things. He can also be considered high and exalted above the cosmos (transcendentally as universal Lord). He may be considered the cause without cause (Psalm 90:2; Isaiah 9:6). As Barth so aptly portrayed it, the Trinity is a self-sustaining being that is the source of all being. The Trinity's people are part of God's creation who need to find their source of life in the Godhead (Acts 17:24-28). But at the same time, according to Moltmann, the nature of the Trinity is defined as relational from before the cosmos was birthed. Hence when Christ incarnated as the Divine, He was simply fulfilling the essence of the Trinitarian nature. According to Barth, and later Moltmann, relational interconnection always defined the Trinity even before They created anything.

The degree of this relationship in terms of how much and how obviously God communicates with people differs across Christian theological traditions. A Trinitarian theology needs to allow for all three persons of the Godhead to be active, if it is to mean anything at all to help the church engage in the sovereign Spirit's leading to reconcile all people to God. The incarnation makes God imminent, with the Spirit of Christ being the abiding catalyst of human interconnection with the heart of the social Trinity, who sends the church out to win new people for Christ.

For a Pentecostal Christian, God may be considered to communicate more often and more directly with believers through prophecy to direct His ongoing mission. For a Christian from one of the Reformed traditions, the Holy Spirit's leading may be considered

---

[288] 'Transcendent' refers to the concept that God is viewed as distant and uninterested in human affairs. Imminent refers to the concept that God is personally involved in human affairs.

249

more subtle – perhaps seeing people who show an interest in Christian things as a sign of the Spirit's action in them. In both cases, the Spirit's sovereign action and leading of God's mission may be assumed.

Is mission evangelism?

There is also another vital distinction to make at this point. It may seem that the description of mission has been to portray it as essentially the same as evangelism. Let us think about this for a moment. What is mission? What is evangelism?

What is mission?

Mission is taken to be the *missio Trinitatis*. It is not simply concerned with evangelising people to accept Christ as Lord and to then consider that its job is done. Mission needs to consider at least:

- the **basic salvation** of the individual

- the **ongoing shaping** of their lives, including a lifetime journey following the God who continues to speak and guide His people on the mission of Jesus to form disciples in every age of human history

- the **intellectual formation** of their understanding about God, and His nature and will for their lives

- the **personal formation** of their character and relational self as part of a community which is unified and diverse

- the **ministry formation** of each believer as one who identifies and exercises their God-given gifts to minister to others

- **missional leadership:** we need to recognise that each of us has a calling to lead others to Christ as we remain open to following the lead of the sovereign Spirit of grace.

Mission is strategic in the sense that the Christian God is said to have a meta-plan for the redemption of creation (Ephesians 1:3-14). To reclaim secular space is by far the largest strategic task facing the church in the West today. So the scope fits with God's cosmic plan spoken of earlier. A lifetime of discipleship formation that seeks to transform people so that their whole lives are focused on the values of

Christian living will be needed, so that their presence in the secular segments of business, education, politics, medicine, engineering and domestic support services, etc will help to desecularise these spheres. This is an important aspect of mission which relates well to the cosmic agenda of Christ. If God is community in His Trinitarian life, then it follows that the Trinity desires to shape disciples to become part of God's family, as responsible sons and daughters who model their lives to daily become more like Christ. Christ is the prototype child of God. Such a view of missional Christian community needs to engage in an ongoing manner with social, ethical, moral and justice issues in society as part of modelling their lives on that of Christ. Social justice and social action also form the compass of *missio Trinitatis* in the sense that Christ envisioned the kingdom of God to transform unjust systems. This He began during His earthly ministry by relieving the suffering of the poor. Environmental redemption is also part of the *missio*, in the more cosmic sense of the reunification of all things under the headship of Christ.

It seems to follow that evangelism is based on the *evangel* (the gospel – good news). The good news is the message of winning people for salvation, based on Christ's atoning death on the cross. It leads to us being discipled for life, to continue being shaped by His life example and to help in the ongoing transformation of society into the likeness of the kingdom of God.

All that has been considered so far helps us to form the basis for a practical theology of the missional church. Newbigin articulated the need for a fully Trinitarian practical theology which is led by the undomesticated Spirit of Jesus. We need to divinely detect God's mission and follow Him into the secular marketplaces in order to transform society. To do this effectively we need to reinvest our spiritual powers by asking God to enable us once again to hear the Spirit's voice and to discern what He is calling us to engage with, as He continues His mission through us inside and outside of the church. This naturally leads to the question, 'How can we hear God's voice more clearly?'

How to discern God's voice

Any Christian seeks to have more than a passing acquaintance with God. The book of Revelation clearly portrays that the apostle John was still passionately in love with the risen Lord Jesus in his old age (Revelation 1:1-10). The book was written towards the end of the first century AD.

Before John had the visions described in this wonderful book, he met his risen Lord in all His glory, and he was once more overcome with awe and wonder at His greatness and mercy. It is often missed that the visions of the book of Revelation have a direct bearing on the mission of God and His people's part in it. The book provides a behind-the-scenes panorama of the cosmic conflict between Christ, Satan and God's people (Revelation 6). At the centre of God's mission is His desire to make clear that the central battle is for people to choose whom they will worship. The symbol of the beast (Revelation 13) forcing men and women to worship it, and the symbol of the worshippers before the throne of God and before the Lamb in chapters 4 and 5 remind us that all mission starts and finishes when people worship God as the only one worthy of our worship. Worship is at the heart of the mission of God, and we must remind ourselves that the early church was forbidden to teach in Jesus' name by the Jewish leaders who had instigated Christ's crucifixion. The believers joined in worship upon their return to the small band of early followers, and the place they were in was shaken and they were filled with boldness to go out and speak in Jesus' name (Acts 4–5). We need to use our spiritual eyes and ears more and more in order to be filled with similar missional boldness.

We want to share with you some pointers that can be experimented with for those who want to develop their capacity to discern God's mission. It is not a one-size-fits-all solution, but we believe it is important to offer some suggestions to help us discern God's voice. It would take another book to really do justice to an exploration of how we can develop our spiritual discernment.

Before we do anything else, it is important to recognise that we all have moments when God's Spirit more obviously communicates with us. It is clear enough from Scripture that believers are filled with the Spirit when they genuinely give themselves over to the lordship of

252

Christ (Acts 2:38, 39). Moreover, we need to encourage ourselves with the recognition that Christ will do what He did for Paul when He guided his mission team to take the gospel to Macedonia and Greece. We trust that our Lord is more willing to give us the Holy Spirit's guidance than we are willing to ask for it (Luke 11:13). And it is notable from this passage that Jesus said that the Father in heaven will not provide a bad spirit for His people. He is not an abusive Father.

With these points in mind, how can we discern the Spirit's guidance more clearly in order to discern God's mission better?

Most of us have probably at some time in our lives heard in a crowded place a voice that we recognise. If it is the voice of someone we know well, we recognise it almost instantly, even if we have not seen the person for a while. Jesus' voice must have been well known to His disciples, and it must have been a great relief to them when they heard it again after the resurrection. If we allow ourselves to imagine what the first disciples might have looked forward to most after Christ returned to His Father, perhaps it had to do with hearing His voice again.

When the Spirit was poured out at Pentecost, the disciples must have understood Christ's words as recorded in John's gospel to be fulfilled (John 14:16-22). He had not left them as 'orphans' but had sent them another 'advocate'. The gospel of John indicates that it is the Spirit's mission to guide disciples to discover Christ's continuing mission (John 3:16). It might be claimed that the disciples instinctively knew the inner voice of Jesus when the Spirit entered their hearts at Pentecost because they knew His earthly voice so well. The mystical inner voice of the Spirit of Christ was probably in actuality a far more intimate means for them to connect with Jesus than had been open to them when He had been with them in the flesh. The mission of Jesus is to be continued by all Christians as they are guided by His Spirit.

The voice of God

If we consider how our own Christian communities relate to the voice of God, we may find a mixed bag of experiences and views regarding the value church members place on hearing it. For instance, some Pentecostal students in one of our classes said that the way they sought to discover God's mission for their churches was by receiving prophetic insights into God's plans for what they should do next. Indeed, this outlook is fairly typical of some charismatic Christians in the UK. Anglo churches more often than not pay some form of lip service to this approach, but in actuality rely more on rational strategies to extend the gospel message into their local communities, as this fits better with a rational Western culture. This is not to downplay strategic thinking as part of the way that the church seeks to fulfil God's mission to the West. However, it does highlight the added value for all Christians, whatever their ethnicity, to learn from each other as part of the multicultural missional conversation to hear God's voice more readily.

It is interesting that Scripture again and again reinforces that Adam and Eve, Abraham, Moses and the prophets were acquainted with hearing God's voice (for example, Genesis 3:8; 15;1-8; Numbers 7:89; Jeremiah 1:4-8; Habakkuk 2:1-2). It is arguable that God's voice is often associated with God's plans and mission for His people. Abraham, the father of many, was sent by God to leave Ur of the Chaldeans and to go to the land God had promised for him and his descendants (Genesis 12:1-3; Acts 7:2-3). Indeed, the whole mission of God was for Israel, and for Christians as inheritors of the promises made to Abraham, to receive an eternal inheritance (Romans 4; Galatians 3). Abraham and his descendants were to be a blessing to the nations so that all might be saved and become part of God's great plan to unite all things in Christ when the Lord returns again (Ephesians 1:10). In other words, God equips His people to hear His voice so that they can discern His plans for them as they engage in sharing in His mission to make new disciples for Christ. Indeed, Christ promised His disciples after His resurrection that He would be with them always to guide them on His mission to make disciples of the nations (Matthew 28:16-20).

Jesus' commission to the disciples to make new disciples is a direct fulfilment of the theological point of view of Matthew's gospel. It begins with Christ's lineage being traced back to Abraham, and ends with Christ sending His followers out to bring the blessing of faith to all the nations as new followers are shaped to worship and serve the Lord Jesus.

Research into the brain through neuro-theology

In much of our research we have explored the importance of discerning God's voice for people in the Christian community. A process of divine guidance for the discernment of God's missional plans and purposes may be considered as part of the spiritual formation that nomadic disciples need to develop. It is important to seek a more nuanced definition for this kind of prophetic gift, given the fears that many leaders and theologians in the Western tradition hold regarding its use, and to cover some biblical, theological and historical territory to prepare the ground for a basic understanding of the biblical basis for this kind of missional spiritual discipline. Strictly speaking, biblical prophetic mysticism is a subcategory of pneumatology (the field of theological study that looks at the work of the Holy Spirit).[289]

By definition, mysticism is related etymologically to the word 'mystery' (Latin *mysterion* – something which remains hidden until revealed).[290] This means that prophetic mysticism is involved in the way God the Spirit may be claimed to guide the local mission of a congregation. This thesis was given broad recognition, as we saw earlier, with Newbigin's call for churches to undomesticate the sovereign Spirit in order that He might lead the missional church as it seeks to follow God's plan to redeem the whole world.

Biblical prophetic mysticism has to do with concepts and experiences that seem to have come to biblical prophets as spontaneous intuitions. It deals with deep encounters with the spiritual world that cannot be reached by the five senses alone. In the early part of the twentieth century, philosopher and theologian Rudolf Otto broke new ground in highlighting the possibility of investigation into this territory.[291] According to neuroscientist (and neuro theologian) Andrew Newberg, the brain *could be* claimed to be hardwired to discern the unseen dimensions of the spiritual world. He particularly emphasises that the brain is set up to work on the basis of

---

[289] Karkkainen, *Pneumatology*, pp.21, 68, 91, 133, 150-151.
[290] Karkkainen, *Pneumatology*, pp.21, 68, 91, 133, 150-151.
[291] Kung, *The Christian Challenge*, pp. 96, 144-150, 205, 717, 718, 755.

belief.[292] It can be the simple belief that what we touch, taste, see and so on is real, or that what we feel deep inside to be evidence of God's presence is equally real, because feeling states are as real as any other phenomenon, in his view, of what we feel compelled to believe.

Newberg asserts that everything in the physical world is based on compelling presences which our minds, through the evidence of our five senses, believe to be real. And this is as true for what we encounter in the material world as in the spiritual, unseen dimension, which theologians term 'metaphysical'. Belief is the foundation to everything we experience, whether material or immaterial.

In Newberg's laboratory work into spiritual experiences and brain states, he used SPECT brain scans to observe changes in brain behaviour when people engage in meditation or speaking in tongues. The results suggest that the brain receives information from a source beyond itself (ie God). Newberg himself does not categorically say that this is the only explanation, but he allows for it. Explanations for brain states observed in these tests do not conclusively reveal that other parts of the brain come into action when people speak in tongues, neither do they clearly demonstrate that an entity (such as God) is giving them a new kind of supernatural language. In our own research we have investigated what seem to be revelations given to prophetically gifted Christians.[293] We are convinced by the consideration of such evidences that prophetically gifted Christians receive revelation knowledge from the Spirit. The research basis is being developed for a later publication.

The evidence suggests that we have a level of neurological programming that helps us to make meaningful contact with the spiritual domain. There are, of course, other less spiritual explanations, taken from assumptions based on non-theistic rationalism. Hence the work of brain researchers such as Newberg may well point toward mechanisms built into our brains that were put there by God, which at least provides interesting testimony to the mind's spiritual abilities that can be developed by those who wish to do so.

[292] Andrew Newberg and Mark Waldman, *How God Changes your Brain: Breakthrough Findings from A Leading Neuroscientist* (New York, Ballantine Books, 2009).
[293] Hardy, *Spiritual and Missional Philosophical Theology*, (2009)

Hay and Nye have tracked the verifiable spiritual capacities of children who, in many cases, have not been taught about God by their parents or at school. It seems that many of them believe God speaks to them, based on evidence taken from experiences reported to Hay and Nye by children in a two-year research project.[294] Interestingly, their evidence is part of the literature which is used by some Religious Education teachers to inform religious education in British schools.

Bearers of the prophetic

It may be said that the Old Testament prophets and Jesus and His apostles all operated as bearers of the prophetic mystical voice. It was by learning to discern the authentic inner voice of God that they were able to receive God's guidance. The Pentecostal and charismatic movements have come to the foreground of Christian missions in the past 100 or so years, as prime examples of the Spirit's potential to bring 625,000,000 people to faith worldwide (ie through varieties of Pentecostalism). Research in the field of psychology and parapsychology has been ongoing for many years into the field of human spiritual experiences and phenomena within the scientific community. This kind of research has been undertaken by some who have a Christian faith and some who do not.

The spiritual theologian Housten comments:

> At the beginning of the twentieth century, psychological investigations (among others, those of George Albert Coe and Robert H. Thouless) into abnormal states of consciousness, which Roman Catholic theologians too often associated with mysticism, treated them as examples of 'hysteria'. James H. Leuba (1868–1946), a critic of religion, saw in them a sexual component. Sigmund Freud (1856–1939) tended to interpret all religion as regressive.[295]

---

[294] David Hay and Rebecca Nye, *The Spirit of the Child* (London, Kingsley Publishers, 2006), pp.5-28.

[295] Partridge, *Dictionary of Contemporary Religion in the Western World*, (Leicester, IVP, 2002), p.39.

These early views have been contested, particularly as more recent investigations have suggested that the whole brain seems to be involved in a person's beliefs and spiritual practices. Modern politicised cultural sensitivities accept spiritual phenomena as part of the postmodern multicultural terrain, and consider spiritual experiences to be normal to humanity. Western governments now make more allowances for religious beliefs in schools and workplaces. Spirituality is seemingly back on the agenda as a real experiential phenomenon within the new terrain of postmodernism, stimulated to some large extent by the arrival of other world religions on the Western doorstep. Oxford scholar and zoologist Alistair Hardy gave the brain's religious programming a position of official credibility in academia by providing evidence of its evolved spiritual capacities.[296]

The Jesuit scholar Marechal accepted psychological investigation into prophetic mysticism as warranted, but maintained it was often distorted by scientific theories which made it some sort of neurosis. Housten states:

> For [Marechal], mystical experience is the form of intuition that senses the presence of God as direct and unmediated in transcendent dynamism.[297]

Moreover, expert in mystical literature Bernard McGinn has significantly contributed to the field by exploring the texts and thoughts of mysticism, seeking to aid contemporary reflection on their contents. He relates Christian mysticism to Scripture:

> Christian mysticism is rooted in the reading of the Bible. The mystic, however, does not seek an academic understanding of the scriptural text; nor is he or she content with viewing the Bible only as a repository of doctrine and moral regulations. The mystic wants to penetrate to the living source of the biblical message, that is, to the Divine Word who speaks in and through human words and texts. This means that the

[296] Hay and Nye, *The Spirit of the Child*, p.22.
[297] Partridge, *Dictionary of Contemporary Religion in the Western World*, p.40.

Bible has been both the origin and the norm for Christian mystics down through the ages.[298]

Given that Scriptural mysticism and the prophetic voice form the historical nexus of this section's contents, it is relevant to note some ways it operated in the experiences of the biblical prophets.

Biblical prophecy and mysticism

The theme of prophecy in the Old Testament is obviously very significant. It represents a large body of material, and would require a book in itself to explore more fully.[299] However, we will consider a few general categorisations to help us understand prophetic phenomena, which are found in both Testaments.

Dreams

The simplest kind of revelatory phenomena mentioned in the Bible is that of dreams, which are often described to have been inspired by God (Genesis 20:3, 6). There are normally visual and auditory aspects which involve the dreamer as a detached observer or as a participant. We have probably all probably experienced dreams like this.

An example of detachment is Jacob's dream of angels going up and down a stairway from heaven to earth (Genesis 28:10-14). Much of the book of Daniel is in some way based on dreams, mostly with Daniel acting as a detached observer (eg Daniel 7:1-8). King Abimelech was a participant in a dream warning him that he had taken Sarah, a married woman, to be his concubine (Genesis 20:3). Each of these examples demonstrates how seriously the ancients took dreams as communications from God, otherwise they would not be preserved as they are in the Bible. Let none of us forget that this is the Bible which is the sacred repository of the most precious documents of the Jewish and Christian faiths. Surely this recognition in itself deserves proper consideration, when we consider how God has guided His people

---

[298] Bernard McGinn, *The Essential Writings of Christian Mysticism* (New York, The Modern Library, 2006), p.1.

[299] J. W. Rogerson and Judith Lieu, *The Oxford Handbook of Biblical Studies* (Oxford, Oxford University Press, 2008), Chapter 22.

throughout history so they can participate effectively in His ongoing mission.

Biblical dreams might be personal messages from God to individuals, or they might have a broader purpose important for others to consider as well. Here are some examples of dreams and visions given for personal reasons, or dreams and visions given for the good of others:

- Genesis 15: Abraham in interaction with God and sleeps = dream about himself

- Genesis 20: Abimelech and God in interaction = dream about himself

- Genesis 28:10-22: Jacob being spoken to by God = dream about himself

- Genesis 31:10-29: Jacob and God in interaction = dream about himself

- Genesis 37:1-11: Joseph and brothers in interaction = dreams about himself

- Genesis 40: cupbearer and baker = dreams about themselves

- Genesis 41:1-49: Pharaoh's dream of seven cows = dream for others

- Genesis 46:1-7: Jacob in dialogue with God = dream about himself

- Judges 7:9-18: loaf of bread hitting camp = Gideon's dream for himself

- 1 Kings 3:5-28 God and Solomon interact = dream for himself

- Daniel 2: statue hit by stone = Daniel's dream for others

- Daniel 7: four beasts = Daniel's dream for others

- Daniel 8: ram and goat = Daniel's vision for others

- Daniel 10–12: terrifying vision

- Matthew 1:20-25 God spoke to Joseph = dream for himself

- Matthew 2:13-15 God spoke to Joseph = dream for himself and his family

- Matthew 2:19-23 God spoke to Joseph = dream for himself and his family[300]

What is important is that a large number of biblical dreams were purely for the benefit of the recipient. If we take seriously the psychologist Jung's research regarding the 'supranatural'[301] content of dreams, he suggested that they reside somewhere in what he called the 'collective unconsciousness'. The 'collective unconsciousness' is defined as visual images that turn up in dreams which have similar meanings in all cultures. It is possible that these images are in some way genetically passed on to children. It has also been suggested that dreams can be 'supernatural' rather than simply 'supranatural', although Jung never went that far. Dreams must inevitably utilise stored images in the brain of collective unconscious 'supranatural' contents, presumably passed on memetically,[302] which the Holy Spirit can utilise to communicate in a language suited to the cultural context of the prophet. This makes perfect sense to us as believers and contextual missiologists. In order for God's revealed messages to make sense to their recipients, they needed to be communicated in a culturally appropriate language using images that the prophets could convey to God's people.

---

[300] Adapted with kind permission from teaching material produced by Dr Mark Virkler.

[301] Supranatural, with *supra* coming from the Latin for 'above' is defined in Jungian terms to be a natural phenomenon rather than a supernaturally derived set of psychological contents of the human psyche, which originate as passed on archetypal memories from past generations as part of what he termed the collective unconscious. Archetypes are taken in Jungian terms to be archaic images which the brain has transmitted from generation to generation, perhaps on a genetic level similar to the ability of migrating birds being able to find their way to and from migration points without having been taught the routes by an earlier generation. A good example of an archetypal image is that of a mother figure appearing in a dream, which would possibly imply generativity, or something about to come to birth in a person's psyche. In Andy's doctoral research he considered dream states and their relationship to spiritual states of being among some case studies he did with Christians.

[302] A meme is thought of as a cultural memory that shapes our identities. It is passed on as part of cultural memory.

Visions

The distinction between dreams and visions might at first seem difficult to make. However, for the purposes of this study, we make a simple distinction. A revelatory dream is that which comes to a recipient when they are asleep. An example is Nebuchadnezzar's dream of a statue (Daniel 2:1-5). A vision may present with visual and auditory phenomena, just as in a dream. It occurs while the subject is in a waking state of consciousness. An example of this is John 's experience on the island of Patmos in Revelation 1. The most obvious point where John actually entered a visionary state is found in Revelation 4:1-2. He described himself as being 'in the Spirit' and seeing a door opened in heaven, and then he was transported in an ecstatic state of mind by the Spirit to behold the heavenly throne room.

A vision may be considered in exactly the same way as a dream might be, yet visual contents are viewed in a waking state. Hence, everything discussed for dreams could be claimed to apply to visions, as potential communications from the inspiration of God's Spirit.

Of course, there may be simple causes for dreams and hallucinations that have little to do with revelation from God. Hence we need to be careful to avoid the conclusion that every dream or vision is from God. What we argue is that just because some brain states may have simple natural explanations without any supernatural communication from God, it is not always the case.

We cannot go into the complex field of psychological states of mind in this short section, and their potential relationship to prophetic mysticism. At this stage our aims are simple, and we would counsel readers to find a good mentor who has much experience with spiritual disciplines of this kind, and who is known for their sound state of mind. We also have to be very careful not to encourage prophetic gifts for individuals if there is good evidence to suggest brain disease or psychotic illness. In these cases, expert medical attention must be sought.

Auditory phenomena

An auditory phenomenon is assumed to be a voice or a set of sounds exterior to the self, thought to be God's voice if no one is nearby to account for its articulation, and as long as there is no illness suspected that can account for it. Of course, there may be psychological and neurological states of mind which cause us to think we have heard a voice when in fact it was an auditory hallucination. Where we would differ from humanistic psychology at this point is to claim that Scripture calls us to take revelations from a real source beyond the self (ie God) to be possible and verifiable. We would counsel leaders to carefully consider the healthy functioning of those who may be spiritually gifted as prophets.

There is biblical evidence of key leaders in ancient Israel who were said to have heard God's voice while they were awake. There is a strong correspondence between Moses' reported experience of God at the burning bush and what he actually heard in a waking state. Moses had a seeming conversation with a real, non-embodied voice (Exodus 3:1-6). An example from the gospels is the voice of God heard at Jesus' baptism (Matthew 3:17).

We are well aware of claims that this sort of language is to be taken as symbolic rather than as a literal historical event. However, we do not accept that this is the only way to think about the use of this kind of language in Scripture, and we are happy to accept that these events really did happen and that the New Testament writers were reporting real memories. When Christ appeared to Paul on the road to Damascus, Paul and his companions saw the bright light and also heard the voice (Acts 9:1-7; 26:12-14). This would seem to suggest that a real physical presence produced the sound waves of the voice that was heard. Of course, this requires us to take the record of Paul's encounter with Christ as a non-mythological account.

Inner voice: pictures, 'video clips', ideas and personal prophecy

Old Testament scholar Chris Wright has done much to nuance the span of God's missional covenant through the Old and New Testament periods, as well as the prophetic passion found in the new covenant.[303] Theologian Scott suggests ways in which prophecy seems to operate in the Christian community.[304] There is also another reality which we have brought together as a category here, which relates to

---

[303] Wright, *The Mission of God*, Chapter 10.
[304] M. Scott, *Prophecy in the Church* (Australia, Word, 1992), Chapter 4.

prophecy. The voice of God may be experienced as a literal flow of words or ideas which come to the mind of the recipient while awake and conscious, in a spontaneous intuitive manner (eg Acts 10:19-20).

This may have been the experience of Habakkuk as he stood waiting on the ramparts of Jerusalem, having made his complaint to God regarding Yahweh's plan to use Babylon to bring His purposes for Israel to fulfilment through Nebuchadnezzar (Habakkuk 2:1-2). The reply that came from Yahweh seems to have been an inner voice, heard while Habakkuk was in a waking state.

What are termed 'words of knowledge' by many modern charismatic Christians may be thought of as an inner voice (1 Corinthians 12:8). This voice can be conversed with while in the conscious waking state (eg Revelation 1). We would assume that many of us experience this kind of phenomenon. Essentially, the book of Jonah offers an example, even if we regard it as a prophetic parable, where Jonah converses with Yahweh.

Moreover, tongues are often interpreted with a notable disclosure of things unknown about another person. Both writers have had verifiable experiences of this type of thing. These tongues are thought to become accessible to a congregation if someone has the gift to interpret the mysterious sounds.

Another category relates to inner visualised pictures, on the screen of the mind, so to speak (eg Acts 10:9-13). These are suggested to occur while the subject is in a waking, conscious state.[305] We would assume that many of us also experience these kinds of things as well. It is hard to give direct evidence of these as such (although Andy investigated reports of this in his doctoral research). This might be suggested in some of Ezekiel's visions, when he saw a plan of the future eschatological temple which was to be restored in the time of the returning remnant of Israel from the Babylonian captivity (Ezekiel 44:5-9). These pictures can be difficult to interpret unless God gives some sense of their meaning to the recipient.

---

[305] Jean-Jacques Suurmond, *Word and Spirit at Play* (London, SCM Press, 1994), Chapter 4.

Catalytic states of mind that can enable readiness to receive revelation knowledge

The biblical prophets appear to have had some basic approaches to catalyse the interface with the mystical prophetic voice. It is hard to be rigid in our claims here, as there is much that they did not report about how they prepared themselves to commune with God prophetically. However, there are some important hints that we may indicate.

Neuro-scientific literature supports a general thesis that there are ways to enable the brain to become more receptive to spiritual states of mind as well as altered states of consciousness. It is possible to deduce preparatory practices that prophets may have used, if we consider Scripture in general.

An example from among the minor prophets illustrates what was probably a popular way of preparing oneself to seek communication with the God of revelation knowledge. Habakkuk utilised four simple steps in order to hear God's voice. These 'Four Steps to appreciate the prophetic voice ' are based on Habakkuk 2:1-2. We acknowledge the spiritual theology of the Virklers, who also speak of four keys to hear God's voice.[306] Here is what Habakkuk did:

> I will stand at my watch
> and station myself on the ramparts;
> I will look to see what he will say to me,
> and what answer I am to give to this complaint.
> Then the LORD replied:
> 'Write down the revelation
> and make it plain on tablets
> so that a herald may run with it.'
> *Habakkuk 2:1-2 (NIV)*

In our own experiences we have had verifiable instances where things have come to our conscious minds which have brought us closer to God, because they have clearly come from a source beyond ourselves. Some colleagues have had precognitive revelations given to them of things that have happened afterwards, without them having taken discernible steps to cause them.

---

[306] Mark Virkler, *How to Hear God's Voice* (USA, Destiny Image, 2005), pp.12-43.

Keeping a dated journal can be an encouraging way of recording things God may have communicated to us intuitively. Essentially, the famous 'We' passages in the book of Acts are probably taken from Luke's travel journal when he accompanied Paul on mission (eg Acts 16:10).

The Semitic world of Jesus' time and earlier took spontaneous intuitions seriously, as either communications from God or at times as the work of evil spirits. Modern rational theology has tended to pour scorn on this idea. Perhaps modern Christians need to go back to receiving revelations that come as intuitions in order to verify the evidence for themselves. It will certainly help new believers to tune into the relational God of our Lord Jesus Christ, if we as disciples know how to recognise the authentic inner voice of God. Once again, we want to caution readers to consider mental health issues which less-stable individuals may develop if they are encouraged to explore this kind of spiritual practice.

The four steps are simple to practice as a spiritual discipline. According to Peter's speech in Acts, God wanted all categories of His people to be able to receive revelations from His Spirit:

'In the last days, God says,
I will pour out my Spirit on all people.
Your sons and daughters will prophesy,
your young men will see visions,
your old men will dream dreams.
Even on my servants, both men and women,
I will pour out my Spirit in those days,
and they will prophesy.
I will show wonders in the heavens above
and signs on the earth below,
blood and fire and billows of smoke.
The sun will be turned to darkness
and the moon to blood
before the coming of the great and glorious day of the
Lord.
And everyone who calls
on the name of the Lord will be saved.'
Acts 2:17-21, quoting Joel 2:28-32 (NIV)

Mostly, the ancient prophets seemed to receive visions that were accompanied by messages that helped to guide them or God's people. Hence we can assume that hearing God's voice often had visual data as part of its impartation. When Paul met Christ on the road to Damascus he saw a bright light and heard the voice of the Lord (Acts 9:1-9). Paul was then given the clear mission to take the gospel particularly to the Gentiles, throughout the Greco–Roman empire.

Paul clearly became accustomed to hearing the inner voice of the Spirit, as he talked of himself exercising prophecy and glossolalia to the Corinthian believers. If you read the passage on tongues and prophecy in 1 Corinthians 14, Paul clearly reminded the believers that the Spirit would be active in their worship gatherings, to bring those who did not believe to repentance and the recognition of God's reality for their lives.

Learning to hear God's voice, which was so normal for Paul and his contemporaries, is clearly closely connected to being able to engage in God's mission to save the whole world. For those of us raised in a more rationalistic and scientific age, some simple steps to help us focus on listening to God's voice will be helpful.

These are the four simple steps we want to recommend to help us hear the inner voice of the Spirit in order to appreciate the voice of God:

Step 1: Still your thoughts and feelings using calm worship music or stress-relief exercises. Become still and allow a space to develop inside your being. Choose a time and place where you will not be distracted. Relaxation techniques are very helpful to stimulate a relaxed frame of mind.

Step 2: Pray quietly to Jesus and wait for Him to spontaneously stimulate your intuitive self to receive ideas, pictures and imaginations. Ask Jesus to protect your time with Him and to quiet all other distractions and wrong influences.

Step 3: You may find that pictures, thoughts, ideas and feelings come into your mind spontaneously. Sometimes whole strings of ideas can come to us. Rather than trying to rationalise these at this point, suspend your critical faculty and just allow the flow of spontaneous thoughts and ideas to manifest themselves to your consciousness. Remember, God can protect you from negative influences. Once a thought or series of ideas seems to have stopped, you might want to ask a question. A good one might be, 'Lord what do want to say to me about what you have just communicated?' Then wait for an answer without trying to make one up or to force one to appear – remain relaxed. (If you find you feel deeply disturbed or destabilised on an inner level at this stage, desist immediately.)

Step 4: A good way to stay calm and focused during these times is to write, describe or draw what comes to you in your personal journal. This is a great way to help your analytical left brain capacity to be engaged while remaining inwardly still, in order to concentrate on what comes spontaneously and intuitively into your mind. You can always analyse your journal later, so don't worry about it right then. Finish with some prayer or praise and then move on to the day's activities.

This, of course, all sounds way too simple – even laughable. As critical theologians we understand rational theology very well, and it can and does clash with systematic theology and certain forms of critical reflective practical theology. We find that these other intellectual capacities and ideas help us to challenge our intuitions. It helps us to maintain what we feel is a healthy balance in our ministries. Scripture contains many examples of prophetic intuition, so it seems strange not to at least experiment to see whether it really brings sceptics closer to the Christ of spiritual experience.

From another point of view, this shows us how many wonderful Christian people we know personally who have embraced a rational theological faith, built on something that was felt at some time in their early Christian lives to have been a real connection with God, only to lose this sense for fear that they might be criticised later for fanaticism by critical academics with whom they work. Of course, we must be careful not to become deluded and believe that everything we experience in dreams or as intuitions is a direct message from God. Neither of us think this is the case, but we do believe God communicates by His Spirit with His people in order to guide the missional church to follow the *missio Trinitatis*. As Trinitarian theology emphasises the relational life that exists between the persons of the Trinity, it also provides the rationale for the person of the Holy Spirit to be the medium through whom the Trinity guides His people on earth. As mentioned in an earlier chapter, nomadic disciples follow the voice of Jesus as He continues His mission to reconcile the world to the Trinity's cosmic family. The Multicultural Trinity is actively seeking to unite people in multicultural missional communities and churches in the multicultural West.

Conclusions

It is important to be cautious with spiritual practices that encourage us to experiment with intuitive experiences. We have both found it very beneficial to be mentored by experienced, balanced people who have spent many years developing a variety of spiritual disciplines (prophecy being one part of a far bigger picture), such as the four-step practice suggested in this chapter. Most importantly, Newbigin's practical theology of mission would have the multicultural missional church actively seek to discern the guidance of the sovereign Spirit. This is vital for each of us to press forward in achieving so that we can engage in God's local mission for our congregations, as well as to help us inform our missional conversations through learning that comes from people conversing as members of the broad multicultural kingdom of God, as we intentionally seek to engage in the multicultural missional conversation together. We wonder what it would look if hundreds of multi-ethnic breakthrough congregations were planted in the West, made up of multiple cultures. What new kinds of richness might the missional Spirit of Jesus bring to the secular debate about the place of religion in the multicultural secular Western public square?

Group exercise

Take about 20 minutes to meditate on a piece of Scripture. Choose a passage that means a lot to you at the moment. Take the following steps.

- Before you start your meditative reading, find a comfortable chair and take a few minutes to relax with slow, meditative breathing.

- When you are feeling relaxed and attentive, read the Lord's Prayer and ask the Lord to be with you during this exercise.

- Read the passage at a pace which allows the words to sink into your consciousness. Try not to analyse the passage but rather ask the Spirit of God to speak to you as He wants to.

- Once you have finished your reading, allow a minute or two of silence. Ask God to quietly bring to your consciousness anything He wishes to draw to your attention. If it feels like something significant is repeating itself in your mind, or you feel a sense that God is speaking on a deeper level about something that captured your attention in the text, ask Him what He wants to say to you about this thing.

- If ideas, words or pictures come back to you, jot them down. Sometimes people have strings of ideas, pictures or feelings coming intuitively to their consciousness. Write, draw or describe what comes to you. Keep going with this process until it feels like it has stopped. Date your entry in your journal. End with prayer.

Chapter 10
The Challenges of Power Theology

In this chapter we will discuss the important area of power theology. For many, the idea that there is such a thing as a theology of power is new to them. The idea of power in a Christian context is often associated with power evangelism and power healing. In this belief system, what Jesus did as He went about delivering people from evil spirits and healing their illnesses is still to be part of the experience of the church and its ministry today. The writers have witnessed many great examples of how Christ is still active by His Spirit today to deliver and heal.

In this chapter, however, we are not talking about this kind of power theology. Rather, we want to consider how leaders and members and their outlooks on life can be shaped and influenced by a kind of power theology which is part of our deeply held beliefs. Put simply, we will be considering how people can use the power they have in church for good or for ill. We want to explore some of the challenges of power assumed by leaders which, from time to time, can be in danger of being used to abuse others without necessarily meaning for this to happen. Too often the way we use power over others is subconscious, and we need to look more critically at our own views of power, and how God exercises His power among us and through us to make sure we are not abusing the power we have over others.

What we mean by 'power theology' is the idea that we all have beliefs about how God uses His power and how He wants us to exercise that power in the way we relate to each other, whether as leaders, members of a church or part of a para-church missional organisation.

The writers have been involved in some wonderful movements of the Spirit in the past 30-odd years. We have witnessed the great benefits that an emphasis on God's power to deliver and heal people from disease and various kinds of oppression has brought to the churches. The renewed emphasis that the birth of Pentecostalism

271

brought with it, starting in the early twentieth century and focusing as it did on those great passages in Scripture that call us to look for the work of Christ to continue in healing and delivering people today, has thrilled us both.

Some of the key passages which remind us of Christ's call for His disciples to engage in a ministry of deliverance and healing like His are found in the gospels, in passages such as Matthew 10:1-6. When Jesus sent His 12 apostles out to engage in a ministry like His, He gave them authority over evil spirits and power to raise the dead and to heal. In Luke 10 we read about Jesus sending out 72 of His followers to engage in a similar ministry. John 14:12 records that Jesus said His followers would do greater works than He had Himself done in His earthly ministry. Many have been confused by this passage, but viewed in its context it makes perfect sense. The Holy Spirit, whom Jesus would send to guide His people, would only do what Jesus would do (John 16:12-16). What we believe Jesus meant in this passage was that the Spirit of Christ would continue to do the works of Christ throughout the gospel age. Moreover, as we saw earlier, in Peter's first sermon on the day of Pentecost, he reminded the crowd that the prophet Joel had promised a time of outpouring of the Spirit which would mean that signs, wonders and the works of God would accompany those who believe in Christ (Acts 2:5-39). The belief and conviction that many charismatic practising Christians hold dear is that the risen Christ is still active in these and many other ways today.

These convictions form some of the assumptions of what we would call a type of power theology. Not all Christian traditions interpret the passages we have just mentioned to mean that Christ is still active in deliverance and healing today to the extent that other charismatic and Pentecostal groups believe He is.

It is important to note that too often the media picks up on the worst kinds of stories where poor practices to do with exorcisms or the like are concerned. This is natural enough for a secular society that is suspicious of the abuse of power which leads to the neglect of individual rights. We must be careful to not turn a blind eye to potential abuses of power theology where there is a keen focus on deliverance and healing ministry. It is important to ensure that we engage in best practice when we pray for others, seeking to bring them to wholeness. To put it another way, we need to be vigilant to avoid making quick-fix decisions about helping people who may need more prolonged professional support and ministry to help them come to greater wholeness in their lives.

All of the above makes it vital for us to be careful not assume that our particular brand of power theology is suited in the same way to each new circumstance to which we seek to apply it. A person with a mental illness like schizophrenia will not respond very well to being told they have a demon that needs casting out if the cause of their condition is brain disease.

Having said this, what we are trying to do in this chapter is to explore how power can be abused in the church. It seems vital to us that we have a frank discussion about power abuse because we have both seen it happen from time to time, and the church does itself no good by denying such things. Moreover, if we are all to engage in conversation for the sake of the coming kingdom of God, we need to be aware of some of the challenges we all face in our use of power. The only being in the universe who can exercise power out of a motive of perfect love is God, and we all need to be reminded that as weak human beings we need to be aware of our limitations and temptations in the way we exercise the authority we have – especially as mature leaders in the church.

What we have discussed so far in this book relates to how different Christian churches can seek to work more closely with others by joining in with the multicultural missional conversation. We have recognised a number of challenges to doing this. We have also suggested some ways to help us overcome the obstacles that too often inhibit our efforts to persevere in getting to know each other better. We mentioned some of the bad press that some Pentecostal and charismatic churches have received regarding abuses of power in an earlier chapter. These abuses are most often focused on exorcism practices which have, in a few cases, ended with the death of a child. Having said this, we also recognise the wide range of news stories that have raised issues such as child abuse among a range of Western churches. Abuses that arise as a result of power theology are not a unique expression of any one churchmanship. We probably all hope that these kinds of cases are few and far between, but it does raise the issue of power theology and how it encodes the way we behave as we engage in spiritual warfare practices like exorcisms. It also raises the issue of the abuse of adult power over children and youth, which is an important justice issue.

It is notable that postmodern Westerners are very suspicious of belief systems that seem from their perspective to give leaders too much power which can be used to manipulate those for whom they are responsible. Moreover, power abuse is common enough in Westernised churches as well. In terms of Pentecostal and charismatic churches, part of public perception has to do with anxieties over the differences in the way power is distributed and exercised between, let us say, a Black African culture and a Western European one. Let us not forget either that white charismatic churches are also prone to power abuse if they are not careful. We want to focus on these matters before moving into an analysis of other types of power which can impede our efforts to work cross culturally in mission together.

There are numerous ethnic groups from the southern hemisphere who come from what cultural psychologists term 'high power distance cultures.'[307] These cultures believe that power needs to be vested in formal positions, and it leads to deference to people in higher positions in societal structures. These cultures are hierarchical in nature. There is exercise of high power and a creation of distance between those higher in the system compared to those lower down the chain. Such cultures tend to be collectivist – in other words, people identify themselves in terms of their rank and position in their society, and people know and accept their predefined positions, for the most part. African ethnic cultures can be predisposed towards high power distance culture, as can Asian and South American ones. The issue at this point is that migrant churches in the West often foster a form of leadership in their congregations that is based on the high power distance culture of their homeland, which they have imported with them to the West.

High power distance cultures are neither worse nor better than low power distance cultures which are typically found in the West (see below for discussion). Culture is broadly neutral, but what we do in our cultural frameworks can be either good or bad. Leaders in a

---

[307] Cardwell, Clark and Meldrum, *Psychology*, p.325.

culture which is high power distance can use their positions for good or ill. The structured hierarchical leadership system of this high power kind of culture can tend to motivate specific behaviours between leaders and those they lead.

In one BMC group we are aware of, the leader is treated with reverence, respect and a degree of awe by his members. He is considered to be the man of God in a special sense. Members give him gifts of money, goods and services in order to show respect to him. His word is final when it comes to settling matters, although it is evident he takes his time to listen carefully to the different perspectives when big community decisions are involved. When he preaches, his messages are treated as significant and as the word of God to His people. He has younger men who follow him and provide him with support, caring for many of his personal needs. Some of them have specific roles to support his ministry. They work hard to maintain his respect and to do what he asks of them.

This example is typical of some BMC congregations. It is a good example of how high power distance cultures can influence the way leadership is exercised in a church. We are not criticising this form of leadership, although it is very different from the way our own native Western culture has shaped us to exercise leadership. The point is to highlight a significant difference of how power is exercised in most Western cultures compared to non-Western cultures. These differences in how power is used and perceived can make it hard for Westerners and non-Westerners to work together in cross-cultural missional collaborations if they are not understood and addressed.

Western culture tends to be 'low power distance'. Low power distance cultures do not respect hierarchical structures to the same degree as high power distance cultures do. Power is only exercised from higher up a system if it is absolutely necessary, otherwise the rights of individuals are maintained to enable them to make choices and to seek their own individual rights. Distance and power are not emphasised, so that all may be considered to be equal. Western cultures tend to be more individualistic in nature, and there is an assumption that everyone has a right to their own opinion and to be respected for who they are.

Anglo churches most often tend to be based on low power distance culture. The leader is held to account by the people he or she leads. Leaders find it harder to win respect in more individualist congregations because they hold their positions by proving themselves capable of leading their churches and paying due deference to the individuals within them. In other words, Western culture tends to focus on leaders serving the needs of the people in their churches rather than the people paying deference to the leaders as in some way superior to them. Power is shared, and there is normally not an emphasis on the power of the leader because of his or her position. Particularly in Protestant and evangelical churches, decisions are made based on democratic principles. This kind of congregational leadership approach is based on a flat structure more than a hierarchical one. Leadership occurs by consensus most of the time. This is less the case in some ecclesiastical traditions like Roman Catholicism, where the priest has certain powers not permitted to the laity. To a slightly lesser extent, this could be said of the high Anglican Church as well.

It is also worth noting that low power distance Western cultures have arisen out of the worldview of the Enlightenment and humanism. In a secular society, where God is no longer at the centre of the worldview, the rights of the individual to autonomy and to do what they want with their own lives is the biggest priority to live by. This tends to lead to a sense of distrust of authority structures and concerns about religious groups that claim the right to ask obedience of their followers. Probably the largest problem with low power distance cultures is the unwillingness of people to live in obedience to God or the laws of the land if they conflict with their own value systems. In the West there is much we can learn from the far greater respect that is given to authority structures in high power distance cultures.

That said, it must not be forgotten that the West is built on a low power distance culture, and non-Westerners will struggle to engage with Western people if they do not seek to contextually engage with them in these cultures – and conversely, Westerners will not be able to appreciate the values and behaviours of non-Westerners from high power distance cultures unless they can form friendships with people from them.

Having said all this, it has hopefully become clear that there are significant differences between the leadership ethos of high and low power distance cultures. The practical outworkings of our theology of power and who is permitted to exercise it is significantly affected by cultural pre-programming, through nurture from our childhood years. It will be hard to find the right leadership approach if people from high power and low power distance cultures try to work more closely together in missional ventures. It will be even harder to plant a multi-ethnic congregation made up of people from these two different kinds of culture. For example, what sort of leadership style would be needed? Would it need to be high or low power distance? Difficulties would inevitably crop up as a result of different expectations from the different types of power cultures. In turn, differences of this type could lead to cross-cultural conflicts, unless a lot of hard work is put into helping people understand their different expectations. And it would be important from the start to consider whether it is possible to work more closely with people from these different cultures. We would have to evaluate the willingness of participants to work together through their differing cultural expectations of others, if there is to be a good chance of forming cross-cultural missional alliances.

For example, the decision as to who is permitted to exercise power in some African cultures has to do with patriarchy. African culture, in general terms, has a more ancient patriarchal cultural system. In such cultures, the power is passed down the male line. These are known as patrilineal cultures. Much more is assumed in patrilineal cultures, such as stratified levels of power assumed in tribes or clans. Those who have a lineage traceable to a chief, king or nobility will be considered to deserve greater power than those with a lesser lineage. This view of inherited power is still part of the cultural memory of African people who trace their roots back to their founding fathers.

We must be careful not to overplay this observation, but believe it would be fair to say that BMCs tend to have strong cultural memories of patriarchy, which lead them to honour highly those with a high lineage who lead them. This draws on some strong cultural sources from their homelands, and the power of the cultural memories underpinning them must not be underestimated. Patriarchy can influence how power is exercised in these churches.

Matriarchal power systems are not so evident in non-Western congregations. However, some cultures are matrilineal, where the family name is passed down the female line. Black female power theology values strong matriarchy in its cultural DNA, and women of power are revered as strong women of God on whom other women should model their lives. Black male leaders have to contend with this kind of power theology, and it is a significant voice found particularly in BMCs.

We need to be aware of these forces so that we can work more sensitively with our brothers and sisters in these churches. We would also do well to examine our own culture. Who are our role models? Let us not forget that Paul called on Christians in his time to imitate his life (1 Corinthians 4:16).

What it is important to explore next is the suggestion that these two kinds of cultures produce their own practical theologies of power. Following the question of cultural power theology will be the question of the differences between a spiritual worldview and a secular worldview, and the views of power or the powers that underpin them. Then we will consider how theologies of power can produce different abuses of power which need to be adjusted by a more rounded biblical picture of how God exercises power. Finally, consideration will be given to how we might work cross culturally with postmodern secular people by providing a new hermeneutic for how our missional congregations exercise their use of power when they relate with each other.

Practical power theology and cultural influences

Walter Wink, one of the pre-eminent scholars of power theology, provided useful views to help us think through the issues of power theology in the light of the ancient worldview compared to the modern worldview.[308] His work may help us all to think through the differences in power theology that come from our cultural differences. Our culture affects our Christian beliefs. We have already considered an example of this related to high and low power distance cultures.

---

[308] Wink, *Naming the Powers*, pp.10-22; Wink, *Engaging the Powers*, pp.24-46; Wink, *Unmasking the Powers*, pp.7-23.

The ways in which our particular cultures shape the structures of the societies we come from also help us to structure our beliefs about the norms and values that we should use to shape our lives.

The culture of the early Christians was in the first place based on Jewish traditions. As the gospel spread to the Gentiles, the Greco-Roman culture had an impact on what the norms and values of the Christian faith should be. It is broadly correct to note that both the Jewish and the Greco-Roman cultures were high power distance. Kings, nobles, rulers, governors and so on were distanced from the ordinary people. People expected to treat their rulers with deference and obedience, which usually meant they had to accept their allotted statuses and places in the social hierarchy. Jesus Himself called His disciples to consider the implications of what His actions as their Lord and Master had on the way they should treat each other (John 13:12-17). The kingdom of God, to some significant degree, assumed that God and His Christ have authority and power over those who are part of Their dominion. We have already noted that Jesus transformed the concept of lordship and power to mean service. However, there was still an assumption by the people of the Jewish and Gentile Christian Greco-Roman cultures that God had the right to expect their obedience, and that to be disobedient could incur His disfavour. Hence the early church came out of a general cultural milieu that was high power distance in terms of the norms and values of that period. Having said this, we will consider how Christ transformed power theology for His followers to something different from the abuse of power by some earthly kings of His time.

A classic example from Scripture regarding the relationship between key beliefs and cultural differences is the conflict that arose between Jews who had accepted Jesus as their Messiah and Gentiles who were not ethnically privileged to be part of the chosen people. The conflict found its epicentre in the question of circumcision. Circumcision was a symbol for the Jews that they were part of the covenant people whom God had miraculously established through Abraham their forefather. The Jewish argument was that Gentiles should do more to become Christ's people than simply have faith in Him: they needed to also be circumcised as a sign that they were accepting the Jewish way of life, which inevitably would include

Torah observance, keeping the festivals and observing the Sabbath. Obedience to the Torah was to be taken by God as a sign of fidelity. Circumcision was more than a simple cutting of the foreskin; it also included the promise to observe the whole Torah. Paul made the case that before Abraham was circumcised, God reckoned him to be in right relationship with Him based on his trust in God (Galatians 3:6-9). In like manner, it should have been enough for Gentiles who had the same sort of faith as Abraham to be included as the people of Christ without being circumcised (Galatians 3:14). Paul stressed that the Torah was no longer the means on which followers of Christ should base their lives (Galatians 4:1-7). The theological implications of this are still significant areas of debate.

The writer of Acts explained to his readers that Paul went to the synagogue on the Sabbath as it was one of his Jewish customs (Acts 17:2). That he felt it necessary to explain this 'custom' shows that Sabbath keeping had ceased for Gentiles by that time. 'Customs' are part of the traditions that form our cultures. The book of Acts suggests that the Christians of the first century had already abandoned the cultural norms and values of Torah observance by the time it was written – between 62 and the 90s AD.

It is enough at this point to suggest that much of biblical testimony is based on cultural norms and values which are not as such the key tenets to the Christian faith. Paul considered the atoning death of Christ to be central to his theology of forgiveness, as was the theology of the resurrection to the Christian hope of eternal life (Romans 6:23). Faithfulness was demonstrated by the development of the fruit of the Spirit and by the confession of Jesus as Lord (Galatians 5:22-26; 1 Corinthians 12:13). The complications of Jewish Torah lifestyle were considered to be of cultural value to Jews but not binding on Gentile converts.

If this kind of assumption is made about the simplicity of the gospel of Christ, then the absolutes of the Christian faith are far fewer than we might expect them to be. At this stage we cannot develop this line of thinking and it will have to be left to the reader to explore this further. However, if we accept that being a disciple of Christ is based on becoming like Him in terms of the qualities He exemplified, as well as faithfully following Him as He leads us, there is much scope to allow the Spirit of Christ to guide our Christian communities to engage in God's mission. The incarnate Christ respects culture, and His Spirit can empower us to form our missional churches so that they can be relevant to different cultures that we find in the multicultural West.

Obviously, though, not everything about culture is neutral, and some of it needs to be transformed by Christ. What we believe is important for differing ethnic Christians in our multicultural Western society is to allow themselves to be open-minded to how our cultural pre-programming tends to bias our interpretations of Scripture.

If we are to learn to fellowship intentionally together, we will need to discuss more openly our differences of interpretation of Scripture. Within the context of our different assumptions about how power is exercised in the approaches we take to working together in mission, it will be important to seek common ground which will help us to avoid potential conflicts. We might find it helpful to use some of the reflective practices suggested earlier in this book to help us to do this.

The ancient vs the secular worldview

There are notably differences of worldview between many non-Western and Western Christians. It is important that we consider these differences as they relate to the views we have about the sources of spiritual power and authority which we call on to justify the actions we take in our churches. In Wink's later theology of power, he identified five spiritual power theologies:

- the ancient worldview

- the spiritualist worldview

- the materialist worldview

- the theological worldview

- the integral worldview.[309]

Cultural anthropologists will probably agree that many non-Western Christians have come to the West from what we might call pre-modern cultures, although globalisation is rapidly changing this

---

[309] Wink, *The Powers that Be*, chapter 2, pp15-19.

reality.[310] A pre-modern culture is one that does not share the Enlightenment and rationalistic worldview. The spiritual outlooks of pre-modern cultures tend to resonate the most with Wink's concept of the 'ancient worldview':

> This is the worldview reflected in the Bible. In this conception, everything earthly has its heavenly counterpart, and everything heavenly has its earthly counterpart. Every event is the combination of both dimensions of reality. If war begins on earth, then there must be, at the same time, war in heaven between the angels of the nations in the heavenly council. Likewise, events initiated in heaven are mirrored on earth. This is a symbolic way of saying that every material reality has a spiritual dimension, and every spiritual reality has physical consequences. There can be no event or entity that does not consist, simultaneously, of the visible and the invisible.[311]

This worldview describes that of many non-Western congregations living in the West. Scripture assumes that the visible earthly challenges and opportunities that believers face have spiritual entities behind them. It is not hard to see how non-Western believers find support for their own worldviews based on their charismatic theologies. Pentecostal Christians who see the world in this way recognise that being part of the kingdom of God means that there will inevitably be conflict with evil forces.[312] According to this worldview, positive opportunities come from God and the negative challenges of illnesses, oppressive social or political circumstances come from the devil and evil angels. All visible reality in this world is engaged in an ongoing cosmic conflict with good and evil forces, which are thought to drive earthly events behind the scenes. This worldview is particularly strong within NPCs (Neo-Pentecostal churches) and some Asian churches. Charismatic Westerners often subscribe to much of this worldview too,

---

[310] Haralambos and Holborn, *Sociology*, p.200.

[311] *Wink, The Powers that Be*, p.15.

[312] Clinton Arnold, *3 Crucial Questions about Spiritual Warfare* (Grand Rapids, Baker Academic, 2008), p.19.

although they carry much of the materialistic worldview with them as well.

It would be too simplistic to claim that all Westernised Christians (or non-Christians) share a simply defined worldview. The materialist worldview, the theological worldview or the integral worldview may draw aspects of their outlooks on God's place and work in the visible and invisible world. However, the materialist worldview still has a powerful influence on Western imagination. Wink defines it:

> This view became prominent during the Enlightenment, but is as old as Democritus (who died about 370 B.C.E.). In many ways it is the antithesis of the world-rejection of spiritualism. The materialist view claims that there is no heaven, no spiritual world, no God, no soul; nothing but what can be known through the five senses and reason. The spiritual world is an illusion.[313]

It is obvious enough that Western Christians do not subscribe to the extremes of materialist philosophy, but the impact of materialism on their thinking must not be underestimated. Generally speaking, the mainline denominations in the West do not subscribe to the ancient worldview to the degree that many non-Western Christians do. It is important to note that not all BMCs have a Pentecostal background. Those who don't will have more in common with the mainline Western denominations.

We particularly need to focus on Pentecostal BMCs and NPCs at this point. Western Christians tend to be less suspicious about the power of evil spirits and the devil over their experiences in the visible world. They have a greater tendency to look for scientific and rational explanations.

The difference in outlook between Westerners and non-Westerners on the power of evil spirits is one area of potential conflict which could stop these groups successfully working together in missional endeavours. Practical theologians McSwain and Treadwell formulated a set of strategies to help churches of just one cultural group overcome

---

[313] Wink, *The Powers that Be*, p.17.

conflicts.[314] Power theology differs between Westerners and non-Westerners, so if we are to work more closely together we need to develop some conflict resolution strategies to help us understand and resolve our differences.

Probably the largest difficulty that native Westerners – both Christian and non-Christian – will have has to do with the spiritual warfare practices exercised by many non-Western Christians. The greater regularity with which these churches identify and deal with demonic oppression and exorcisms is a cause of concern to many Western church leaders. Moreover, the degree of perceived power that prophets and leaders have in Pentecostal ethnic churches and Western charismatic churches is often considered to be fanatical, if not downright misguided. These kinds of judgements are very real, but they are often gross over-reactions to perceived differences rather than real differences.

The popular writer Devenish discusses the need to overcome the power of cultural strongholds that cause people to develop superior attitudes when comparing their own cultures to others.[315] His observations are to be welcomed if we are to work more closely together.

It would be too easy at this stage to assume that we are criticising Pentecostal groups because we are Western church leaders. However, this is not the purpose of identifying our worldview differences. On the one hand, it can be argued that Christians who frame their beliefs with reference to the ancient worldview are more true to the biblical worldview than more materialistic Western outlooks allow for. However, on the other hand, Western Christians tend to think that there is a lack of criticality exercised by Pentecostal and charismatic Christians about the degree of influence of evil forces. In this case, a critical reflective approach to assessing how believers should seek to engage with and overcome temptations or oppression is thought to protect people from potential abuse. Moreover, many Western Christians argue that God has provided the West with wealth and an

---

[314] Larry McSwain and William Treadwell, *Conflict Ministry in the Church* (Nashville, Broadman Press, 1981), pp.12-30.

[315] David Devenish, *Demolishing Strongholds: Effective Strategies for Spiritual Warfare* (Milton Keynes, Authentic, 2005), p.16.

abundance of scientific medical knowledge in order to do away with much of the need for people to seek miraculous healing. We would argue that there is merit in both perspectives that we all can learn from as we engage in the multicultural missional conversation.

Enlightenment materialism and rationalism still does much to define the outlooks of postmodern people. It is true that there is more openness to a variety of spiritual experiences, including interest in the supernatural in television programmes. Moreover, there is more openness to rational explanations concerning the meaning of life and the place of science in how we explain and address the challenges of modern life. Non-Westerners bring the ancient worldview that causes them to recognise the need to engage the powers of secularism and postmodernism on a spiritual level too often forgotten by Westerners.

The missiologist Wagner identified the need for Christians to pray for the power of God's kingdom to overcome the forces of godlessness and evil. He spoke of the need to engage in Strategic Level Spiritual Warfare (SLSW) prayer.[316] If we are to learn from this approach to overcome the powers behind postmodernism, we will need to be careful how visibly we do this: secular people will not welcome overt and visible use of SLSW when we build friendships with them for missional purposes.

The greatest concerns of postmodern people are likely to concern perceived fundamentalism, where a particular Pentecostal power theology assumes that people with whom they work need to become recipients of their ministry and to subject themselves to their leaders. Any claims by black or white Pentecostal charismatic leaders to have authority to deliver postmodern people from evil forces would probably be viewed with great distaste because of the general lack of confidence that they have in absolute claims to authority or the exercising of it. This is a very important insight to bring into the missional conversation with non-Westerners, in order to help them to adapt their practices if we are to work together and obtain a hearing.

---

[316] Wagner, *Warfare Prayer*, pp.161-180.

Domination systems and the dominion of the kingdom of God

It is correct to suggest that every person in this world is subject to some level of domination being exercised over their life. Governments establish policies which dictate how our economies function, how laws are constituted and defined, what parents must do to educate their children, the requirement to pay taxes and the requirement to perform services to employers for payment. From childhood we are indoctrinated and socialised to accept and cooperate with dominant systems which require behaviours of submission.

Wink had a highly developed theology of how domination systems work and their influence on our views of how God's kingdom exercises power on believers' lives. We cannot do justice to his theology in a short section, but we will consider an example which will help us to grasp a little of Wink's theology of power.

Stated as simply as possible, every human being is indoctrinated into accepting the rights of society to exercise authority over them. Within mature democracies, particularly, there are strong ethical guidelines enshrined in laws to protect society from the abuses of power. Because human beings can never be claimed to exercise power over others for purely unselfish reasons, it is open to abuse in some societies that do not have mature protective structures in place or where these structures break down. The height of this selfishness is seen when totalitarian regimes give power to one group at the expense of others who are weaker.

Abuse of power can manifest itself in numerous ways. Obviously the Holocaust is a terrible testament to the abuse of power, with six million Jews murdered under the Nazi regime. The genocides that happened in Rwanda and in the former Yugoslavia are also part of the horrifying reality of the abuse of power over others. The recent death of Nelson Mandela reminds us all of the sacrifices that those who seek justice for the downtrodden have to make. His long imprisonment and then his broadly gracious rise to power after his release did not find him taking revenge on those who had imprisoned and persecuted him.

These examples are extreme, but palpable enough to show that the modern world has not overcome the basic forces of selfishness that lead to the abuse of power.[317] Figures like Mandela, Gandhi and Christ Himself are strong examples of men who did not waver and who did not use their power to harm those who sought to harm them. Often the extermination of one people group or minority group has been justified as a necessary sacrifice because of perceived wrongs that the victims have done to the regime that persecutes them.

However, the kingdom of God is based on another kind of use of power. This means that we as subjects of this kingdom need to base our fellowship on different principles. Kingdom authority is based on the power of God's love, defined in the death of Jesus on the cross as sacrifice for the sake of others (1 John 4:9-10). Jesus spoke of this type of love, which puts the good of the other before itself as the basis of the Christian lifestyle (1 Corinthians 12:27-31). Christ led the way by denying Himself and taking up His cross of self-sacrifice. He calls His followers to do likewise (Luke 9:23). Jesus as the representative human being sets the example of how to exercise the power of leadership.

We are essentially talking of servant leadership, which puts others ahead of ourselves (Philippians 2:7). This is, of course, open to abuse in the Christian community unless each member puts the needs of others before themselves. The practical implications of putting others first will mean that we look after each other's needs through acts of loving service. Missional leaders as servants seek to equip those they lead to serve others, from the starting point of using the gifts they have from God to help others. Such leaders need to lead by example as they seek to serve the community. Simply stated, the reign of God is based on gift-love, which can be defined as sacrificial service exercised by all the people in the Christian community out of love for God and others. This love cannot be limited to just the people in the church, as the missionary God exercises His love to all people and seeks His lost sheep ahead of the church in every possible segment of secular society. This becomes a very subversive antidote to the other forms of power, which in itself is uniquely attractional and motivational.

This language of servanthood is obviously idealistic, and in reality it is not always possible for everyone in the church to give equal

---

[317] Paul Beasley-Murray, *Power for God's Sake: Power and Abuse in the Local Church* (Milton Keynes, Paternoster, 1998), pp.1-12.

amounts of service at all times. However, it remains to aspire to the principle of love in an imperfect world which awaits the final establishment of the new heaven and new earth where the ideal will become real. It is Christ who is the model person who gives us everything as a gift of sacrificial grace, and keeps the principle of service at the centre of the beliefs and practices of our communities. When it becomes part of the genuine fabric of our souls, the power of this kind of love, shaped within us by the example of Christ, will be a compelling testimony to the power of the gospel to unite people.

This view of how the example of Christ transforms us to support each other obviously requires that people commit themselves to becoming more like Christ every day. It also requires a lot of patience and forgiveness when we are let down by others, or when we let them down. This commitment to model our lives on sacrifice and service reshapes the way communities can live together more harmoniously. It also requires tolerant and sacrificial love towards those we find it hardest to love, especially when they are culturally very different from us. In order for diverse Christian groups to work together as part of the multicultural missional conversation, the mind of the humble Christ needs to be developed in our efforts to fellowship with each other. It is at the points of greatest strain that the love of Christ needs to be sought, or our efforts to work together will be fraught with disappointment and failure. The kind of gift-love that Christ exercised in His ministry can only come into our lives by supernatural infusion. Like salvation and life itself, it is a gift, not a product that is ours to generate or create for ourselves.

Conclusions

A practical theology of power has to be based on the model of Christ's sacrificial love. However, the example of Christ is not enough in and of itself. It is vital for the Christian community to keep seeking deeper intimacy with the Christ who lives in the hearts of each of us to enable Him to provide us with the power of His gift-love to transform the way we live with cultural diversity. This infuses love and commitment for us to be able to treat each other as Christ treats us by His all-encompassing grace. This kind of power theology needs to come from a connected intimacy with the Christ who lives in our hearts by faith (Ephesians 3:17). It requires a new kind of spiritual formation based on the power of the love bond of God, who is the Holy Spirit, sent into every heart that welcomes Him.

If we wish to plant multi-ethnic breakthrough congregations together, this kind of spiritual power theology will need to be central to their formation. The kinds of leaders who can help form these kinds of communities have to be willing to be the first to offer service to others, rather than exercising their power and position to make things happen as they want them to occur.

Paul's analogy of the body of Christ is very informative here as we consider the place of each person in the Christian community (Ephesians 1:23). Each of us is to be a vital contributor to the continuing shaping and formation of Christ in one another in the body of Christ – not because any one individual is more precious than another, but because we all need each other to help form the whole missional body of Christ as described by Paul in 1 Corinthians 12:27-31. The body of Christ in Paul's thought is not an individual who stands alone, but it is all believers who look after each other and are far less rounded if they try to stand alone. Left to ourselves, we do not have all the resources to sustain our Christian lives (1 Corinthians 12:12, 13). It is only as we give and receive service from others, based on love and trust in them, that we receive the resources of the whole ministry of the body of Christ.

This wholeness must never be assumed to be more the possession of leaders and less that of members. Rather, we all need to equip each other to become more whole as Christ pours His gift-love out through each of us. We need each other in the kind of body fellowship described so well by Paul in 1 Corinthians 12–14. People with strengths in one area will be weak in others, and in these, others who are stronger will be able to provide for the strengthening of the weaker. Christ's kingdom keeps on coming as he brings the whole of His body to fullness as He pours out different gifts which, when they are exercised in love towards each member in the body, make up the fullness of the healthy functioning body of Christ (Ephesians 4:10-16).

All members of the body of Christ are essential to representing the fullness of Christ to those who as yet are to join their fellowship, and no one is more important or more deserving of special reverence than any other member of the body is. All of us are vital to the full representation of Jesus to the world that looks on. The body of Christ which functions in this way exercises the power of Christ's sacrificial love, which will be a witness to those outside of the church who will notice the difference that gift-love makes to a community. We believe this is infectious, and provides the narrative for those who do not believe in Christ as yet to come to join with us to experience the love of Christ in action as it is poured out through each of us to the world around us.

Reflective exercise

Take a few minutes to reflect on the following questions.

- What is your theology of power?

- What is your church's theology of power?

- What areas of abuse of power can you identify in how others are treated?

- How is power abused in your church (even in unconscious ways)?

- How is power used well in your church?

- How does the concept of grace effect and affect the way power is practically used in your life and in the life of your church?

- What has challenged you in this chapter and why?

- What could you or your church do differently in the way power is exercised in the light of this chapter?

- What steps need to be taken to address abuses or misuses of power in your church?

Comments

Chapter 11
Religious Pluralism and Mission

August Comte, the French functionalist sociologist, formulated an interesting perspective on the development of secular society. It is important to understand his ideas because they have influenced thinking about the so-called secularisation thesis, which we will explore a little more below. He argued (published 1830–42) that history passes through three phases which change people's religious values in the context of the driving forces of each stage.[318]

He conceived firstly of a theological stage where religious and superstitious beliefs tend to dominate the imaginations of people in society. However, with developments in thought and education and exposure to other cultures, the power of these superstitions is weakened as societies evolve, leading to a metaphysical stage. In this stage, philosophical thought plays a larger role in forming beliefs and opinions and consequently leads to the questioning of received superstitions and traditions. Doubts also increase regarding the reliability of one system of belief compared to another.

A third stage, which comes to dominate over time – termed the 'positive stage' by Comte – has to do with science and rational thought. Science and reason come to dominate the outlooks of people in societies, thus removing their need to turn to superstition or religion for explanations of life. During this stage, what were once thought of as forces beyond the understanding and control of human beings come to be understood from a naturalistic point of view. The laws that govern these natural forces of nature can be manipulated and controlled much better through human science.[319] In this third phase, Comte argued, people no longer need gods or religion to help them cope with the difficulties of life because they feel in control of the forces they once feared as capricious gods or demons working against them. In an almost classical sense, Comte developed the basic rationale for the so-called secularisation thesis.

---

[318] Auguste Comte, *The Positive Philosophy*, (London, Bell & Sons, 1986).
[319] Haralambos and Holborn, *Sociology*, pp.429-430.

This thesis suggests that as society becomes more enlightened and scientific in its outlook, people no longer need to form beliefs that focus their attention on divine beings for answers to their troubles. Others have thought differently. The sociologist Durkheim did not agree that secularisation means the complete cessation of the significance of religious beliefs but rather that fewer people would adhere to them. Sociologist Max Weber predicted a progressive reduction in the scale of the importance of religion to society, whereas the communist philosopher Marx suggested that capitalist societies tend to promote the significance of religion. This is caused by the inequalities these societies produce, making religion the opiate of the people to help them cope with their lower status.[320]

European nations have particularly witnessed a rapid and alarming decline in church attendance. This began with the Great War, and has been particularly evident since the end of the Second World War.[321] It is hard to judge how radical the decline has been throughout the West, but some European nation states have gone as low as about 3% of the population attending church, whereas the figure is about 8–10% in the UK, depending which statistics are consulted.[322] Christian leaders and missiologists who focus on mission in the Western hemisphere would almost certainly agree in general terms that the importance of official religions has decreased in line particularly with Durkheim's predictions. However, the question we need to start by asking in this chapter on Christian mission to Westerners is whether official religious affiliation to a church is actually the best measure of the spiritual beliefs of people in society. Moreover, what alternatives to attending formal religious services do postmodern people consider to be meaningful? How do they alternatively express their faith or devotion to a higher power if not in established religious settings? These questions are crucial to consider when thinking about joining in the multicultural missional conversation regarding sharing the gospel with non-religious groups, ie secularised and postmodern people.

---

[320] Haralambos and Holborn, *Sociology*, p.430.
[321] Martin Robinson, *Winning Hearts, Changing Minds*, p.58-75.
[322] See the statistics mentioned in chapter 1.

After all, it is important to note that postmodern people do not find religion attractive.[323]

Religious pluralism is a recognised facet of Western society, as is the greater acceptance by younger people of multiculturalism as a normal part of living in our diverse free Western democracies. American missiologist Garces-Foley comments on the reasons for this more accepting outlook in terms of her research in the US, but her comments are equally true for the most part for British society:

> American attitudes toward diversity have changed dramatically in the last fifty years, but not uniformly. Among young, urban, college-educated Americans, a 'cosmopolitan ethos' is particularly apparent. I attribute this to the combination of being educated in the ideology of multiculturalism and being surrounded by diversity during formative years in urban environments. The insistence on embracing diversity in the schools and in the culture at large has instilled in these young people a high value for diversity. When young adults join churches, they look for congregations that reflect the diversity in which they live, work, and go to school. Multi-ethnic churches do not seem countercultural to these young people who have been reared in diverse settings, but within the larger United States few voluntary institutions have managed to create inclusive communities across ethnic boundaries.[324]

It is not hard to agree with much of what Garces-Foley says here. Young people engaged in multicultural schools and urban environments in a number of UK cities and towns consider multicultural diversity to be normal. Where there is a real difference is in her comments about what 'these young people' look for when they go to church in the UK compared to her studies in the US. Probably just under 50% of Americans go to church, and there are therefore higher numbers of young adults raised as believers who assume

[323] Stanley Grenz, *A Primer on Postmodernism* (Cambridge, Eerdmans, 1996), pp.72, 73.
[324] Garces-Foley, *Crossing the Ethnic Divide*, p.11.

church-going is normal,[325] which then leads them to seek out multi-ethnic churches that value multicultural diversity when they leave home. Churches in the UK struggle, like the 'voluntary institutions' in the US do, to 'create inclusive communities across ethnic boundaries'. Garces-Foley's research was carried out in New York and has provided her with good examples of multi-ethnic churches that do attract young people who welcome diversity.

The question of what it will take to reach the 40% of our population of Generations X and Y who have never been to church has to take into account the UK's more advanced decline in church attendance by parents and therefore their young people. Moreover, 1,000 fewer children aged 10–12 attend church every week with their parents. This decrease has remained constant for the last 30 years.[326] So, in the first place, the majority of young people who have never attended church regularly, or at all, do not consider church attendance to be normal. In the second place, the 10–12-year-olds who are no longer going to church with parents who go regularly undermines Garces-Foley's thesis in terms of available numbers of young people who may look for multicultural churches in Europe. This deficit in numbers means that the practice of worshipping regularly in a church has not been passed on to the majority of Generations X and Y in the UK and much of Europe.

Having said this, secular young people in the UK are similar to their peers in the US as they, too, are being shaped to welcome diversity. Perhaps successful mission ventures that welcome diversity as part of their outreach strategies will create a contextual bridge that will attract younger adults of this type, who value communities that welcome multicultural diversity. This may provide us with a strong argument for forming the missional practices of newly planted multi-ethnic breakthrough congregations that seek to provide environments which welcome diverse peoples. In this respect, multicultural breakthrough missional groups may perform a service that first-

---

[325] However, this seems to be rapidly changing. See David Kinnamann, *Unchristian: What a New Generation Thinks About Christianity, and Why It Matters* (Grand Rapids, Baker Books, 2007), pp.13-40.
[326] Peter Brierley, *Reaching and Keeping Tweenagers: Analysis of the 2001 RAKES survey* (London, Christian Research, 2002), p.3-4.

century Jewish synagogues offered. These synagogues often welcomed people in order to dialogue about the Jewish faith (see Acts 18:4). Indeed, many Gentile proselytes of this era would have been shaped to some significant extent by these opportunities of dialogue. It is noticeable that community churches that open their doors to local people for activities like mother and toddler groups, pensioners' groups, cafe services, dance groups, youth clubs, etc tend to promote opportunities for dialogue .

Having said this, it is noticeable that religious services are not attractive to those who have never attended them. The word 'religion' has a bad press with many young people, who associate it with a restrictive and boring pursuit that strange people with old-fashioned beliefs do together, or more recently with fear where religious abuses have taken place. This has certainly been our experience, having worked around young people who have never attended church. Native secular Western young people are very different to migrant young people, whose Christian cultures see the majority of them attending first- and second-generation ethnic churches.

This difference makes it hard for migrant parents to understand Western culture, where the majority of young adults have no experience of church life. This is a challenge we need to discuss together if we are to successfully engage in missional partnerships, where new approaches can be imagined into being which will help ethnic churches to fulfil their desires to bring Western converts into their religious services to learn about Christ.

The difficulty in this case has to do with the acceptance of religion as a normal part of many ethnic cultures outside the West. People in non-Western societies expect to participate in religious services and festivals. How will non-Western Christians bridge the gap with Westerners who lack affinity with religion? Young Westernised adults do not generally find church services appealing, hence it may be better to think of ways to plant multi-ethnic community groups that welcome diversity, where friendships can develop outside of formal religious services.

The move from religion to experience and friendship

Religion in the West, particularly for those under the age of 35, is a distant to non-existent memory of yesteryear. However, interest in the spiritual and supernatural is on the increase among many in Generation Y. The Pentecostal theologian Gordon Fee made the important observation that current postmodern society is similar in some aspects to the first-century Greco-Roman world. This gives him reason for hope, even though he recognises that secular culture has largely disavowed itself from its Christian roots:

> But there is reason for hope as well since contemporary postmodernism looks much like the culture of the Greco-Roman world into which the gospel first appeared some two thousand years ago. The secret of the success of the early believers in their culture lay first with their 'good news' centred in the life, death and resurrection of Jesus. Immanuel had come, bringing both revelation of the character of God ('Have you been with me for so long and don't know who I am? The one who has seen me has seen the Father' John 14:9) and redemption from our tragic fallenness ('You shall call his name Yeshua, for he will save his people from their sins' Matt. 1:21). But their success also lay with their experienced life of the Spirit who made the work of Christ an effective reality in their lives, thus making them a radical alternative within their culture.[327]

The likeness he refers to between the present postmodern culture and the ancient one relates to the search of the people for meaningful experiences of the transcendent and divine. The first-century mystery religions, with their participative spiritual dramas by which people were inducted into their mysteries, put participants through powerful emotional rites that they felt deeply and could embrace as significant rites of passage.[328] Moreover, many peoples were in transition because

---

[327] Gordon Fee, *Paul, the Spirit and the People of God* (London, Hodder and Stoughton, 1997),pp.xiii, xiv.
[328] Charles Barrett, *The New Testament Background: Selected Documents* (San Francisco, Row Publishers, 1989), pp.120-134, 265, 267.

of the deportation policies of the Roman war machine that had moved many from their homelands to serve as slaves throughout the Empire. Furthermore, Roman armies often mobilised soldiers to serve in new regions, and after soldiers retired from active service they were settled in new lands rather than in their original places of birth. This meant their families and children were raised in new regions where life was uncertain and new social systems needed to be established.

This sense of insecurity also meant that there was an over-abundance of people who were looking to form their identities in the contexts of their new situations. All this led to a search for new experiences and ways of establishing themselves with their gods or other local gods upon whom they called to protect them. In the context of the early Christian missionary movement, as Fee notes, the 'experienced life of the Spirit' was attractive for those seeking encounters with the divine which could be grounded by deeper spiritual connections with the God of Christ. What also proved increasingly attractive for some of the more educated classes was a faith that claimed to be verifiable through experiencing the Spirit's presence. Roman thinkers had cynically given up on the idea that the gods really existed, but they were open to the idea of one god as an intellectual theory based on the ideas of middle Platonism. At the same time, the idea of a monotheistic faith which brought meaningful experience as well as intellectual rationale was not unattractive. The possibility of accepting the Christian faith had come about partly because of Plato's philosophy, which removed the avarice of untamed gods by hypothesising the existence of a transcendent deity who was broadly uninterested in human affairs. It is interesting that some of the early Christians who were part of the Roman Emperor's household came to faith in the context of the intellectual need for belief in one god. Fee is quite right to draw comparisons with postmodern society, which, too, is cynical of claims to absolute truth, or religious claims which call for complete devotion to the Christian God or to any other absolute system of belief.

At the same time, this cynicism does not mean there is not openness to explore faith claims. For some postmodern individuals known to the authors who have come to a committed Christian faith, the crucial thing in making this decision was the importance of forming deep friendships with believers. It is also noticeable that they are interested in the strengths that faith will bring to their lives, so it takes them much longer to reach the conclusion that the Christian faith makes good pragmatic sense for them to frame their lives around. Postmodern converts are probably more convinced by observing Christians whose lives are more deeply satisfied than their own.

This is the critical point for non-Western and Western missional churches to grasp if they really want to share the gospel with postmodern Westerners. The questions raised by postmodern people have to do with the pragmatic value of the Christian faith in terms of how it satisfies a person's need for meaningful experiences, which can sustain them for the long term. The kinds of friendships needed to help them to form these conclusions cannot happen in church services alone, if at all.

The postmodern need for an existentially satisfying belief system is more important than going to a church which may or may not motivate people to adopt a satisfying spirituality. A typical Protestant and evangelical aim is to encourage people to attend church services in order to hear the gospel preached by professional clergy. Yet the way these services are often conducted does not provide the type of relational atmosphere which helps deeper fellowship to take place.

It is not just reverse missionary churches that are challenged by postmodern religious pluralism; it is the same for Western Christians. The churches that are the least successful in reaching non-Christians in the West are those that are still trying to get people to come to their religious services to explore faith through the preaching of the professional minister. Some new ideas are much needed.

Multi-ethnic breakthrough community churches may be a good way to form relationships with local secular people. If people from a range of ethnic backgrounds form such community congregations, and the local communities are made up of the same kind of ethnic diversity, offering community meeting points in a well-resourced community church building will hopefully help people to get to know believers better. This will not necessarily offer the best solution for reaching Westerners who value the spiritual pluralistic opportunities that the New Age movement represents. However, community churches that welcome diversity can offer opportunities for

299

postmodern people who value harmonious living in a diverse multicultural society; this will include the provision of the right environment to get to know Christians on a more personable level.

We turn our attention next to New Age spiritualities. Then we will spend a short time thinking about the missional opportunities which ethnic migrants from other world religions represent to our churches to win new people for Christ in the West.

Missional opportunities presented by New Age spiritualities

Paul Heelas and his colleagues conceive of the postmodern search for meaningful spiritual experiences by discussing the different approaches people take to exploring the possibilities.[329] They talk of those who are finding their answers in so called 'New Age' spiritualities, of which there are many. They share in a spiritual movement which they term the 'holistic milieu.'[330] Haralambos comments:

> The holistic milieu contrasts with the congregational domain in which people attend places of collective worship on a regular basis, typically once a week. The holistic milieu is less visible than the congregational domain, but involves one-to-one encounters (for example between a healer and a client) and small group activities (for example, yoga groups).[331]

Heelas and his colleagues offer other crucial insights into four themes found among most New Age participants:

Theme 1 – Self-spirituality: This emphasis involves individuals looking deeply inside themselves to discover self-healing, rather than attending traditional religious services to seek answers outside of themselves through others or God.

---

[329] Paul Heelas, et al., *The Spiritual Revolution: Why Religion is Giving Way to Spirituality* (Oxford, Blackwell, 2005).
[330] Haralambos and Holborn, *Sociology*, p.420.
[331] Haralambos and Holborn, *Sociology*, p.420.

Theme 2 – Finding the inner god or goddess: Each person can find their own god or goddess within themselves. Indeed, in some systems of New Age spirituality, the individual needs to discover that they themselves are a god.

Theme 3 – Detraditionalisation: Postmodern people have turned away from traditional sources of influence and power. Instead, the individual is thought of as the source of truth and understanding for spiritual matters. Formal religion is not considered to have any bearing on the decisions individuals make.

Theme 4 – Personal responsibility: The individual is responsible for his or her own beliefs, actions and spiritual practices. Each has the right and freedom to determine what truth is for themselves. The kind of truth that each individual embraces can be their own special version of truth, which might be different to other truths. Collective authority expressed through official bodies such as churches is not valid. The only kind of valid truth is that which a person finds for him- or herself.

Some theological commentators like John Drane argue that New Age adherents have turned to it because the scientific modern worldview has not provided personal spiritual satisfaction. He points out that many Westerners are deeply disillusioned with the inability of churches to satisfy cravings for spiritual fulfilment on an experiential level.[332]

Conversely, sociologist Steve Bruce argued that the arrival of the New Age movement is better defined as a result of modernity rather than an as a postmodern phenomenon.[333] New Age mysticism in this case is just a heightened form of individualism, the result of the Enlightenment which puts the individual in a new place of power with the concepts of humanism. Humanism looks away from non-scientific sources of knowledge towards the rational sciences to provide answers to life's questions, and does not require divine beings to explain the world around us.

---

[332] Drane, *Do Christians Know How to be Spiritual?* Chapter 1.

[333] Steve Bruce, *No Pope of Rome: Militant Protestantism in Modern Scotland* (Edinburgh, Mainstream, 1995), pp.40-65.

The next inevitable stage in the evolution of this perspective is for individuals to reject the authority claims to truth of science itself, and instead to take authority for themselves to decide what truth is. It is philosophically impossible to prove that any one truth is more certain than another, therefore individuals have the right to choose the truth they think is best for them to follow. Science's empirical method excludes the possibility of confirming the reality of the metaphysical spiritual dimension of the human psyche or the existence of supernatural beings like God because claims of God's existence cannot be demonstrated on an observable level, or as a repeatable occurrence which the method requires in order for findings to be checked. Self-verification of the supernatural is deemed to be more authentic to postmodern people than the authority claims made by science to be the only real approach to experimentally demonstrate the reality of observable phenomena.

It is the power of this kind of hyper-individualism which the philosopher Bauman claims brings the threat of disintegration to modern society. If every individual forms their own version of truth, the forces of pluralism will inevitably lead to chaos.[334]

Migrant Christians come with a passion to bring the gospel back to Westerners, but they are not well equipped to understand this kind of hyper-modernism. The reason for this is that most often they come from pre-modern collectivist cultures which do not provide an understanding of post-Enlightenment ideology. In these cultures, a person has a prescribed place in the community's hierarchy. Individual rights are less important than basing one's beliefs and practices on accepted truths.

Migrant churches in the West often bring these ideas with them, and their people find it very difficult to relate to the hyper-individualism of Western people. This makes it vital for Western Christians to join the multicultural missional conversation in order to help their non-Western brethren to understand this individualist approach to spiritual life. The conflict that might arise from a migrant Christian's view of spirituality based on received views compared to

---

334 Bauman, *Liquid Modernity*, Chapter 1, pp.40-57. This view is one of the points Bauman makes in this very informative work.

Western individualism as the source of individual spiritual authority is not easy to discern. The question is, 'How can migrant reverse missionaries join in partnership with Western Christians who understand how to work in mission with Western individuals?' And let us be clear: many Western Christians do not know how to convey the Christian message effectively to postmodern people.

One solution is for experienced Western missional leaders to mentor and coach migrant leaders so that they can learn how to engage with postmodern New Age seekers. The missiologist Jehu Hanciles highlights that non-Western forms of Christianity have their own pluralism which, we would argue, provide hope that migrant reverse missionaries come to the West somewhat prepared to understand the West's pluralistic nature, including the pluralism of varieties of New Age spiritualities. But before we turn to this, let us consider his comments in support of this thesis:

> The old heartlands [of the former Western Christian nations] exemplified political domination, territorial control, national religion, cultural superiority, and a fixed universal vision. In sharp contrast, the emerging heartlands of the faith [outside the West] embody vulnerability and risk, religious plurality, immense diversity of Christian experience and expression, and structures of dependency. The forms of Christianity that now flourish in the non-western world are not only post-Christendom, they are anti-Christendom.[335]

This 'post-Christendom' form of non-Western Christianity has been brought by migrants to the post-Christendom West.[336] Migrant Christians might be helped to share their rich experiential versions of Christian spirituality in a language which, at its heart, will appeal to New Age adherents who themselves have reacted against the claims of Christendom to provide absolute authoritative belief systems. Further research is needed to find out how non-Western Christian approaches to spirituality might resonate with some forms of New Age spirituality.

---

[335] Hanciles, 'Migration and Mission', p.135.
[336] Murray, *Post-Christendom*, pp.5-11.

However, it must be recognised that there is a very broad range of interests within the New Age category. Some will not easily resonate with a Christian belief system, and neither will some adherents welcome friendships with missional Christians. New Age beliefs might include interest in clairvoyance, communicating with aliens, seeking the help of spirit guides or masters, transcendental meditation, meditation, psychotherapy, renascent paganism, renascent Gnosticism, tarot, self-healing, Ouija, astrology, witchcraft, Wicca, reflexology, natural remedies, Gaia, aromatherapy or yoga. There are opportunities for migrant Christians to understand some of the forms of spirituality of New Age practitioners; many come from cultures that appreciate the spiritual worldview, which help them to understand the more mystical bent behind New Age beliefs.

For example, some migrant Christians come from cultures that value forms of spirituality that seek balance with the forces of nature. Those who call themselves pagans, or those who practice Wicca (white magic), value living in harmony with the natural forces of nature as well. There will be important resonances with these forms of New Age values for migrant reverse missionaries if they can learn to suspend their judgement of those who call themselves pagans in order to build meaningful connections with them for Christ. Because many non-Western Christians view things like paganism and Wicca as being under the power of demonic forces, it will be a great temptation to engage in spiritual warfare practices early on, which would turn New Age people away from them. Here, once again, it is important for reverse missionary leaders to be mentored by experienced Western missional leaders who have had experience with converting New Age peoples to the Christian faith.

Pluralism and world religions in the West

We believe that a large piece of learning for Western Christians to engage in with ethnic migrant congregations has to do with lessons they have learnt from sharing their faith with people in their homelands from other world religions. We know of numerous migrant Christians who converted to Christianity when they were still in their homeland, before they migrated to the West. This is where much learning can also take place as part of the multicultural missional conversation.

Anthony Giddens provides graphic evidence of the importance given to religion among a selection of world nations and their cultures. What is useful about his graphic representation is that it captures the value attached by different migrant ethnic groups to religion. It is important to remember that some people from the nations highlighted below now live in the West. Giddens' graph also captures the values attached by Westerners to religion, which will hopefully provide some understanding of the comparative differences between the values of more and less developed industrial nations regarding religious affiliation.[337]

Percentage of Population who say 'Religion is Very Important'

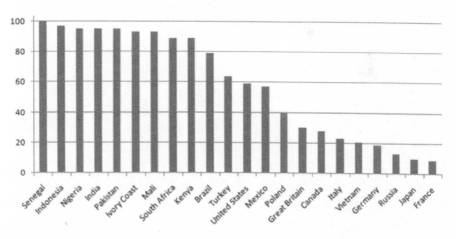

Giddens discusses the diagram above in terms of offering an index of how secularisation has led to lower levels of Westerners perceiving the importance of religion in their lives compared to non-Western nations:

> Secularization can be evaluated according to a number of aspects or dimensions. Some of them are objective in nature, such as the level of membership of religious organizations.

---

[337] Giddens and Sutton, *Sociology*, p.697

Statistics and official records can show how many people belong to a church or other religious body and are active in attending services or other ceremonies. As we shall see, with the exception of the USA, most of the industrialized countries have experienced considerable secularization according to this index. The pattern of religious decline seen in Britain is found in most of Western Europe, including Catholic countries such as France or Italy.[338]

The hope is that migrant Christians in the West can help Western Christians share their faith with those who come from nations that still have high religious values. What is encouraging is that engagement in multicultural missional conversations will help us all to understand and try new approaches to sharing the gospel with non-Christian migrant groups or secular postmodern groups. It is important that we celebrate the opportunities together and seek realistic solutions to the challenges which inhibit our ability to engage in successful missional ventures with the large varieties of people in the multicultural pluralistic West.

Comparative missional theology

It is important to consider the power of comparative theology to be brought into the multicultural missional conversation. Comparative theology is highly practical in helping us to compare and contrast different belief systems. As the missional conversation requires different ethnic groups to engage in communication, it useful to understand where our theologies agree and where they differ. Moreover, this tool will help us to understand the beliefs and practices of other world faiths, as well as some of those found among postmodern people, such as paganism or Wicca. Comparative theology is very useful, particularly in the context of a pluralistic society, as it provides insights into other practical theological points of view.

---

[338] Giddens and Sutton, *Sociology*, p.696.

Gavin D'Costa,[339] a Catholic theologian, makes six important points about the challenges and advantages of adopting this kind of approach as part of our attempts to work with other Christians from other cultures, as well as to understand those not of the Christian faith so that we can share the gospel with them too. We will briefly outline some of his views here. We would add that some comparative theologians have a very liberal faith which more conservative evangelicals like ourselves would not embrace as fully. However, this is not a reason not to use some of the good insights of this field of study to help us in our missional endeavours.

1. D'Costa suggests, 'It is time to lose our fixation of simply trying to understand other faiths in order to just evangelise them.'[340] This is a question of authenticity. It seems unethical to us to build strategic friendships with people of other faiths with a hidden agenda to convert them to our own faith. If we are to be genuine in our desire to form lasting relationships with those who do not embrace our outlook on the world, we need to be genuine in our approaches to them as well, which includes the need for an honest desire to get to know them as people in their own right. Too often, friendships with those of other faiths, or of no faith, lack genuine Christlike love which seeks to serve others despite their choices. This then leads to churches dropping those who do not respond fairly quickly to their efforts to convert them after first meeting them.

2. D'Costa adds, 'Dialogue must precede theology of religions, for dialogue is "a process or practice, not a theory" and thus we "must first learn about non-Christians" "from" them, before theorizing "about" them.'[341] This makes sense without the need to comment, except to note that missional dialogue can occur between Christians and non-Christians alike.

---

[339] Gavin D'Costa, *Christianity and World Religions: Disputed Questions in the Theology of Religions* (Chichester, Blackwell Wiley, 2009), pp.35-36.
[340] D'Costa, *Christianity and World Religions*, p.37.
[341] D'Costa, *Christianity and World Religions*, p.37-38.

3. D'Costa makes the point that comparative theologians in the academy tend to specialise in just one particular world faith, such as Hinduism or Buddhism.[342] However, in terms of forums that develop around the multicultural missional conversation, ethnic Christians who have converted from other world faiths can provide others with knowledge that will help them form meaningful missional friendships with non-Christians from these other faiths now living in the West.

4. He continues, 'There is a need for closer comparative readings of the source texts which other faiths use to form their beliefs and practices.'[343] It has too often been the case that Christian evangelistic strategy has required non-Christians to get to know Christian source texts thoroughly without regard for trying to more deeply understand the source texts of those we seek to convert. Proper contextual missional practice requires that we also understand the core texts of those with whom we form friendships in order to build incarnational bridges of understanding.

5. D'Costa further adds that the process of comparative theology requires, 'theological engagement with the other as well as a theological self-transformation in light of this engagement with the other.'[344] Anthony Gittens makes a similar point that those who engage in reverse mission find themselves transformed by the perspectives of those with whom they are engaging in another kind of reverse mission back towards themselves. D'Costa and Gittens aver the value of getting to know the richness of the faith perspectives of those we seek to convert to Christianity.

6. Some of those who deeply engage in obtaining comparative understandings of other faiths develop 'multiple identities'.[345] This is by far the largest concern for more conservative evangelical

[342] D'Costa, *Christianity and World Religions*, p.38.
[343] D'Costa, *Christianity and World Religions*, p.38.
[344] D'Costa, *Christianity and World Religions*, p.38.
[345] D'Costa, *Christianity and World Religions*, p.38.

Christians, as it smacks of compromise and the loss of a specific evangelical Christian identity. However, this is not necessarily the specific challenge of the formation of 'multiple identities' implied by D'Costa. Rather it has to do with the way in which a believer is transformed by another culture and its traditions, which enables them to become an accepted member of a group at a deeper level. Through this 'deeper' engagement we can seek to transform the subculture of which we are now a part by leading its members to discover Christ, who by His Spirit will make something new within their own cultures. Within the multicultural context, first and second generation migrants who come to the West from the other world faiths carry their homeland cultures with them. These homeland cultures become subcultures in the context of the multicultural West. In order for missional leaders to engage with these subcultures, they need to go some way towards forming 'multiple identities' – other than that identity they had in their originating Christian subculture.

Conclusions

In this chapter we have discussed the challenges that multiculturalism and pluralism generate in the West, in the context of engaging in mission with numerous groups who have different worldviews to our own. The challenge of sharing the Christian faith across diverse cultural traditions and faith perspectives is complex, and no one group can hope to share the gospel with all of the subcultures that surround us, particularly in cities where many different people groups live. We have noted that New Age spiritualities are by far the most complex to engage with in contextually relevant ways because there are so many expressions of them. Notwithstanding these challenges, it is argued that strengths will be brought by the development of new forums, where different ethnic and subcultural groups can learn from each other through missional conversations how to build bridges to reach into new communities.

Perhaps one of the best ways to model God's mission is to join Him in His work with diverse peoples. One way we could do this could be by the planting of multi-ethnic or multicultural breakthrough community churches. The term 'breakthrough' is important here as it has proved very difficult, if not impossible, for these kinds of churches to be formed in some Western nations. We know of some churches that are multi-ethnic. However, the cosmopolitan flavour of such congregations brings many challenges because of cross-cultural differences. It takes sacrifice to be part of such a fellowship because important cultural differences need to be understood, and it takes much longer to get to know people because of this. However, accepting these challenges and planting multicultural ethnic community churches will provide a way for non-Christian community members themselves living in multi-ethnic cities and towns to witness the transformation that the gospel brings when Christians from diverse backgrounds successfully fellowship and worship together.

Disciplines like comparative theology applied in the right way may help us to understand our differences better. It will certainly provide some of the tools to help us understand others, whether they be Hindus, Muslims, Pagans, Wicca, etc. The writers recognise that what we have been saying is somewhat prophetic as these kinds of churches do not as yet really exist in large enough numbers to make a national difference. However, the very nature of our multicultural Western societies challenges us to do what the gospel commands – to take it to all nations and cultures. Paul iterated it in terms of the goal of the gospel:

> In Christ Jesus you are all children of God through faith. As many of you as were baptized into Christ have clothed yourselves with Christ. There is no longer Jew or Greek, there is no longer slave or free, there is no longer male and female; for all of you are one in Christ Jesus. And if you belong to Christ, then you are Abraham's offspring, heirs according to the promise.
> *Galatians 3:26-29*

The book of Acts conveys what deeper kinds of multicultural fellowships such as community churches will need to discover and adopt by the power of the Spirit of Jesus:

And all who believed were together and had all things in common; and they sold their possessions and goods and distributed them to all, as any had need. And day by day, attending the temple together and breaking bread in their homes, they partook of food with glad and generous hearts, praising God and having favor with all the people. And the Lord added to their number day by day those who were being saved.

Acts 2:44-47 (RSV)

It is too often forgotten that this group of believers represented the multicultural diaspora communities spread around the Roman Empire. They were made up of Galileans, Parthians, Medes, Elamites, Jews, Hellenists and proselytes (Acts 2:1-8). Luke's gospel plays on the sending of the 70 disciples to spread the good news (Luke 10), and the peoples he mentions as being present at Pentecost were probably to be taken as a symbol that God wanted to restore the 70 categories of peoples mentioned in the Genesis table of the nations of the world, reversing the separation by language barriers at the time of Babel (Genesis 10). This provides us with the prophetic rationale which calls for us all to join together in the multicultural missional conversation.

We now, like at no other time in history, live with the opportunity of sharing our faith with numerous people groups who live on our doorsteps, because of globalism and international migration. The challenge is for us to join together as the one people of the one Christ to show the world that we are part of the one kingdom of God. This is surely what Jesus calls us to do together as we continue to pray, 'Your kingdom come. Your will be done, on earth as it is in heaven' (Matthew 6:10).

Reflective exercise

Take a few minutes to reflect on the following questions.

- What kind of spirituality does your church have – charismatic, liturgical, traditional, etc?

- Who has been converted from another world faith in your church? What faith did they convert from? In what ways do they engage in mission with those from their former faith group to share the gospel with them? How successful have they been in sharing their faith in this way?

- Which kinds of postmodern spiritualities can you identify in your locality from the list offered in this chapter? Name them and locate them.

- How could you engage with these postmodern faiths?

- What has challenged you in this chapter and why?

- What new mission opportunities can you identify for yourself and your church from this chapter?

Comments

Chapter 12
How to Engage in the Multicultural Missional Conversation

Let's get practical. How can we start to engage in the emerging multicultural missional conversation? Tom Sine is a missional thinker who seeks to help the church of Christ to engage in missional conversations in the postmodern context. He comments on a common lack of strategic vision which we must avoid:

> Most Christian churches, denominations and mission organizations do long range or strategic planning. The irony is that they plan as though they are frozen in a time warp – as though the future will simply be an extension of the past. Pastors in both conventional and experimental churches are often unaware of the challenges facing their members in our new global society. So it shouldn't be surprising that they offer little help in dealing with those challenges. Similarly, those who work with Christian college students at Christian colleges or through campus ministries seldom alert them to new challenges or creative alternatives facing them upon graduation. As a consequence, students are not adequately prepared to live and serve God in a rapidly changing world.[346]

In order to engage in the multicultural missional conversation, we suggest five principles to guide us in exploring how to be open to the way God wants us to serve Him 'in a rapidly changing world'. As is the case with all principles, they will only help us if we actively and intentionally engage in investigating how to apply them. In the case of the missional conversation, it is obvious that we need to be motivated to take part in conversations with other leaders and groups. This will inevitably mean a significant time investment. Missional conversations

---

[346] Sine, *The New Conspirators*, pp.130-131.

are the bread and butter of keeping in touch with this 'rapidly changing world'.

We will offer some practical suggestions in this chapter. We hope they will prove helpful.

Principle 1: Understand your own mission related to your vision and calling

To do this well, you need to understand from the beginning that this is a three-step process that involves careful listening.

A. Listening to empower others

Before we pay attention to actively listening to others' stories with a view to helping them think through how they can more effectively go about their ministries, it is important firstly to prioritise our own listening to God. We need to gain a clear understanding about His missional heart and purpose for us in the journey He has set us upon. It is vitally important to understand that our missional journey is just one important expression of the wider kingdom agenda. This recognition should keep us from believing that what we are involved in is the most important thing happening, thereby helping us to avoid becoming too self-focused. In addition, it will help us to channel our efforts into the specific missional contribution we will be making, as suited to our specific context. We won't then be tempted to try to do too many different things, thereby making our contribution ineffectual.

Secondly, it is about actively listening to each other. This is quite foundational to a missional understanding of the nature of being church together. Listening is very hard work, and it takes time to build the space and trust required to hear what each person is really trying to contribute to the missional conversation. We would recommend taking time as a church to intentionally engage in some process work to assist clear understanding of what God's vision is. This will usually mean spending some time away from the normal rounds of church life and spending time together to listen, discern, explore, reflect, debate and agree what this vision and mission really is for you as a Christian community.

The danger is that some types of leadership approaches are founded on the view that the senior leader is required to bring all of the creative vision and imagination into the church with no intentional consultation with others. This often leads to hierarchical leadership and disempowerment of the creative work of the Spirit in the lives of others, and it can sometimes mean missing the greater contribution that God wants to bring into the church through inspiring the hearts and minds of different people.

A third aspect is learning to listen to the community where the gospel is to be incarnated as a new kind of church expression suited to the context. It includes listening to the various people groups that are part of the community where a new church is to be planted. Learning the local language and how it reveals the life situations of its people is a vital aspect of engagement for the development of authentic expressions of missional communities which meet the needs of the people on the ground. This again means time investment. The best and enduring expressions of church plants tend to explore this fundamental approach to contextualising the gospel. The worst examples are often those that fail to take this seriously. This can lead to a wide disparity of what the planting team compared to the locals they hope to serve consider to be important. This inevitably leads to a clash of cultures, and the good intentions of the church planters can often be dashed as a result of this fundamental lack of careful listening to what people feel their lives are all about in the local area.

One way to help a church planting team to be informed is to read stories from Scripture that express this type of learning. One such story comes from the apocalyptic writings of Daniel. Here we have a people group who are forcefully displaced into exile and find themselves in a strange new land. The significance is not only the way they experience the passion and compassion of Yahweh in aiding and protecting them in this alien environment, but also that four young Jewish males are used to show the readers how they had to work to engage within this new community. They had to find ways to relate to their new neighbours and needed to pay careful attention to contextualising their faith so that they could help their new neighbours understand why it was so important to them, and indeed to Babylon. The amazing part of the story is found in what they retained of their own culture (eg food laws, spirituality) and what they were willing to do to adjust to their new circumstances (eg their names and their dress). These were hard and challenging issues that these four young faithful believers faced, and yet they persevered and found new ways of engaging with God in His mission among the Babylonians.

Sharing these stories, noting the things that are encouraging and challenging and how they relate to your own contribution can be a very good way of assisting the formation of a team to engage effectively in a new church plant.

B. Engage in local ethnographic research

Another vital piece of work that church planter needs to be encouraged to adopt is local ethnographic research. This more 'academic' approach provides core data about the community and introduces vital research to enable the best engagement so that the whole team can effectively participate with the new community.

The importance of demographics[347]

Demographics can be described as the process by which we come to know who lives where, what they are like and why. Any or all of the above models require a basic understanding of demographic patterns in the target area.

Until relatively recently, the task of discovering who lives where was a time-consuming process. The following major sources of information figured heavily: Census information, the electoral register and local authority planning office data. Today it is possible to access Census information by purchasing a compact disc and using a computer to process it. The information can be used to provide a considerable variety of mapping patterns.

Why does it matter who lives where?

Information about the socio-economic and ethnic groups in a neighbourhood, together with figures on the number of people in each grouping, can help to establish a detailed picture of the kinds of needs

---

[347] This section is based on Springdale College: Together in Mission BA church-planting materials, originally written by Martin Robinson.

that a church might be called to meet in a given area. It can assist planters to see which areas or districts require church plants and, in particular, which are the most needy areas.

Beyond statistics

Even when we have built a detailed picture of how many people belong to particular groups in a given area, we need to know more about them. For example, how long have the majority of people lived where they are now? Do people move in and out of the neighbourhood? What facilities are available? What major social trends are there? What are the employment factors?

These and many other questions help us to see beyond mere figures to obtain a 'feel' for the issues that a church plant might be called to address. The answers will help to determine the kind of model that will be appropriate. For example, if it becomes clear from the data that there is a marked difference between the people who live in the area where the new church is to be planted and the people who will be doing the planting, then it might be necessary either to review the model or to select a different area for the plant.

Why are people the way they are? In addition to demographic information, it is important to understand something of the history of the area. The 'why' questions are just as important as the 'how many' questions. For example, although it is good to know how many people attend church and whether that number is growing or declining, it is just as vital to know why these patterns are occurring. This will allow 'spiritual mapping' to take place. By this we mean the social and cultural factors that give rise to certain patterns of resistance and receptivity to the gospel. For example, when we look at the United Kingdom as a whole, we see marked differences in percentages of people who attend church depending on the type of neighbourhood. It is important to understand the historical reasons for these differences and to begin a process of prayer for change.

C. Nurture self-awareness of our own history

It is important to be intentionally aware of our own 'history'. None of us lives in a vacuum, and we all have been socialised within certain constructs of culturally accepted norms and values that we are often blind to, but which are highly important to us in order to support the ways we think people should live together and behave. We can 'assume' things because they are part of our inherited framework of what identifies us and our faith community, but others will not necessarily assume or understand these when we try to plant what we think are suitable community churches among them. This includes what we accept as appropriate behaviour and, conversely, what we reject and think of as inappropriate.

For many church planters, there is a received religious culture that supports certain aspects of particular denominational distinctives that are based upon theological understandings, hermeneutical interpretations, past and current experiences that have helped form our views of what churches should be like, and expectations from the governing body of a denomination or network. Adding the histories from other ethnicities or subcultures to the melting pot of what can be contradictory views of what the norms and values should be for a group can challenge people to rethink these as part of the journey of discovery.

Additionally, there are 'controlling stories' and key narratives that shape our understanding of our own unique history. These include the way we tell and are informed by the significant and important ones. For the Jews, the story of the Passover is one such story, told from the perspective of a displaced and oppressed people and the miraculous engagement of Yahweh to deliver them from the oppression of the Egyptians. This is a story we know well. We have been informed by our reading and rereading of Scripture and by our theology, which have informed and shaped us to think and behave in the ways we do. But there is also the story of the Egyptians and their engagement with this experience, which would likely provide a very different telling and understanding of the story of Israel! The point here is to help us become more aware of the assumptions that our history has produced within us.

It is good to embrace and be honest about our histories and their influences on our approaches to missional engagement. After all, these will be working in us and through us as we seek to engage with our local communities.

Principle 2: Relationally network with others on the missional journey

One of the great advantages of the present Western missional context is the realisation that no singular denomination, church, organisation or person has all the understanding, wisdom and skills needed to express the missional heart of God our Father and thereby to fully engage in the kingdom of God. We need to partner together in order to express more fully the kind of missional community that God is seeking to develop in our world. This is more than just rhetoric; it is a reality of how God is seeking to develop His church.

While this is an admirable aspiration, the reality is often less than what is hoped for. The demands of local ministry and the missional engagement of our work, the need for active involvement within our own denominations or networks, the opportunities locally and nationally, all make great demands on our time. To add the intentional involvement of working with others who are not part of our interests and groups can be a real challenge. It needs to be more than just scheduled meetings in order to really to get to know people, although these are also helpful. Discernment in seeking who we should be working with is part of our exploration in this kind of missional engagement. Who is God calling us to work with, and what will be needed in order to engage with them in the best ways possible?

Local and regional churches

One of the great benefits of working with others is learning together. Having the time and commitment to partner enables us to experience and reflect together on what have been good and bad practices and expressions of mission. Learning to identify those who have been on the journey longer than we have and coming alongside them is one way of exploring the needed partnership that will keep us on track. This will obviously be time consuming, as it is vital to take time to build meaningful relationships with others if working together is to be sustainable.

The challenge is how do we find them? Not all expressions of church planting understand and embrace what it means to be a missional community. There are real theological, social and cultural

319

differences that we cannot ignore. Even within our own denominational frameworks there will likely be a variety of experiences and expressions of church planting and how we should go about it. Seeking advice from others, consulting and learning from them is a great practice to adopt as part of our ongoing learning and reflective practice. Not only will it potentially save us from wasting valuable time, funds and energy, but it could also be a great opportunity for our vulnerability to be expressed as new partnerships are formed based more on friendship and a common passion for this type of mission, rather than simply hoping our existing church history and hierarchy will be the things which enable us to do church planting well.

Other denominations and networks

It is often easier to work with those we know, or those with whom we share a common set of values and objectives, for obvious reasons. These are often those within our own church family, as it is much easier to get on with those we do not have to work so hard to relate to. Even where there is a wider divergence of church planters who join together, often there is a shared history and understanding of 'how we do things in our network/s'. To move beyond our own support structures to other expressions of being church, of leadership, of how God works, is more challenging but equally more rewarding.

Locally, there are, of course, councils of churches and other gatherings (often more expressly evangelical and/or charismatic) which provide one place of engagement. There are valuable things to be learnt from these expressions, even if it helps us to think about how we might not wish to express something. Their wide appeal is also the limitation to be useful arenas for learning about the missional context. The varieties of theology which express what truly constitutes being church and God's mission can easily be lost without careful discernment of what such arenas are trying to achieve together. For example, there is the question of appropriate involvement in the work of other church planting groups. It is one thing to learn from each other, but at times it can defeat the point of networking with other planters if it is not clear that these are learning forums rather than membership groups where everyone is expected to see things in similar ways.

One of the best aids is to listen intentionally to other Christians as they speak about what is at the heart of their denomination. Those whose aim is essentially mission will be speaking, writing, teaching and living it, because it is part of their very DNA. Their passion will be focused more on mission than just on maintenance of existing church structures. They will have energy and insights into the greater mission of God than just what they are doing in their own local contexts. Spending time developing these relationships can be a great asset in the growth of your own understanding. Equally, your story and journey should be welcomed as part of the learning.

Other key influencers

There are developing movements and key leaders that are focusing more intentionally on the multicultural missional conversation. Quite often they will be found more on the margins, finding their influence through blogs and podcasts and other forms of social media. There are equally, of course, books, seminars, lectures and more traditional expressions of influence. Some of these are noted in the list of resources at the end of this chapter.

One of the people who has been highly influential within the wider debate is the late Bishop Lesslie Newbigin. His work, firstly as a missionary in India, then his re-engagement with mission in the Western world upon his return to Britain, has set the standard for much of the wider missional conversation. He sought to take the missionary principles learned in India and to contextualise them for active engagement in the UK in order to help bring the Christian story back more centrally to secular society. He asked the pertinent question, 'Can the West be won?' It is the same question we are still asking and exploring today. Newbigin knew part of the answer lay in the missional nature of the local church. That is what gave him hope for the future, and that is why this exploration is not just about adding another church to the mix, but rather expressing a new kind of human community of the Spirit, together as the people of God.

There are other voices of influence that need to be heard. We need to find those who will fully inform and challenge us in this great endeavour that God has called us to and to drink from the wells of their lives, their experiences, their learning and their involvement.

Principle 3: Stay informed

The sheer volume of information that each of us is now faced with every day is staggering. We can become overwhelmed by the sheer overload of all of this data and thereby miss the really important resources that will aid us in the important journey of being attentive to God's voice and what He is doing to transform the world.

The key question to ask ourselves is, 'What are the most important things for me to be focusing on?' It is all too easy to know much of what is happening in the world without really knowing very much of what God wants us to know, suited to His call on our lives and work for Him. Millions of bits of information, often quite contradictory, loom on the horizon of our web browsers and bookshops. How can we stay clearly informed to nurture and develop our thinking and practice?

Educational provision

For many, the traditional route is within education. Today there are a number of very good theological and Bible colleges that are aware of the key influences and discussions around the missional conversation. Many offer degrees that have part or even all of their work relating to key missional issues. However, at present very few have much focus on the multicultural issues we have been discussing in this book.

Both of the authors currently teach at Springdale College: Together in Mission.[348] We know this organisation and so are using it as an example, but not in an exclusive way, as the list of resources demonstrates. Within this college the BA students learn in all the modules about the missional nature of God and how this informs and supports our reading of and practical engagement in mission to the Western world. One of the newly developed pathways relates to reverse mission. Part of the learning of this pathway is a growing awareness and understanding of how this might find expression within multicultural church planting.

---

[348] See http://springdaleweb.sdcol.org.uk.

Seeking to partner with training or education bodies can help resource your existing and potential leaders. These bodies can also help grow awareness of the missional conversation because of their experience, knowledge and expertise of the bigger picture.

Movements, conferences and seminars

While doing a degree course is an important aspect of staying informed, not everyone can or needs to do this to engage in the process of learning. Many church networks and denominations offer learning within their own structures. These might be day seminars or weekend conferences; each is a valuable contribution to the overall shaping of thinking and practice. Finding out from your own denomination what is on offer is a good way of staying abreast of recent ideas and developments.

In addition, there are specific movements that have been developing, often around church planting, and which have developed key resources for learning and participation. Some of the more well known within the UK are Fresh Expressions, the Church Planting Forum, Urban Expression, Forge UK. These and various others provide learning, training resources and key influences that encourage and enable continued input into our own development of these newly formed missional communities.

Even within all of this, there is still a dearth of resources for multi-ethnic church planting. This is an area where much work in sharing good practice, writing training materials and developing courses and seminars needs to take place.

Online resources and social media

The greatest volume of resources can be found through the web and social media platforms. Whereas with a book or journal, one can often work out the theological slant or perspective that the author is conveying, often by the named publisher, this is not usually the case with the internet. The vast ocean of information, some of which can be quite contradictory, is instantly available, but these are not always the best resources for engaged learning since anyone can publish anything. This is in no way a complaint; just an observation.

Websites are often the starting point of discovery. We have learned much from even a cursory trawl of some of the key ideas presented. Reading our own denominational websites can also offer an understanding of how missional issues are being considered.

Other resources include online journals, blogs, podcasts, news feeds, and the growing use of social media such as Facebook, Twitter, Instagram, Google+ and many others. Each of these offers some very helpful resources to further develop our thinking and awareness. At the end of this chapter we have included a short list of resources that we have made use of and can recommend.

Even with all that is readily available, more is required. The specific engagement of the key issues around multi-ethnic church planting is still very new, so we would like to encourage readers to find new ways to share their experiences and offer new resources so we can all continue to learn how to work well together.

Principle 4: Invite significant influencers into your life

One of the inherent dangers of leadership is the inability to continue to receive significant input into the leader's life and expression of leadership. None of us have all the abilities, skills, understandings and insights that are required to bring us to maturity. Some stop growing after gaining a particular insight or experience and then live off of that event for the reminder of their ministry. Others can become threatened by their perceived lack of insight, or may feel insecure around others of differing abilities. We need the voice and input of significant others who are able to add value to our leadership.

The starting point is to inculcate a lifelong attitude to learning. This may be formal or informal, but it is more a mindset than purely an outcome. Leaders who are willing to intentionally develop this kind of approach are usually the ones who are the most creative and flexible, and who find it easier to deal with change, since they exercise their own ongoing change process as part of their professional practice.

A variety of training organisations and denominations invest in developing and releasing significant others to become mission accompanists to aid leaders in their quest towards greater maturity and effectiveness. These might be coaches who bring experience and often coaching systems to help pioneer church planters and new leaders to feel supported and encouraged. One training coach recently suggested that church plants are much more effective where there is a coach who helps a planter to reflect on his or her work, compared to those who are left on their own. They might also be mentors, who work to grow and develop the leader in their relationship with God, with their family, with themselves and with their work. Our own experience of being mentored has proven to be invaluable to our leadership and ministry development.

Others can include more structured leadership support systems, such as one's own denominational leadership mentoring schemes, or colleagues and friends who provide mutual support and peer observations. Sharing our journeys, the highs and lows, the things that have been good and those that have been great blunders, is part of this process of action–reflection learning which is so vital to our continuing growth as leaders.

Finally, having people who partner with us as prayer supporters and warriors, or as financial supporters, is an incredible source of strength and blessing which can help us to keep on growing because of the presence of God being focused in our lives and ministries.

The important thing is to keep on intentionally growing so that we can help grow other leaders by investing ourselves into their lives as well. The New Testament letter to Timothy suggests a helpful pattern where Timothy is encouraged to teach others who will then teach others (2 Timothy 2:1-2). Thereby everyone continues to be supported and challenged to grow in their leadership.

Principle 5: Build relationships with unchurched people

For many of us, the work of ministry is mostly a work among the people of God, often at the expense of those who are not part of our local Christian community and are thereby unaware of the love of God found in Christ Jesus. William Temple, in a rough paraphrase, suggested that the church should be an organisation that exists primarily for its non-members. Many church planters begin with a clear engagement with unchurched people, but soon find that all their time is taken up in running the church.

One tool that can be helpful within our postmodern context is the Engle scale. Engle took the view that not only is sharing our faith about saying certain words and looking for particular responses, but that our spiritual journeys are works of progress. The original scale began at −10 and worked its way to conversion at 0. The revised scale goes back even further, recognising that for many adults and children there is no clear Christian memory to draw on (such as for a prodigal, who would return to God as their Father). Rather it is more likely a strong secular or other faith perspective, or even none at all, that is characteristic of many ordinary British and European women and men today. The scale encourages a wider read of how our faith story is shared and received.

There are, of course, important people who can bring new possibilities and resources to our communities. These are the gatekeepers, those who have great influence, whose lives are important, whose views are listened to. Coming alongside them in partnership can be instructive of how God can open new opportunities. We have had important such experiences where local community leaders (such as local councillors and others in authority) have given their voice to aid the work of mission in local communities. They are often known as people of peace, who will make a way ahead in the communities among which we are called to work.

The ultimate multicultural missional conversation is not with other Christian leaders but with people who do not know Christ and who can form friendships with local believers, which can lead to them joining a Christian community. The missional conversation goes back to the roots of the word 'mission' itself. It comes from a Latin root which means 'to send'. If we follow God's guidance to be the 'sent ones' who share life with those who are not yet believers, then we are engaging in the highest possible meaning of the missional conversation.

List of resources

Here is a selected list of current key resources that support this chapter and will aid you in your life and ministry:

Books

Adogame, Afe, *The African Christian Diaspora: New Currents and Emerging Trends in World Christianity* (London, Bloomsbury, 2013).

Chike, Chigor, *African Christianity in Britain: Diaspora, Doctrines and Dialogue* (Milton Keynes, Author House, 2007).

Croft, Stephen, *Transforming Communities: Reimagining the Church for the 21st Century* (London, Dartman, Longman & Todd, 2002).

DeYmaz, Mark, *Building a Healthy Multi-Ethnic Church* (San Francisco, John Wiley & Sons, 2007).

Garces-Foley, Kathleen, *Crossing the Ethnic Divide: The Multi-ethnic Church on Mission* (Oxford, Oxford University Press, 2007).

Gibbs, Eddie, *Church Next* (Leicester, IVP, 2001).

Hirsch, Alan, *The Forgotten Ways* (Grand Rapids, Brazos Press, 2006).

Jones, Lee F., *Pastoral Leadership Skills For the Multicultural, Multi-ethnic Church* (Bloomington, XLibros.com, 2010).

Gerardo, Marti, *A Mosaic of Believers: Diversity and Innovation in a Multi-ethnic Church* (Bloomington, Indiana University Press, 2005).

Monyagh, Michael, *Church For Every Context* (London, SCM, 2012).

Murray, Steven, *Planting Churches: A Framework for Practitioners* (Milton Keynes, Paternoster, 2008).

Newbigin, Lesslie, *Foolishness to the Greeks* (London, SPCK, 1996).

Newbigin, Lesslie, *The Open Secret* (London, SPCK, 1995).

Olofinjana, Israel, *Turning the Tables on Mission: Stories of Christians From the Global South in the UK* (Watford, Instant Apostle, 2013).

Robinson, Martin, *Planting Mission-Shaped Churches Today* (Oxford, Monarch Books, 2006).

Sandiford, Gilbert, *Multi-ethnic Church: A Case Study of an Anglican Diocese,* (Cambridge, Grove Books, 2010).

Smith, Efrem, *The Post-Black and Post-White Church: Becoming the Beloved Community in a Multi-Ethnic World* (San Francisco, Wiley Josey Bass, 2012).

Spenser, Linbert, *Building a Multi-Ethnic Church* (London, SPCK, 2007).

Williams, Rowan, (ed.), *Mission-Shaped Church* (London, Church House Publishing, 2004).

Yancey, George, *One Body One Spirit* (Downers Grove, IVP Books, 2003).

Blogs

Café Vista: http://togetherinmission.co.uk/caf-conversations-2/ (accessed 1st November 2014).

Journals

Urban Theology online Journal: http://www.urbantheology.org/journals (accessed 1st November 2014).

Podcasts

Nomad: http://www.nomad.libsyn.com (accessed 1st November 2014). Also on iTunes.

Movements with Steve Addison (found on iTunes: https://itunes.apple.com/au/podcast/movements-that-change-world/id323810890?mt=2

The Multi-ethnic Church Podcast: http://toginet.com/podcasts/themulti-ethnicchurch/?s=themulti-ethnicchurch (accessed 1st November 2014).

Educational institutions

Cliff College: http://www.cliffcollege.ac.uk (accessed 1st November 2014).

London School of Theology: http://www.lst.ac.uk (accessed 1st November 2014).

Redcliffe College: http://www.redcliffe.org (accessed 1st November 2014).

Springdale College: Together in Mission: http://springdaleweb.sdcol.org.uk/ (accessed 1st November 2014).

Spurgeon's College: http://www.spurgeons.ac.uk (accessed 1st November 2014).

Organisations

Anglican Church Planting Initiatives: http://www.acpi.org.uk/Joomla/ (accessed 1st November 2014).

Forge: http://forgescotland.com (accessed 1st November 2014).

Oasis: http://www.oasisuk.org (accessed 1st November 2014).

The Eden Network: http://eden-network.org (accessed 1st November 2014).

The Missional Network: http://www.themissionalnetwork.com (accessed 1st November 2014).

Together in Mission: http://www.togetherinmission.co.uk (accessed 1st November 2014).

Urban Expression: http://www.urbanexpression.org.uk (accessed 1st November 2014).

Urban Neighbours of Hope: http://www.unoh.org (accessed 1st November 2014).

Denominations/networks

Many denominations in the UK have expressions of multicultural churches. Those that intentionally work to express multi-ethnic church planting include:

Churches in Communities International:
http://www.cicinternational.org (accessed 1st November 2014).

The Baptist Union of Great Britain: http://www.baptist.org.uk (accessed 1st November 2014).

The Fellowship of Churches of Christ in Great Britain and Ireland: http://www.fellowship.co.uk (accessed 1st November 2014).

Appendix – Journal Sample

Welcome to your electronic journal

This is a simple document that you can set up as a table in Microsoft Word or a similar programme, which allows you to input your entries on your chosen days. You will notice that it is set up by month, with dated daily entry points. It does not have a requirement for daily entries, but it is expected that you make significant entries at least twice a week.

Alternatively, if you are more comfortable with a notebook and pen, that's fine too!

A coach could help you to reflect on your learning. Reflect also on your learning with a few peers. After a short time, keeping your journal will become second nature.

Name:

Church:

What is expected

September 2012	Activities Today – What happened: Be specific giving precise details about what you did or what happened, i.e. context, events	Reflectic it? In what w face this sitc missional pi what ways h strengths ar
Mon 17th	1. Started the course today – we covered New Testament studies. I could see from the start how the learning from the biblical interpretation session could be useful to help me explain difficult bits of the Bible better 2. I met with my coach and we discussed how to set up my placement task for BIB101. We decided that I would prepare two presentations to be given at our beyond belief course for new Christians	1. I felt chal the Bible is sense to me what I believ
Tues 18th	Today was my first full day in the placement. I met the church leaders when I was invited to join them for a meeting about the preaching themes for the month of October.	I felt warmly Jesus – foct good to be I planning for preaching tc
Wed 19th	I was introduced to the beyond belief team today. I have been invited to the meeting with the new believers on Thursday at 7pm. They seemed a bit concerned about me attending the	I felt rather I an idiot. My protective o

In the second column you will see you are asked to give precise specific details of what you did in a given day, or over a couple of days in a week. You will notice from the sample how this person has written about their first few days of engaging with journalling. Notice how they describe carefully what they did in the first column. You need to be specific rather than general in these entries.

xcific d,	**Reflections on Activities:** Why did this happen? What does it mean? How should I respond to it? In what ways did it stimulate or challenge me spiritually? What interpersonal skills did I have to use to face this situation? What interpersonal skills do I need to further develop? What are some of the key missional principles that I have had to use or learn? What new ministry skills have I explored use of? In what ways have my beliefs been challenged? What am I weak in and how can I improve? What were my strengths and how can I keep on building on these?
e re for	1. I felt challenged by the first session on hermeneutics. I have tended to think interpreting passages from the Bible is quite straight forward. I realised though that I have only been focussing on passages that make sense to me. There are passages I have been avoiding because they make me question some aspects of what I believe about God's goodness.
rch t the	I felt warmly accepted by the team. I had one or two ideas about a series focussed on the parables of Jesus – focussed on the Kingdom of God. They felt that they had done this not that long ago, but it felt good to be listened to and that my ideas were taken seriously. It feels quite different to be part of the planning for church services. I have often felt that I did not understand how decisions were made about preaching topics. This has helped me to see that some careful thought goes into planning topics.
een at e or	I felt rather low this evening. It wasn't nice to feel like a burden for the Beyond Belief group. I felt like a bit of an idiot. My coach heard about the mood at the meeting and told me that one or two of them are very protective of this group. It seems like their might be some hidden tensions. I feel a bit worried that things might not work out with this group.

In the third column you are to reflect on the specific activities of the first column. It is important to reflect on precise things as opposed to generalisations, as this will help you to obtain insights into ways of improving how you react and deal with situations. Notice the range of questions you can use to get you started.

Take time to carefully consider the challenges you are facing and how you can improve your responses and approaches. Identifying and building on your strengths and working on your weaknesses will remain a common theme for you to focus on.

February 2014	Activities Today – what happened: Be specific, giving precise details about what you did or what happened – context, events, etc.	Reflections on activities: Why did this happen? What does it mean? How should I respond to it? In what ways did it stimulate or challenge me spiritually? What interpersonal skills did I need to use to face this situation? What interpersonal skills do I need to develop further? What are some of the key missional principles that I have had to use or learn? What new ministry skills have I explored? In what ways have my beliefs been challenged? What am I weak in and how can I improve? What were my strengths and how can I keep building on these?
Mon 3		
Tues 4		
Wed 5		
Thurs 6		
Fri 7		
Sat 8		
Sun 9		
Mon 10		
Tues 11		
Wed 12		
Thurs 13		
Fri 14		
Sat 15		
Sun 16		
Mon 17		
Tues 18		
Wed 19		
Thurs 20		

Bibliography

Books

Adams, Edward, *Parallel Lives of Jesus* (London, SPCK, 2011).

Akrong, Abraham, 'Deconstructing Colonial Mission – New Missiological Perspectives in African Christianity', in Adogame, A., R. Gerloff and K. Hock, (eds.), *Christianity in Africa and the African Diaspora* (London, Continuum, 2008).

Altcock, Craig, *The Shaping of God's People: One Story of How God is Shaping the North American Church Through Short-term Mission* (USA, Lulu, 2006).

Arnold, Clinton, *3 Crucial Questions about Spiritual Warfare* (Grand Rapids, Baker Academic, 2008).

Bailey, Rayna, *Immigration and Migration* (New York, Infobase Publishing, 2008).

Baker, Colin and Sylvia Prys Jones, *Encyclopedia of Bilingualism and Bilingual Education* (Clevedon, Multilingual Matters Ltd, 1998).

Barrett, Charles, *The New Testament Background: Selected Documents* (San Francisco, Row Publishers, 1989).

Barrett, Charles, *The Acts of the Apostles* (Vol.2, 15-12, T&T Clark, 1998).

Barker, Chris, *Cultural Studies: Theory and Practice* (London, Sage, 2008).

Bauman, Zygmunt, *Liquid Modernity* (Oxford, Blackwell Publishers, 2000).

Beasley-Murray, Paul, *Power for God's Sake: Power and Abuse in the Local Church* (Milton Keynes, Paternoster, 1998).

Bonhoeffer, Dietrich, *The Cost of Discipleship* (New York, Touchstone Books, 1995).

Bonk, Jonathan, *The Routledge Encyclopedia of Missions and Missionaries* (London, Routledge, 2010).

Bosch, David, *Transforming Mission* (London, Orbis, 1991).

Branson, Mark and Juan Martinez, *Churches, Cultures and Leadership: A Practical Theology of Congregations and Ethnicities* (Downers Grove, IVP Academic, 2011).

Brierley, Peter, *Reaching and Keeping Tweenagers: Analysis of the 2001 RAKES survey* (London, Christian Research, 2002).

Bruce, Steve, *No Pope of Rome: Militant Protestantism in Modern Scotland* (Edinburgh, Mainstream, 1995).

Burnett, David, *Clash of Worlds What Christians Can Do in a World of Cultures in Conflict* (London, Monarch Books, 2002).

Cameron, Helen, John Slater and Victoria Slater, *Theological Reflection for Human Flourishing* (London, SCM Press, 2012).

Cardwell, Mike, Liz Clark and Claire Meldrum, *Psychology* (London, Harper Collins, 2004).

Charles, Talbert, *Reading Acts: A Literary and Theological Commentary* (revised edition, Macon, Smyth and Helwys, 2004).

Collins, Francis, *The Language of God: A Scientist Presents Evidence for Belief* (London, Pocket Books, 2007).

Comte, Auguste, *The Positive Philosophy* (London, Bell & Sons, 1986).

Conzelmann, Hans, *The Theology of St Luke* (London, Faber & Faber, 1960).

Croft, Steven (ed.), *Mission-shaped Questions* (London, Chichester House Publishing, 2008).

Crouch, Andy, *Culture Making: Recovering our Creative Calling* (Downers Grove, IVP Books, 2008).

D'Costa, Gavin, *Christianity and World Religions: Disputed Questions in the Theology of Religions* (Chichester, Blackwell Wiley, 2009).

Devenish, David, *Demolishing Strongholds: Effective Strategies for Spiritual Warfare* (Milton Keynes, Authentic, 2005).

Dorr, Donal, *Spirituality of Leadership: Inspiration, Empowerment, Intuition and Discernment* (Blackrock, Columbia Press, 2006).

Douglas, James (ed.), *Let the Earth Hear His Voice: International Congress on World Evangelization, Lausanne, Switzerland* (Minneapolis, World Wide Publications, 1975).

Drane, John, *Do Christians Know How to be Spiritual? The Rise of New Spirituality and the Mission of the Church,* (London, Darton Longman and Todd, 2005).

Dunn, Richard and Mark Senter (eds.), *Reaching a Generation for Christ* (Chicago, Moody Publishers, 1997).

Eidse, Faith and Nina Sichel, *Unrooted Childhoods: Memoirs of Growing Up Global* (London, Nicholas Brealey Publishing, 2004).

Esler, Phillip, *Community and Gospel in Luke–Acts* (Cambridge, Cambridge University Press, 1987).

Fee, Gordon, *Paul, the Spirit and the People of God* (London, Hodder and Stoughton, 1997).

Flett, John, *The Witness of God The Trinity, Missio Dei, Karl Barth, and the Nature of Christian Community* (Grand Rapids, Eerdmans, 2010).

Garces-Foley, Kathleen, *Crossing the Ethnic Divide: The Multiethnic Church on a Mission* (Oxford, Oxford University Press, 2007).

Gibbs, Eddie and Ryan Bolger, *Emerging Churches: Creating Christian Communities in Postmodern Cultures* (London, SPCK, 2006).

Giddens, Anthony and Anthony Sutton, *Sociology* (Cambridge, Polity, 2012).

Goodhew, David (ed.), *Church Growth in Britain 1980 to the Present* (Farnham, Ashgate, 2012).

Green, Joel, *Practicing Theological Interpretation: Engaging Biblical Texts for Faith and Formation* (Grand Rapids, Baker, 2012).

Greene, Colin, and Martin Robinson, *Metavista: Bible, Church and Mission in an Age of Imagination* (Milton Keynes, Authentic Media, 2008).

Grenz, Stanley, *A Primer on Postmodernism* (Cambridge, Eerdmans, 1996).

Halteman, R. F., *Of Widows and Meals: Communal Meals in the Book of Acts* (Grand Rapids/Cambridge, Eerdmans, 2007).

Haralambos, Michael and Martin Holborn, *Sociology: Themes and Perspectives Seventh Edition* (London, HarperCollins, 2008).

Hastings, Adrian, *African Catholicism Essays in Discovery* (Philadelphia, Trinity Press, 1989) .

Hay, David and Rebecca Nye, *The Spirit of the Child* (London, Kingsley Publishers, 2006).

Hecht, Richard and Vincent Biondo, *Religion and Culture: Contemporary Practices and Perspectives* (Minneapolis, Fortress Press, 2010).

Heelas, Paul, et al., *The Spiritual Revolution: Why Religion is Giving Way to Spirituality* (Oxford, Blackwell, 2005).

Hiebert, Paul, *Transforming Worldviews: An Anthropological Understanding of How People Change* (Grand Rapids, Baker Academic, 2009a).

Hiebert, Paul, *The Gospel in Human Contexts: Anthropological Explorations for Contemporary Missions* (Grand Rapids, Baker Academic, 2009b).

Hiebert, Paul and Eloise Hiebert Meneses, *Incarnational Ministry: Planting Churches in Band, Tribal, Peasant, and Urban Societies* (Grand Rapids, Baker Book House, 1995).

Hogg, Michael and Graham Vaughan, *Social Psychology,* (Harlow, Pearson Education Limited, 2011).

Jentsch, B. and M. Simard, *International Migration and Rural Areas: Cross-National Comparative Perspectives* (Farnham, Ashgate, 2009).

Jervell, Jacob, *The Theology of the Acts of the Apostles* (Cambridge, Cambridge University Press, 1996).

Karkkainen, Veli-Matti, *Pneumatology: The Holy Spirit in Ecumenical, International, and Contextual Perspective* (Grand Rapids, Baker Academic, 2002).

Kim, Kirsteen, *Joining in with the Spirit: Connecting World Church and Local Mission* (London, Epworth, 2009).

Kinnamann, David, *Unchristian: What a New Generation Thinks About Christianity, and Why It Matters* (Grand Rapids, Baker Books, 2007).

Kirk, Andrew, *What is Mission? Theological Explorations* (London, Darton Longman and Todd, 2006)

Kraft, Charles, *Christianity in Culture: A Study in Dynamic Biblical Theologizing in Cross-Cultural Perspective* (Maryknoll, Orbis Books, 2002).

Kung, Hans, *The Christian Challenge* (London, Collins, 1979).

Livermore, David, *Leading with Cultural Intelligence* (New York, AMACOM, 2010).

Long, Norman, *Development Sociology Actor Perspectives* (London, Routledge, 2001).

Longenecker, Richard (ed.), *Patterns of Discipleship in the New Testament* (Grand Rapids, Eerdmans, 1996).

McGinn, Bernard, *The Essential Writings of Christian Mysticism* (New York, The Modern Library, 2006).

McSwain, Larry and William Treadwell, *Conflict Ministry in the Church* (Nashville, Broadman Press, 1981).

MacCulloch, Dairmot, *A History of Christianity* (London, Penguin, 2010).

Marshall, Howard, *The Acts of the Apostles* (Tyndale Commentaries, Eerdmans, 1980).

Marshall, Howard, *New Testament Theology* (Nottingham, IVP, 2004).

Matthewman, Jim, *The Rise of the Global Nomad* (London, Koganpage, 2011).

Mellor, Howard and Timothy Yates, *Mission and Spirituality: Creative Ways of Being Church* (Sheffield, Cliff College Publishing, 2002).

Moreau, Scott, *Evangelical Dictionary of World Missions* (Carlisle, Paternoster Press, 2000).

Moynagh, Michael and Philip Harrold, *Church for Every Context: A Theology for Every Practice* (London, SCM Press, 2013).

Murray, Stuart, *Post-Christendom: Church and Mission in a Strange New World* (Milton Keynes, Paternoster, 2005).

Nadler, David, Robert Shaw and Elise Walton, *Discontinuous Change Leading Organizational Transformation* (San Francisco, Jossey-Bass, 1995).

Newberg, Andrew and Mark Waldman, *How God Changes your Brain: Breakthrough Findings from A Leading Neuroscientist* (New York, Ballantine Books, 2009).

Newbigin, Lesslie, *The Gospel in a Pluralist Society* (London, SPCK, 1989).

Newbigin, Lesslie, *The Open Secret: An Introduction to the Theology of Mission* (London, SPCK, 1995).

Niebuhr, H. Richard, *Christ and Culture* (Grand Rapids, Harper Torchbooks, 1975).

Olofinjana, Israel, *Reverse in Ministry & Missions: Africans in the Dark Continent of Europe – An Historical Study of African Churches in Europe* (Milton Keynes, Author House, 2010).

Partridge, Christopher, *Dictionary of Contemporary Religion in the Western World* (Leicester, IVP, 2002).

Payne, J. D., *Strangers Next Door: Immigration, Migration and Mission* (Downers Grove, IVP, 2012).

Peskett, Howard and Vinoth Ramachandra, *The Message of Mission* (Leicester, IVP, 2003).

Pfremmer de Long, Kindalee, *Surprised by God: Praise Responses in the Narrative of Luke–Acts* (Berlin/New York, Walter de Gruyter, 2009).

Phillips, David, *Peoples on the Move: Introducing the Nomads of the World* (Carlisle, Piquant, 2001).

Pinnock, Clark, *Flame of Love: A Theology of the Holy Spirit* (Downers Grove, IVP Academic, 1996).

Pollock, David and Ruth van Reken, *Third Culture Kids: The Experience of Growing Up Among Worlds* (London, Nicholas Brealey Publishing, 2001).

Proctor, John, *Acts of God: The Message and Meaning of the Book of Acts* (Grove Booklets B49, Cambridge, Grove Books Ltd, 2008).

Qureshi, Sairah, *Bullying and Racist Bullying in Schools: What are we Missing?* (USA, Xlibris Corporation, 2013).

Robinson, Martin, *Winning Hearts, Changing Minds: When the Western World Ignores the Gospel – What Should Christians Do?* (London, Monarch Books, 2001).

Robinson, Martin and Dan Yarnell, *Celebrating the Small Church* (London, Monarch, 1993).

Robinson, Martin and Dwight Smith, *Invading Secular Space* (London, Monarch Books, 2009).

Rogers, Carl, *On Becoming a Person: A Therapist's View of Psychotherapy* (London, Constable, 1991).

Rogers, Glenn, *Holistic Ministry and Cross-cultural Mission in Luke–Acts* (Mission and Ministry Resources, 2003).

Rogerson, J. W. and Judith Lieu, *The Oxford Handbook of Biblical Studies* (Oxford, Oxford University Press, 2008).

Roxburgh, Alan, *Missional Joining God in the Neighbourhood* (Grand Rapids, Baker Publishing Group, 2011).

Samuel, Vinay and Chris Sugden, *Mission as Transformation: A Theology of the Whole Gospel* (California, Regnum, 1999).

Schilderman, Hans, 'Quantitative Method' in *The Wiley-Blackwell Companion to Theology* (Chichester, Blackwell Publishing Ltd, 2012).

Scott, M., *Prophecy in the Church* (Australia, Word, 1992).

Sine, Tom, *The New Conspirators: Creating the future one mustard seed at a time* (Downers Grove, IVP, 2008).

Smith, Peter, *Global Warming: The Fire of Pentecost in World Evangelism – An Anecdotal History of the Work of Elim Missions (1919–1989)* (Antrim, Antrim Printers, 2007).

Stoddard, Chris and Nick Cuthbert, *Church on the Edge: Principles and real life stories of 21st century mission* (Milton Keynes, Authentic, 2006).

Stott, John, *The Message of Acts* (Leicester, IVP, 1991).

Sugarman, Leonie, *Life-Span Development Frameworks, Accounts and Strategies* (Hove, Psychology Press, 2001).

Suurmond, Jean-Jacques, *Word and Spirit at Play* (London, SCM Press, 1994).

Swinton, John and Harriet Mowat, *Practical Theology and Qualitative Research* (London, SCM Press, 2006).

Thiselton, Anthony, *Hermeneutics: An Introduction* (Grand Rapids, Eerdmans, 2009).

Thompson, Joseph, *How the Spiritual Explosion Among Nigerians is Impacting the World Out of Africa* (Ventura, Regal Books, 2003).

Verlag, Brunner, *Religion in the Public Sphere I* (Switzerland, Forum Mission, 2012).

Verstraelen, Frans, and F. J. Camps (eds), *Missiology An Ecumenical Introduction, Texts and Contexts of Global Christianity* (Grand Rapids, Eerdmans, 1995).

Virkler, Mark, *How to Hear God's Voice* (USA, Destiny Image, 2005).

Vlassopoulos, Kostas, *Greeks and Barbarians* (Cambridge, Cambridge University Press, 2013).

Wagner, Peter, *Spreading the Fire Vol. 1* (Ventura, Regal Books, 1994).

Wagner, Peter, *Warfare Prayer: How to Seek God's Power and Protection in the Battle to Build His Kingdom* (Venture, Regal Books, 1992).

Wainwright, Geoffrey, *Lesslie Newbigin: A Theological Life* (Oxford, Oxford University Press, 2000).

Watters, Ethan, *Urban Tribes: Are Friends the New Family?* (Edinburgh, Bloomsbury, 2003).

Wink, Walter, *Naming the Powers: The Language of Power in the New Testament* (Philadelphia, Fortress Press, 1984).

Wink, Walter, *Unmasking the Powers: The Invisible Forces that Determine Human Existence* (Philadelphia, Fortress Press, 1986).

Wink, Walter, *Engaging the Powers: Discernment and Resistance in a World of Domination* (Minneapolis, Fortress Press, 1992).

Wink, Walter, *The Powers that Be: Theology for a New Millennium* (New York, Galilee Doubleday, 1999).

Witherington III, Ben, *Women in the Ministry of Jesus* (Cambridge, Cambridge University Press, 1984).

Witherington III, Ben, *The Acts of the Apostles: A Social-Rhetorical Commentary* (Grand Rapids/Cambridge, Eerdmans, 1998).

Wright, Christopher, *The Mission of God: Unlocking the Bible's Grand Narrative* (Nottingham, IVP, 2006).

Wright, Christopher, *The Mission of God's People: A Biblical Theology of the Church's Mission* (Grand Rapids, Zondervan, 2010).

Wright, N. T., *The New Testament and the People of God* (London, SPCK, 1993).

Wright, N. T., *Paul: Fresh Perspectives* (London, SPCK, 2005).

Wright, Tom, *Jesus and the Victory of God* (London, SPCK, 1996).

Yohannan, K. P., *Revolution in World Missions* (Carrollton, GFA Books, 2004).

Articles and journals

Cathcart, Rochelle and Mike Nichols, 'Self-Theology, Global Theology, and Missional Theology, in the Writings of Paul. G. Hiebert', *Trinity Journal*, November 2009, Nos. 209-221.

Davis, Pamela, Pamela Suarez et al., 'Re-entry program impact on missionary kid depression, anxiety, and stress: a three year study', *Journal of Psychology and Theology*, 41 No. 2, Summer 2013.

Gittins, Anthony, 'Reflections from the Edge: Mission-in-Reverse and Missiological Research', *Missiology: An International Review*, Vol. 21, No. 1, January 1983.

Greenwood, Chris, 'Boy, 15, 'tortured to death with hammer and chisels on Christmas Day because relative thought he was a witch', *Mail Online*, 6th January 2012. Available at: http://www.dailymail.co.uk/news/article-2082618/Kristy-Bamu-15-tortured-death-witch-claim-Christmas-Day-Newham.html (accessed 2nd November 2014).

Hanciles, Jehu, 'Migration and Mission: Some Implications for the Twenty-First-Century Church', *International Bulletin of Missionary Research*, Vol. 27 No. 4, November 2003.

Hazelden, Paul, 'The Modified Engle Scale: Working with God in Evangelism': http://www.hazelden.org.uk/pt02/art_pt068_modified_engel_pt1.htm (accessed 2nd November 2014).

Houreld, Katherine, 'African Children Denounced as "Witches" by Christian Pastors', 25th May 2011: http://www.huffingtonpost.com/2009/10/18/african-children-denounce_n_324943.html (accessed 2nd November 2014).

Hudson, Alex, 'The Age of Information Overload', BBC News, 14th August 2012: http://news.bbc.co.uk/1/hi/programmes/click_online/9742180.stm (accessed 2nd November 2014).

Jaffarian, Michael, 'Are There More Non-Western Missionaries than Western Missionaries?' *International Bulletin of Missionary Research*, Vol. 28, No. 3, July 2004.

Maysh, Jeff, '"We're not like normal teenagers": Meet the exorcist schoolgirls who spend their time casting out DEMONS around the world, *Mail Online*, 11th August 2011. Available at http://www.dailymail.co.uk/news/article-2024621/Meet-exorcist-schoolgirls-spend-time-casting-demons-worldwide.html

Moon, Steve, 'The Recent Korean Missionary Movement: A Record of Growth, and More Growth Needed', *International Bulletin of Missionary Research*, Vol. 27, 1 Jan. 2003.

Newbigin, Lesslie, 'Can the West be Converted?' (1985): www.newbigin.net/assets/pdf/85cwbc.pdf (accessed 2nd November 2014).

Powell, J. R., 'Families in missions: a research context', *Journal of Psychology and Theology*, No. 2, Summer 1999.

Ralter, M. and M. K. Wilson, 'Culture, human identity, and cross-cultural ministry some biblical reflections', *Journal of Psychology and Theology*, No. 2, Summer 1999.

Sharp, L. W., 'How Missionary Children Become World Christians: The Role of the MK School', *Journal of Psychology and Theology*, 18 No. 1 September 1990.

Turner, Max, 'The Work of the Holy Spirit in Luke–Acts', *Word and World*, (Vol. 23, No. 2).

Tienou, Tite, and Paul Hiebert, 'Missional Theology', *Missiology and International Review*, Vol. 34, No. 2, April 2006.

Turner, M. (2003), 'The Work of the Holy Spirit in Luke-Acts', *Word and World*, Vol. 23, No. 2.

van Gelder, Craig, 'Postmodernism and Evangelicals: A Unique Missiological Challenge at the Beginning of the Twenty-First Century', *Missiology and International Review*, Vol. 30, No. 4, October 2002.

Congressional Record, (V. 151, Pt. 10, June 20 to June 27, 2005).

The Sunday Times, 1st July 2000.

'The make-up of modern Britain: 70% of us claim to be Christians... and only 1.5% are gay', *Mail Online*, 29th September 2011: http://www.dailymail.co.uk/news/article-2043045/Modern-Britain-70-claim-Christians-1-5-gay.html (accessed 2nd November 2014).

'"British whites" are the minority in London for the first time as census shows number of UK immigrants has jumped by 3million in 10 years' *Mail Online*, 11th December 2012: http://www.dailymail.co.uk/news/article-2246288/Census-2011-UK-immigrant-population-jumps-THREE-MILLION-10-years.html#ixzz2sefOvQap (accessed 2nd November 2014).

'UK Census: religion by age, ethnicity and country of birth' *The Guardian*, 16th May 2013. Available at www.theguardian.com/news/datablog/2013/may/16/uk-census-religion-age-ethnicity-country-of-birth (accessed 2nd November 2014).

Britain's Black Church Leaders Unite to Speak Out Against BBC Documentary', *Christian Today*, 8th April 2006: http://www.christiantoday.com/article/britains.black.church.leaders.unite.to.speak.out.against.bbc.documentary/5898.htm (accessed 2nd November 2014).

Websites

Business Matters: http://www.businessmattersedinburgh.com/about/ (accessed 2nd November 2014).

Springdale College: http://springdaleweb.sdcol.org.uk (accessed 2nd November 2014).

Micah Challenge: http://www.micahchallenge.org.au/about-us (accessed 2nd November 2014).

2011 Census: http://www.ons.gov.uk/ons/guide-method/census/2011/index.html (accessed 2nd November 2014).

UK Data Service: http://discover.ukdataservice.ac.uk/catalogue?sn=6695 accessed 2nd November 2014).

Office for National Statistics, 2001 Census Data: http://www.ons.gov.uk/ons/guide-method/census/2011/census-data/2001-census-data/index.html (accessed 2nd November 2014).

Sunday Night Live': http://sundaynightlive.org.uk (accessed 2nd November 2014).

Transform Work UK:
http://www.transformworkuk.org/Groups/208894/Transform_Work_U
K/Resources/Alpha_in_the/Alpha_in_the.aspx (accessed 25th
November 2014).

Mosaic: http://mosaic.org (accessed 2nd November 2014).

WL Academy: http://www.wlacademy.org.uk/about.php (accessed 2nd
November 2014).

World Missionary Conference 1910:
http://archive.org/details/1936337.0004.001.umich.edu (accessed 2nd
November 2014).

http://archbishop-cranmer.blogspot.co.uk/2012/10/uk-border-agency-
obstructs-path-of.html (accessed 2nd November 2014).

Television

Reverse Missionaries, BBC 2 (2012).

Unpublished dissertations

Hardy, Andrew, *Spiritual and Missional Philosophical Theology*, (Doctoral
Dissertation, 2009).

Hardy, Andrew, *A Critical Study of the Challenges Faced by Reverse
Missionaries in the West* (MA Dissertation, 2013).

Kumbi, H., *The Development of Ethiopian and Eritrean Evangelical Churches in
the United Kingdom: Missional Movement or Cultural Dead-End*
(Birmingham: Springdale College, MA Missional Leadership).